The Logic of Japanese Politics

Leaders, Institutions, and the Limits of Change

Gerald L. Curtis

COLUMBIA

UNIVERSITY PRESS

NEW YORK

Columbia University Press
Publishers Since 1893
New York   Chichester, West Sussex

Copyright © 1999 Columbia University Press
Library of Congress Cataloging-in-Publication Data
Curtis, Gerald L.
    The logic of Japanese politics / Gerald L. Curtis.
        p.   cm.
    Includes bibliographical references.
    ISBN 978-0-231-10842-3 (cloth : alk. paper).
    ISBN 978-0-231-10843-0 (pbk.)
    1. Japan—Politics and government—1989– 2. Political culture—Japan.   I. Title.
JQ1631.C87 1999   99–19910
320.952'09'049—DC21

Casebound editions of Columbia University Press books are printed on permanent
and durable acid-free paper.
Printed in the United States of America
c 10 9 8 7 6 5 4
p 10 9 8 7 6

For Midori

Studies of the East Asian Institute, Columbia University

The East Asian Institute is Columbia University's center for research, publication, and teaching on modern East Asia. The studies of the East Asian Institute were inaugurated in 1962 to bring a wider public the results of significant new research on modern and contemporary East Asia.

Contents

Preface to the Paperback Edition

This book provides an analysis and interpretation of Japanese politics, as it has evolved over the past half century, and focuses particularly on the 1990s, a decade of economic troubles and political uncertainties. I argue that the political developments that have occurred during this past decade signal a new period of fundamental political change, one that will lead to new patterns of political party competition and important changes in policy-making processes. I also argue that the shape of a new party and policy-making system will be contingent upon a host of variables, and that the transition itself is likely to be prolonged.

Events that have transpired since the initial publication of this book only reinforce this argument, and they have underscored especially the prolonged nature of Japan's political transition. The weakening of many of the key features of the postwar political system that is discussed in chapter two—the loss of a public consensus on national goals, the decline in the authority and prestige of the bureaucracy, the fragmentation of interest groups, and the erosion of the LDP's support base—continues unabated. The volatility in voting behavior that is discussed in chapter six in the context of the 1997 upper house election became evident once again in the lower house election held in June 2000. Instability in the party system, characterized by the fragmenting of parties and shifting alliances among them rather than the consolidation of a new party system, remains the most salient feature of party politics in the first years of the twenty-first century.

There is no question that Japan's political system is in the midst of the most profound transformation since the early years following the

Second World War. Yet the transition is painfully slow and the resistance to change impressively strong. Although there are elements in the LDP that believe party practices and policies need to change, those who currently lead the party have been resistant to change in their response to challanges. Instead, they have tried to sustain the kind of politics that developed decades ago, an effort that is producing new and complex political tensions within the LDP and accelerating the LDP's loss of support among the urban middle class and the growing number of floating voters who support no political party and account for at least half of the electorate.

How these political tensions are ultimately resolved and what kind of new party system will eventually emerge will be contingent on how key political leaders respond to perceived changes in the political structure. At some point the LDP may well turn to a reformist leadership and once again expand its support among the urban electorate. It is also conceivable that the LDP will split, as it did in 1993, and spark a total realignment of political forces and the creation of a new party system. It is also possible that other parties will continue to increase their representation in the Diet and drive the LDP out of office, although the results of the June 2000 lower house election suggest that this is not likely to happen for at least another two or three general elections. We cannot predict in what exact form change will come to Japanese politics, but we can understand the forces propelling political change, and stalling it as well, and discern the political opportunity structure within which Japanese political leaders will make the choices that will decide the future of Japanese politics.

The political narrative presented in the following chapters concludes with the LDP's defeat in the July 1998 upper house election, the subsequent selection of LDP faction leader Keizo Obuchi as prime minister, and the LDP's formation of a coalition government with Ichiro Ozawa's Liberal Party. In terms of policy-making processes, I point out in the concluding chapter that as the 1990s came to a close, the Diet and its committee system seemed to be gaining in importance as a site for policy making because the coalition lacked a majority in the upper house and had to compromise with the opposition Democrats in the Diet in order to get needed legislation passed.

This expansion of the role of Diet committees in the policy-making process was quickly aborted. In July 1999, contrary to what I expected to happen, the Komeito joined the LDP–Liberal Party coalition. This gave the coalition parties nearly two-thirds of the seats in the lower house and a solid majority in the upper house, making it possible for LDP leaders to remove policy formulation from the Diet and to revert to long-established patterns of policy making with which they were more comfortable. This meant avoiding compromises openly arrived at in Diet committees, and instead centering the decision-making process in ruling-party councils and in consultations among coalition party leaders. Although the postwar Diet's committee structure draws heavily on the American Congressional model, Japanese politicians do not accept American assumptions about the role that parliamentary committees should play in policy making. In Japan's parliamentary democracy, ending up in opposition literally means to go "down to the wilderness" (*geya suru*); only those who are in parties that are in the government are regarded as having a legitimate role to play in policy making. The combination of these assumptions with the practical need to make some concessions to opposition demands in order to avoid their using boycotts and other tactics to paralyze the legislative process is what gives rise to the *kokutai* politics explained in chapter three.

The LDP's decision to bring the Komeito into the coalition was unpopular with most voters. LDP leaders apparently concluded, however, that they had to risk incurring the ire of voters at the polls in order to have a government that could command strong majorities in both houses and thereby avoid becoming hostage to the demands of the Democrats. Moreover, Prime Minister Obuchi came into office with a record low level of public support and no doubt feared that he would quickly be driven out of power if he did not move forthrightly to counter an image of being weak and indecisive. Bringing the Komeito into the coalition and excluding the opposition parties from a role in policy formulation would mean that Obuchi would be able to manage the political process in a more traditional manner for which his training in LDP factional politics had well prepared him.

The Komeito's decision to become a partner in the LDP government was rather more surprising than the LDP's desire to align with the Komeito. The Komeito had a casting vote as long as it remained outside of the government. This gave it a seemingly golden opportunity to leverage its position to demonstrate to voters who were not part of its Soka Gakkai supporting base that it could be a constructive force in policy making.

But party leaders concluded otherwise. They saw an opportunity to demonstrate to the public that they could be a responsible partner in government. Most importantly, they believed that being in government would strengthen their position in the coming lower house election. In late 1994 Komeito leaders had decided to disband their party, at least with regard to its lower house members, and to become part of the Shinshinto, the New Frontier Party. After that party collapsed at the end of 1997, the Komeito had to regroup as an independent party and develop a new strategy for survival under an electoral system that severely penalizes small parties. That strategy was to tie its fate to the LDP.

In April 2000 Prime Minister Obuchi suffered a massive stroke. He died a few weeks later. The Chief Cabinet Secretary assumed the prime minister's responsibilities, while a small group of party leaders conferred on who should succeed Obuchi. Their decision was to select Yoshiro Mori, who had recently taken over as leader of the faction formerly led by Hiroshi Mitsuzuka. LDP leaders came under a great deal of criticism for the opaque process by which they managed the succession. But criticism notwithstanding, on April 5, 2000, Yoshiro Mori became Japan's new prime minister.

The coalition government under Mori was comprised of the LDP, the Komeito, and a small number of former Liberal Party members who had regrouped into a new Conservative Party. Just prior to suffering his stroke, Obuchi had a tense meeting with Liberal Party leader Ozawa, who demanded a number of policy concessions from the LDP if he were to remain in the coalition. It may well have been the case that Ozawa calculated his group would do better in the lower house election if it were not part of the government. In any case, Obuchi rejected Ozawa's demands, and Ozawa led his party once again into the opposition. Those who did not follow him and decided to remain part of the coalition government formed the Conservative Party.

A month after coming to power, Prime Minister Mori dissolved the lower house and called elections for June 25. Nearly four years had passed since the previous lower house election in October 1996. Not surprisingly, the LDP entered the election campaign in a defensive mode. Prime Minister Mori's popularity was at a low ebb. He had stirred controversy with a comment that Japan was "a country of the gods centered on the Emperor" and was taken to task by the press for suggesting that it would be good for the LDP if unaffiliated floating voters stayed in bed and away from the polls on election day. The great majority of LDP voters were unhappy about the party's coalition with the Komeito, and public support for the cabinet was no more than 18 percent. Economic conditions had not improved significantly despite massive government deficit spending on public works projects, and there seemed to be growing public concern about mounting government deficits and excessive public works spending.

Yet, as the election approached, public opinion surveys conducted by the major newspapers all suggested that the LDP was headed toward a major victory and that it would probably secure a majority of lower house seats on its own. The LDP was expected to do well, especially in the single-member districts where its incumbents traditionally had strong personal bases of support. A week before the election, the *Asahi Shimbun*, based on its most recent nationwide public opinion survey, predicted that the LDP would win 257 seats, with only 241 seats needed for a majority. All the other national newspapers came out with similar projections.

As it turned out, the polls were as inaccurate in predicting the electoral outcome in the lower house election in June 2000 as they had been in predicting the outcome of the upper house election in July 1997. Many voters made up their minds about what party to vote for either late in the campaign or changed their minds after reading what the polls predicted. The election did not particularly spark a lot of excitement among the electorate. The 62.4 percent voting rate was the second lowest for a lower house election in the postwar period, surpassed only by the even lower rate in the previous 1996 election. That the results were at such variance with mass media predictions is an indicator of the volatility evident in recent voting behavior in Japan. It is reasonable to assume that there is a prospect for even greater voting behavior volatility if the voting rate were to increase in future elections.

The LDP went into the election with 271 lower house incumbents and came out of it with only 233. Although it managed to surpass its own stated minimum goal of securing 229 seats, it sustained substantial losses, especially in urban areas. This, coupled with its falling so far short of what the surveys had predicted it to win, resulted in media coverage that emphasized the LDP's "defeat." Newspaper pictures of grim faced LDP leaders and beaming Democratic Party ones made a similar point.

June 25, 2000 Lower-House Election Results					
PARTY		VOTES	% OF VOTE	SEATS	CANDIDATES
LDP	Single-member	24,945,806	40.97	177	271
	Proportional representation	16,943,425	28.31	56	326
Democrats	Single-member	16,811,732	27.61	80	242
	Proportional representation	15,067,990	25.18	47	259
Komeito	Single-member	1,231,753	2.02	7	18
	Proportional representation	7,762,032	12.97	24	63
Liberal	Single-member	2,053,736	3.37	4	61
	Proportional representation	6,589,490	11.01	18	82
Communists	Single-member	7,352,843	12.08	0	300
	Proportional representation	6,719,016	11.23	20	66
Socialists	Single-member	2,315,234	3.80	4	71
	Proportional representation	5,603,680	9.36	15	76
Conservatives	Single-member	1,230,464	2.02	7	16
	Proportional representation	247,334	0.41	0	3
Minor Parties	Single-member	1,973,831	3.24	6	141
	Proportional representation	911,634	1.52	0	39
Independents	Single-member	2,967,069	4.87	15	79
	Proportional representation	—	—	—	—

The above chart provides basic data on the election's results. There are three points in particular to be made about this election's outcome. The most important one is that the LDP won the election. The second is that support for the LDP among voters in urban centers declined. And the third is that the leading opposition Democratic Party benefited from an anti-LDP vote but was unable to generate much public enthusiasm for making it the ruling party.

The LDP came through the election with its position as the dominant party in the governing coalition intact and with its leader as the country's prime minister. Although LDP leaders greeted the results with pained expressions, they had to be relieved at the outcome. The LDP fell seven seats short of a majority, but it actually secured an effective working majority—if one considers that the seven Conservative Party members represent little more than a faction of LDP members who, for the time being, are outside the formal party organization, and that some of the twenty-one independents elected to the lower house quickly joined LDP factions even though they remain outside the LDP itself for the time being and may eventually join the LDP *kaiha*, an important intraparliamentary institution that is discussed in chapter five.

The LDP performed as well, or as poorly, in the 2000 election as it did in the previous election in 1996. It won 239 seats in a house of 500 members in 1996 and 233 seats in a house of 480 members in 2000. It had 271 incumbents at the time the house was dissolved in June 2000 because of the large number of New Frontier Party lower house members that joined the LDP when that party collapsed in 1997.

As for the New Frontier Party, of the 156 NFP members elected in 1996, 138 ran for reelection in June 2000, of whom 100 were successful. Twenty of the twenty-four former NFP members who ran as LDP candidates won. Twenty-eight of the thirty-six who ran on the Komeito ticket were elected. There were thirty former NFP members among the successful Democratic Party candidates. There were eleven who won as members of the Liberal Party, including, of course, the NFP's founder Ichiro Ozawa. Seven former NFP members were elected on the Conservative Party ticket, and another four won without party support.

It is important not to underestimate the significance of the LDP victory in this election. The party lost seats, but what matters most is that it won the election. That has given it four more years to try to build its popular support and to keep the opposition parties out of power before it has to call another election, assuming that it remains unified and is able to defeat inevitable opposition party attempts to pass nonconfidence motions in the government.

Although it remains in power, the LDP had to be alarmed by the election's results. Once again, as in the two previous lower house elections, it failed to win a majority of seats. And this was the case even though it had many more incumbents in the election (thanks to the disintegration of the New Frontier Party) than it needed to secure a majority. Once again, as in the 1997 upper house election, its losses were concentrated in the most urban and most populous districts in the country. The results of the June

2000 lower house election left no doubt that the LDP would have to make a concerted effort to broaden its appeal to urban residents and to the nonparty supporting electorate in order to prevent the further erosion of its support base.

Whether alliance between the Komeito and the LDP was beneficial for either party in the 2000 lower house election is not entirely clear. Roughly 60 percent of the LDP's candidates received the support of the Komeito. That party's ability to turn out Soka Gakkai supporters to vote for LDP candidates is reflected in the large gap in the LDP's vote in the single-member and proportional representation districts. The LDP garnered nearly twenty-five million votes in the single-member constituencies, two million more than in 1996 even though it ran fewer candidates than it did in that earlier election, and eight million more than it won in the proportional representation districts in the June 2000 election. No doubt there were LDP supporters and nonparty-affiliated voters who cast ballots for LDP candidates in single-member districts and for a different party in their proportional representation district. But there is no doubt that most of the eight million more votes the LDP obtained in single-member districts than in proportional representation ones came from the Komeito. That number corresponds closely to the Komeito's own vote in the proportional representation districts.

Komeito support did not necessarily benefit all single-member district LDP candidates who were offered it, however. According to exit polls, in at least some districts a considerable number of LDP supporters voted against LDP candidates in single-member districts because of their opposition to the Komeito. In Tokyo, for example, two prominent LDP incumbents, Kaoru Yosano and Takashi Fukaya, lost. According to one exit poll, Yosano received the votes of 90 percent of Komeito supporters and Fukaya got 73 percent of the votes of Komeito members who voted. But Yosano won only 72 percent of the votes of LDP supporters and Fukaya only 69 percent.[1]

The Komeito ran candidates in eighteen single-member districts. The LDP withdrew its own candidates in fourteen of them in order to support the Komeito. Komeito candidates won in only half of these districts. In five of the fourteen districts, LDP members who had been denied their party's endorsement ran as independents against the LDP-supported Komeito candidate. The Komeito won seats in only two of these five districts. (The LDP also abstained from running candidates in another twelve single-member districts in order to support Conservative Party candidates. Seven of those candidates were successful.) The last time the Komeito ran as an independent party, in 1993, under the old electoral system, it won fifty-one seats. In the 1996 election it did not field its own candidates since it had become part of the New Frontier Party. In the 2000 election it won only thirty-one seats even though its nearly eight million votes in the proportional representation districts compared to only five million votes that its candidates won in 1993 under the multimember district system. The fact that it won twenty fewer seats in 2000 than in 1993, while increasing its popular vote by three million, is an indicator of how severely the single-member district component of the current electoral system disadvantages small parties.

With the disappearance of the New Frontier Party, the Democratic Party stood alone as the major challenger to the LDP in the June 2000 election. It ran 261 candidates in the 300 single-member districts, compared to only 143 Democratic Party candidates in the previous 1996 election. In theory, at least, it fielded enough candidates to win a majority of seats, which was only the third time ever that a party other than the LDP had done so. The Socialists had run more candidates than needed for a majority once under the previous electoral system, and the New Frontier Party did so in the 1996 election.

The headlines in the morning editions of the major national newspapers the day after the election all reported the Democrats' "advance" (*yakushin*) and the LDP's sharp decline in seats, and carried pictures of the broad smiles of the Democratic Party's leaders Yukio Hatoyama and Naoto Kan. The Democrats had won 127 seats, compared to only fifty-two seats it won in the 1996 election and the ninety-five seats it had at the time the house was dissolved. (The larger number of incumbents it had at election time than were elected on the Democratic Party ticket in 1996 was the result of the entry into the party of New Frontier Party members.) It won thirteen of the twenty-five seats at stake in Tokyo's single-member districts, leaving the LDP with only eight. Democratic Party candidates took seats away from LDP incumbents in three districts in Saitama prefecture, another three in Kanagawa, four in Chiba, and two in Aichi, all major urban areas. In terms of the popular vote, the Democrats outpolled the LDP in single-member districts in Tokyo, Aichi, and Osaka, and in the proportional representation districts it beat out the LDP in Saitama, Kanagawa, Tokyo, Nagano, Aichi, Osaka, Hyogo, and Fukuoka. Overall, the Democrats garnered 25.17 percent of the proportional representation vote, only three points behind the LDP's 28.31 percent.

These successes notwithstanding, the picture of smiling Democratic Party leaders and newspaper headlines focusing on the party's "advance" in the election were a reminder of how much influence a mindset that was formed over the long years of LDP one-party dominance continues to exert over the thinking of politicians and political analysts in Japan. In an era when the victory of the LDP in lower house elections was a foregone conclusion, the issue of how much the Socialists or other opposition parties were able to erode LDP support carried some importance. It affected the factional balance of power within the LDP, and it provided some indication of what changes might occur over the long term in relative party strength.

To treat the results of the June 2000 election as a victory for the Democrats and a defeat for the LDP only makes sense if one assumes that LDP control over the government was unchallengeable, a way of thinking that prevailed during the so-called '55 system but one that seems at odds with Japan's current political realities. Focusing on the Democrats "advance" obfuscated the more important fact that the Democratic Party failed to drive the LDP out of power in the June 2000 election despite having a golden opportunity to do so. It lost not because the LDP was popular but because the Democrats were unable to generate any noticeable enthusiasm among the electorate for giving it the reins of power. The party leadership was unable to articulate a policy program to deal with the nation's economic problems or a vision of Japan's role in the world that was distinguishable from the LDP's or that captured the imagination of a public that seemed only too ready to vote against the LDP if an attractive alternative presented itself. The one economic policy reform advocated by Democratic Party chairman Hatoyama that drew a lot of attention was a proposal to lower the threshold at which income would be taxed. LDP leaders quickly jumped on this proposal as an effort to make poor people pay for the nation's economic problems. Despite the dramatically successful summit meeting in Pyongyang between South Korean President Kim Dae-Jung and North Korean leader Kim Jong-Il that concluded only days before the election campaign began, the Democrats had nothing to say about how Japanese should think about foreign policy given the possibility that major changes might be occurring in the international situation in Northeast Asia.

The increase in seats that the Democratic Party achieved was largely due to the disappearance of the New Frontier Party. It should be remembered that the NFP won more seats in 1996, even though it had to compete with the Democrats as well as the LDP, than the Democrats won in 2000. Even in urban Japan, the Democratic Party's performance was not as strong as some commentators suggested it had been. It won more seats than the LDP in single-member districts only in Tokyo and Aichi and tied the LDP in Saitama, Shizuoka, and Hyogo. In every other prefecture, urban as well as rural, the LDP won more seats than the Democrats or any other party. The singular exception was rural Iwate prefecture, Ichiro Ozawa's home base, where the Liberals won three of the four seats at stake, and the LDP won the other one.

All available evidence suggests that the Democrats did as well as they did because there was a considerable number of voters who wanted to vote against the LDP rather than because there was an outpouring of support for the Democrats. Given the volatility of voting behavior in Japan today and the virtual collapse of strong bonds of loyalty to any of the established political parties, the Democrats were in a position to take power away from the LDP, or at least to have come much closer to doing so than they did, if they had generated greater excitement for that possibility among the voters. That they failed to do so, not their supposed success in increasing the number of seats they hold in the lower house, was the important story of this election's outcome.

Even though it failed to unseat the LDP, by significantly increasing the number of seats it commands in the lower house and because of the favorable reporting it got from the Japanese press, the Democratic Party got a considerable postelection boost in public approval ratings. An *Asahi Shimbun* tracking poll found that 25 percent of the 1,421 people it monitored supported the Democrats three days after the election, up from 12 percent in March and May. The *Yomiuri Shimbun's* monthly poll of 1,987 people, taken in early July 2000, gave the Democrats a 20.6 percent support rate, double the 9.6 percent they rated in May, while support for the LDP fell from 34.2 percent to 29.9 percent. Asked in the *Asahi Shimbun* survey which party gives them greater hope for the future, 43 percent picked the Democrats, and only 38 percent said the LDP. Among nonparty-affiliated voters, support for the Democrats was 43 percent to only 16 percent for the LDP.[2]

These numbers are certainly not firm. A similar surge in Democratic Party support followed the 1997 upper house election as well, only to dissipate later. What they do reflect is a fluidity in Japanese voting attitudes and an opportunity for parties to bring about significant and potentially dramatic and far-reaching changes in Japanese politics if they can figure out how to inspire the electorate with an attractive program and a dynamic leadership.

The other noteworthy aspect of the election's results was the surprisingly strong showing by both the Social Democratic Party and the Liberal Party and the lackluster performance by the Japan Communist Party. Ozawa's Liberal Party obtained 11 percent of the proportional representation vote, eighteen seats in proportional representation districts, and another four seats in single-member districts. The Social Democratic Party did surprisingly well, winning fifteen proportional representation seats and another four in single-member districts. That these two parties, which stand at opposite ends of the spectrum on many if not most important issues such as constitutional revision and economic liberalization, drew as much support as they did is an indicator of voter dissatisfaction with the LDP and the Democrats. The Communist Party, which most observers believed would grow in strength as a result of the election, apparently lost a lot of the anti-LDP protest vote to the other parties that competed in this election. Its percentage of the vote in the proportional representation districts declined by two percentage points from the previous 1996 election, and it was unable to elect anyone in single-member districts, even though its absolute vote total in the single-member districts was higher than it was in the 1996 election.

There are two points to stress with respect to the consequences of the outcome of the June 2000 election. One is that the LDP, having managed to come through the election still holding onto power and no doubt frightened by the contracting of its urban support, is almost certain to try to avoid holding another lower house election until the term of the current house expires in 2004. In other words, the chances that the LDP will be voted out of office anytime soon are minimal. That suggests that if a reorganization of the party system is to occur during this first decade of the twenty-first century, it is most likely to occur as a result of a split within the LDP, sparked by a leadership struggle in the party. This is how political change came about in the 1990s, as described in the pages of this book. However, the failure of the events of the 1990s to force a fundamental realignment of political forces has left many politicians understandably more cautious about provoking a party split now than they were a decade ago.

The other point is that the election has not only left the LDP in power, but it has also set the stage for what may turn out to be an intense competition and complicated battle for seats in the upper house election that

will be held in July 2001. Given the party's terrible performance in the latest upper house election and its poor performance in the June 2000 lower
house election, LDP leaders undoubtedly are going to be arguing with
each other over strategy, especially about whether to go into the election
in alliance once again with the Komeito. And this will be interwoven with
a factional struggle for power within the party.

Factions remain the key institution within the LDP in terms of structuring the competition for party power and mediating the recruitment of
cabinet ministers and key party officials. Factional leadership is in considerable flux, however, and the current factional lineup in the LDP is
considerably different now than it was when the first edition of this book
was published. Former Prime Minister Hashimoto is now the titular
head of the party's largest faction, with ninety-four lower and upper
house members, that had been led by Prime Minister Obuchi. The former Mitsuzuka faction, now headed by Prime Minister Mori, has sixty-
one members. The next largest faction of fifty-nine members is headed
by Koichi Kato, who at the moment stands as the most likely challenger
to Mori for leadership of the party and appears to be the most likely
LDP member to be prime minister after Mori. The Eto–Kamei faction,
which is a group of fifty-two Diet members that came out of the Mitsuzuka and Nakasone factions, is the other major factional group in the
party. The factional picture is rounded out with the twenty-two-member
Yamazaki faction made up of former Nakasone faction members, a
grouping of thirteen Diet members in a leaderless faction that is still
identified by the name of its former leader Komoto, and a group of
eleven Diet members that are close to the current foreign minister Yohei
Kono. There are twenty-seven LDP Diet members currently without
factional affiliation. Changes in the electoral system appear to be weakening the factional system, but it is still too soon to see how the LDP's
organization will evolve in response to the new electoral system and to
the generational and other changes that are taking place in the party and
in the society at large.

My intention in writing this book was not to predict the future course
of Japanese politics but to understand how it has arrived at its current
state. Throughout the discussion I stress the interaction of particular institutional constraints and individual choice. That dynamic, of course, continues to drive Japanese politics today and into the future. By understanding how that dynamic has operated in the past, we will be better
positioned to understand the significance of developments in Japanese

politics to come. To assist the reader in gaining an understanding of these dynamic qualities of the Japanese political system is the overriding objective of this book.

Notes

1. *Asahi Shimbun,* June 26, 2000.
2. *Asahi Shimbun,* July 4, 2000; *Yomiuri Shimbun,* July 4, 2000.

Preface

Over the last half of the twentieth century, Japan emerged from wartime defeat and devastation to become a stable political democracy with a powerful economy second in size only to the United States. Success not only made it a key leader in global economic affairs, but also led to predictions in the 1980s, by Japanese and foreigners alike, that Japan was on track to becoming the world's dominant economy.

Now, not much more than ten years later, as it stands at the threshold of a new millennium, Japan is faced with formidable problems. Its economic performance in the 1990s was the worst in half a century. Its political stability, a hallmark of the long period in which governmental power was dominated by the conservative Liberal Democratic Party, has given way to political uncertainty and to a rapid succession of weak coalition governments. Even Japan's elite government bureaucrats, long accustomed to being admired and treated with respect, are now roundly attacked for corruption and blamed for policy mistakes that made a bad economic situation worse.

With the end of the cold war and the development of a society in which nearly the entire adult population saw itself as middle class, the ideological underpinnings of nearly four decades of one-party dominance in Japanese politics collapsed. The politically relevant ideological spectrum contracted, making possible political alliances across a conservative-progressive divide that would have been unthinkable only a few short years earlier. The LDP lost power in 1993, only to return a year later in alliance with its longtime rival, the Japan Socialist Party. Politics subsequently has been punctuated by party splits and shifting party alliances, low voting rates, and short-lived coalition governments that hesitate to make bold policy choices. This political pattern seems likely to continue at least into the early years of the new century.

As Japan stumbled through the 1990s, Japanese public opinion became increasingly nervous about the future, yet it remained deeply skeptical about reform proposals that would cause fundamental, wrenching changes in the nation's economy and in the Japanese way of life. Japan's very success in catching up with the West economically and in achieving social stability and political democracy clearly had created new problems that required new solutions, while it had created at the same time a society that was profoundly risk averse. Japanese political leaders became caught in the cross-currents generated by this contradictory impulse in the body politic—by the desire to stick with the tried and true on the one hand and by a deep and growing anxiety about the future if things did no change on the other. They responded by adopting slogans of reform while the politics they pursued were cautious in the extreme and invariably fell far short of what the situation demanded.

Economic development, demographic shifts, value change, and the transformation of the international political system had profoundly altered the context for political action in Japan. Ambitious politicians in the 1990s, confronted by a changed structure of opportunities and constraints, improvised new strategies and formed new alliances, invariably insisting to the public, as they did so, that they were motivated by a desire to bring about reform. The consequent political battles were complex, with important decisions often resulting not from careful strategic calculations but as ad hoc responses to events as they unfolded.

Yet the struggle among politicians seeking to obtain or hold on to power did not take place in a vacuum; it occurred within and was constrained by Japan's particular institutions. In this book I have sought to analyze the evolution of contemporary Japanese politics by focusing on the actions of politicians taken within particular institutional constraints. My purpose in doing so has been to explore Japanese political dynamics and the inner logic of the contemporary Japanese political system and to explain the ways in which political leaders are limited in their ability to bring about change.

So many people were unstinting in helping me as I did the research for this book that it is not possible to thank each of them individually in these pages. This is especially the case because this book, although concerned primarily with the political events of the 1990s, is a product of more than thirty years of involvement with Japan. I knew many of the politicians whose names appear in these pages for many years before they became leaders in the 1990s. As will quickly become obvious to the reader, they gave generously of their time to answer my questions and were remarkably candid in doing so. I want to express my gratitude to each and every one of them. I must also address a collective thank you to the scholars, journalists, and the many others without whose help I could not possibly have written this book. Many foreigners hold an image of Japan as a society peculiarly difficult to penetrate. My own experiences, however, have convinced me that scholars, journalists, and people who may find themselves doing business in Japan, if they approach Japan with curiosity and genuine interest, and strive to overcome the language barrier, will not only be able to learn a great deal about this society but will also have a good time in the process.

Several friends who read earlier drafts of the manuscript provided comments that have made this book far better than it otherwise would have been. They include Michael Blaker, Merit Janow, Hugh Patrick, Cheol-hee Park, and Bob Uriu. My wife, Midori, and our daughters, Elissa and Jennifer, gave me support and encouragement without which I could not possibly have written this book. To my family and friends and all the many people in Japan who taught me what I know about Japanese politics belongs the credit for what is valuable in this book. I alone bear responsibility for its shortcomings.

The Logic of Japanese Politics

The Logic of Japanese Politics

Miki's Story

In early September 1976, while a research scholar at the University of Tokyo, I received a message that the prime minister, Takeo Miki,[1] whom I had known for several years, was available to speak with me if I called him at his home later that day. Not having seen Miki since he had become prime minister nearly two years earlier, when a corruption scandal forced Kakuei Tanaka to resign, I was looking forward to this conversation, especially since it came at a time when the LDP was in crisis and Miki's future as prime minister was uncertain.

Miki had begun his political career before the war, was elected to the Diet without the endorsement of the government's Imperial Rule Assistance Association in the one wartime election in 1942,[2] led his own party after the war, and was a faction leader in the ruling Liberal Democratic Party. He was a veteran of postwar Japan's political struggles and held many important party and government posts, including LDP secretary-general and foreign minister. Under normal circumstances, however, he would not have been able to win the LDP's support to become party president and the nation's prime minister. His faction was too small and other LDP leaders regarded him as too liberal.

But those were not normal times. Miki had a reputation as a clean politician. He was a well-known and longtime advocate of political reform. With the LDP trying to contain the damage created by the corruption charges leveled against Prime Minister Tanaka, Miki's image of incorruptibility seemed just what the party needed to quell public criticism. Miki's weak power base made the party bosses confident they could control him.

In deciding to make "clean Miki" prime minister, these LDP leaders got far more than they had bargained for. Miki pressed the party to support political-reform legislation, proposed a strengthening of the antimonopoly law that was opposed by important leaders in the business community, and did nothing to slow the investigation or stop the arrest of former Prime Minister Tanaka on suspicion of having received bribes from the Lockheed Corporation. Miki's refusal to do anything to help Tanaka infuriated party leaders and convinced them to oust him from office as quickly as possible. Their "down with Miki" *(Miki oroshi)* campaign dominated Japanese politics through the second half of 1976.

Miki finally resigned that December, taking responsibility for the party's loss of more than twenty seats in a lower-house election held earlier that month. A couple of weeks later, during the New Year's holidays, I visited him at his country home in Manazuru, on the Pacific coast a few hours' drive south of Tokyo. I was eager to hear Miki's retrospective on his two years in the prime minister's office. However, the struggle to defend himself against the down-with-Miki campaign, the strain of the election campaign, and the disappointment at having to relinquish the prime minister's post had taken their toll, leaving him too tired to do very much talking. He would drift off in midsentence, leaving his wife and his private secretary Masao Kunihiro (a University of Hawaii–trained anthropologist, an accomplished translator and simultaneous interpreter, and later a maverick Socialist Party member of the upper house) my wife, and me to sit there talking in hushed tones until he would open his eyes, say a few words more, and nod off again.

That was not Miki's condition the day I telephoned him in September. He was in the middle of fending off the LDP's efforts to drive him out of office, intent to open a new Diet session, and determined not to resign. He told me on the phone that LDP faction leaders Fukuda and Ohira, who would follow Miki into the prime minister's position one after the other, had come to see him a few days earlier to ask him to step down. They had warned him that if he did not, Miki said, they would have no choice but to join the moves that were underfoot in the LDP to remove him as party president.

Miki was an ardent admirer of British parliamentary democracy. He also was a crafty politician who knew how to play the Japanese power game as well as anyone. He enjoyed a reputation as a "Balkan politician" because of his demonstrated ability to leverage his position as head of a small political faction to maximum advantage in the shifting alliances of LDP factional politics.

Miki reminded Fukuda and Ohira that he held two separate positions, president of the LDP and prime minister of Japan. While the party could remove him as president if its leaders wished, only the Diet was empowered to remove him from the prime ministership. If Fukuda and Ohira and other party leaders wanted to replace him with a different prime minister, he suggested, they should submit a nonconfidence motion to the Diet. That would accord with the rules of parliamentary democracy.

Miki did not have to spell out for them what might happen if the LDP moved forward with a nonconfidence motion. He might exercise the constitutional prerogative of his office to dissolve the house and call new elections, which would effectively split the party into pro- and anti-Miki camps and leave it to the voters to decide which they preferred. Or he might try to forge an alliance with centrist forces in the Socialist and Democratic Socialist parties, split the LDP, and precipitate a basic realignment of the party system.

On the telephone, Miki recounted to me his meeting with Fukuda and Ohira in what sounded like a tone of both amusement and victory. He knew that party leaders would not risk a nonconfidence motion. He not only had called their bluff but in the process had given them an important civics lesson in parliamentary democracy. "Curtis-san," Miki told me, "I don't wish to be prime minister indefinitely. . . . But my responsibilities are to the Diet, not to the LDP. I, not the LDP, am prime minister of Japan."

The Opportunity Structure

This incident is a parable for some of the themes explored in the pages that follow. The analysis provided here about Japanese politics in the 1990s is about political skill, political institutions, and political reform— precisely the elements in the story of Miki and the LDP's attempt to drive him from office. It is a story of the tactics and strategies used by political leaders trying to obtain or hold onto political power within a particular institutional context.

The story's details are important. Politicians have an autonomy of choice. No two politicians will necessarily make the same decision when placed in the same situation. Theories that assume they do miss most of what is interesting, and important, about politics. Miki responded in a particular way to the efforts by other LDP leaders to force him to resign. Another politician might not have demonstrated the same steely resolve and accepted the demands of party leaders that he step down. Decisions made by individuals, as I emphasize throughout this book, are the direct cause of what happens in politics.

The tactical and strategic choices that individuals make in pursuit of their political objectives, what makes sense in terms of individual behavior, are not determined in a vacuum, however. They are constrained by a particular context: by the institutional framework, by domestic economic and social circumstances and the international environment prevailing at the time, and by historical experience, custom, and precedent. Taken together, these contextual factors create a particular complex structure of opportunities and constraints.

Opportunity structures obviously vary from one country to another. In different places, institutions differ,[3] and even where formal institutional structures are similar, there is a different history within which those institutions have evolved. There is no theory or methodology that offers a short cut to avoid grappling with the effects of complex and distinctive opportunity structures on the dynamics of political action. Much of the focus of the discussion in this book is on the interactions among politicians as they pursued their political objectives inside a particular Japanese structure of opportunities. It is a story of how politicians maneuver to exploit opportunities and how the context of their actions constrains the choices they make.

One theme that is emphasized in this book is how formal institutions, those that are stipulated by law, and informal institutions, those that are the product of custom and precedent, are linked in providing a context for political action. Linkage involves the use of informal institutions to circumvent constraints of formal ones, and of formal institutions to validate decisions made in the context of informal ones. The manner in which the Diet adopted electoral-system reform, analyzed in chapter 4, is an example of the latter—how formal institutions, in this case Diet committees, were used in an opportunistic way to validate decisions taken in informal settings. The development of *"kokutai* politics" explained in chapter 3 is an example of how systematized informal negotiations among government and opposition party leaders to manage the legislative agenda substitute for, or supplement, institutions bearing formal responsibility for dealing with such matters.

Japanese politics is characterized by an elaborate array of informal institutions. Yet, the formal structure of Diet committees, and for the most part the formal institutions established in the immediate postwar years when Japan was occupied by the United States, remain in place.

These formal institutions are neither irrelevant nor superfluous. Unlike other more legalistic societies, the Japanese have dealt with the problem of formal institutions that do not function as expected or as needed not by replacing them, but by innovating informal institutions to compensate for their inadequacies. Formal and informal institutions then become part of an integrated system, producing a complex matrix of institutions that is in some ways opaque. In Japan, this system facilitates adaptation to changed circumstances without necessarily going through the time-consuming and contentious process of legal reform.

Structure and History

Political action is constrained not only by a political system's particular institutional features, but by broad, historically evolved structural factors as well. When the Liberal Democratic Party came to power in 1955, Japan was a society divided into progressive and conservative camps, as discussed in the following chapter. Leaders of these two camps advocated antithetical policies on issues relating to the constitutional order and Japan's positioning in the bipolar international system of the cold war. They stood not only for different policies but also for different values. The quest to catch up with the West economically provided a powerful unifying national goal and a source of social cohesion in what was an ideologically divided polity.

By the time the LDP lost power in 1993, there was no cold war. Political competition no longer revolved around conflict between progressives and conservatives. Public attitudes were characterized by ambivalence about goals rather than by a consensus that the nation's energies should be concentrated on fostering rapid increases in the GNP. Political, bureaucratic, and intellectual leaders appeared incapable of defining new goals that the public found appealing and that could serve as a basis for political mobilization. Optimism that the twenty-first century would be Japan's had given way to a profound pessimism that Japan's best years were behind it and that the future would be worse than the present.

These shifts, across half a century, in basic features of Japanese society of course provided a changed context for political action. Broad, historically evolved structural change in Japanese society meant that how individuals perceived their environment and the political choices available to them would change. But these structural changes did not determine *how* individual behavior would change. Structures do not determine behavior, as Marxists and non-Marxist "structuralists" argue they do,[4] but behavior is determined within structures. Structures differentiate the "possible from the impossible and the likely from the less likely."[5]

This book is about autonomous individual action, institutional constraints, and structural pressures in shaping Japanese politics in the 1990s. Causation is a complex matter, however, and it is often impossible to specify the relative importance of institutions, the weight of history, or individual choice in determining particular outcomes. Distinctions can be fuzzy. Little is gained by an analysis that rigidly demarcates boundaries between individuals, institutions, and structures. The context within which individuals act can be so constraining that little room is afforded for the exercise of individual choice: structures themselves appear to have causal consequences. Under such circumstances, trying to have the last word on whether individuals caused something to happen or whether structural or institutional factors caused it to occur can degenerate into a rather pointless academic exercise in search of "independent" variables. It is one I avoid in favor of accepting the intrinsic complexities of causation and the need for an eclectic, synthetic approach.

Politicians and Politics

In the fall of 1975, about a year before my telephone conversation with Prime Minister Miki, I spent several months at the Royal Institute for International Affairs, Chatham House, in London. While I was there, a delegation of Diet members from the Japan Socialist Party visiting London came to Chatham House for a discussion with several of their British Labour Party counterparts.

The meeting came at a time when the LDP was reeling from scandals involving former Prime Minister Tanaka and worried about losing seats in the next lower house election. Several of the Socialist Party members talked about Japan's domestic political situation, explaining that the progressives would continue to close the gap with the conservatives, and that the Socialists would come to power in the relatively near future.

One British MP, after listening to the Socialist Party members' presentation, said he had only one piece of advice, if in fact the Socialists found themselves in control of the government: that was to be prepared to deal with a bureaucracy that would try to thwart every attempt they might make to bring about fundamental reform. That was the experience of the Labour government when it came to power after the Second World War, and it was the experience of every Socialist party on the Continent that came to power with the intention of reversing the policies of previous governments.

Bureaucrats everywhere are experts at defending their prerogatives and resisting efforts by their supposed political masters to impose new policies, he said. Japan, he assumed, was no different. "Whatever you try to do that breaks with precedent, the bureaucracy will try to sabotage," said this Labour MP. I do not recall much else about that meeting, but the bitterness with which this Labour Party member spoke of bureaucratic intransigence and in particular his use of the word "sabotage" left a powerful impression on me.

Sabotage in Tokyo

Almost twenty years later, I was in Tokyo having breakfast at a restaurant in the Hotel New Otani with a cabinet minister in the coalition government then led by Prime Minister Tomiichi Murayama, the Socialist Party chairman. Like many successful politicians in Japan and elsewhere, this cabinet minister was a terrific raconteur. He had an uncanny ability—another trait common among successful politicians—to analyze the political situation in which he was deeply enmeshed with a kind of outsider's detachment and wry humor. He now spent more than an hour telling me one story after another of the difficulties he was having trying to get control over the ministry he ostensibly headed.

If British ministers have trouble controlling senior bureaucrats who are adept at saying "Yes, Minister" while they resist implementing the changes that the minister has called for,[6] the situation is many times more difficult for ministers in Japan. There is no system of junior ministers or of political appointees to bureaucratic positions in Japan: the only politicians in government ministries are the minister and, depending on the ministry, one or two parliamentary vice-ministers. Ministers do not bring their own staff with them, but depend on the bureaucracy for expertise and support.

Bureaucrats in Japan (as elsewhere) as a rule try to avoid confrontations with their ministers, assuring them with the Japanese equivalent of "Yes, Minister" that the politician's wishes will be carried out while using their control over the bureaucratic machinery to thwart policies of which they do not approve. But in the unsettled politics of the 1990s, Japanese bureaucrats, sensing a policy-making vacuum, openly pressed their own policy agenda, as we shall note in later chapters.

The cabinet minister who was sharing with me his frustration in dealing with the senior bureaucrats in his ministry remarked: "I argue with them, but they have an argument to counter everything I say, and I have no one on my side whom I can call upon to help me out." On one occasion, after several meetings and long hours of debate, the minister told his senior bureaucratic staff that even if their position on the issue they were discussing had intellectual merit, there was no way that it could be sold to the political leadership. Whereupon one official spoke up to say that he had called on one of the LDP's senior politicians, a former prime minister, just the day before and the LDP veteran had expressed complete agreement with the position the bureaucrats were insisting upon. Another official followed by saying that he met with the LDP secretary-general. A third recounted his meeting with the head of the LDP's Policy Affairs Research Council, and yet another mentioned his discussion with one of the key leaders in the Socialist Party. The bureaucrats informed their minister that all these political leaders had indicated their understanding of the wisdom of the ministry's position. The officials had done their *nemawashi*, their informal consultations with key people in the political world, in their effort to isolate the minister and force him to change his position.

This minister then said to me that anyway he was not about to cave in; he would persevere and show the bureaucrats who was boss. He added that he was certain that they would do everything in their power to sabotage what he was trying to do. Although we were speaking in Japanese, he used the English word "sabotage," bringing back to me memories of the episode in London two decades earlier.

A few days after this breakfast meeting, I was on a bullet train to Nagoya with a well-known commentator on public affairs who is host of a Sunday morning television news-entertainment program. We were to have a discussion before an audience in Nagoya that was being taped for broadcast on a radio network and had agreed to meet on the train to plan what we would talk about.

No sooner had the train left Tokyo Station than this man said he had a curious meeting that very morning with two officials who worked for the minister with whom I had had breakfast only a few days earlier and who was scheduled to appear on his television program the following Sunday. When a cabinet minister is scheduled to appear for an interview, he said, bureaucrats from the ministry sometimes visit him ahead of time to brief him about the issues the minister is involved with and provide background materials. Their hope is that the interviewer will steer questions in a direction that the minister will feel comfortable with and that will make him look good. That morning, however, the bureaucrats who called on him did so in order to explain why the policy positions the minister was advocating were wrong. He took from his briefcase a sheaf of newspaper articles and other papers he said the officials had left with him. They were critical of the minister and supported the policy positions being advocated by the ministry's bureaucrats. It was the first time he could recall that bureaucrats had tried to influence him to make their minister look bad rather than look good. Ministry officials had been busy trying to sabotage their minister not only with the leaders of the parties in the coalition government but with the mass media as well.

The Logic of Politics

This episode was very much on my mind as I decided what themes to emphasize in this book. In today's writing about Japan by political scientists and foreign journalists, so little deals with politics. The popular press in particular conveys an image of Japanese politics in which bureaucrats dominate or where harmony and consensus prevail and policy making is little more than a process of collusion among the LDP, the bureaucracy, and the big-business community. Such stereotypes fail to capture what are intensely political relationships, whether between politicians and bureaucrats, the state and organizations in civil society, or within and between political parties and party factions.

The Japanese state, I suggest in the next chapter, can be characterized as "refractive," absorbing and responding to demands emanating from groups in civil society and from the electorate, but trying in the process to bend those demands into a shape that conforms as much as possible to the interests and the preferences of the managers of the state themselves. The "state," however, is hardly a unitary actor. There is competition within and among agencies in the bureaucratic establishment and among politicians as well as between politicians and bureaucrats. Social demands are not processed through corporatist arrangements in which peak organizations aggregate demands and negotiate government policies with representatives of the state. The structure on the demand side of the political market in Japan is pluralistic. In such a political system, tracing the policy process requires paying attention to power relationships, strategies, and trade-offs between relevant actors in society and in the state and within the state structure. Popular stereotypes of Japan, Inc. or of a "strong" state managed by like-thinking bureaucrats fail to capture the political quality of what is after all a political process.

Much writing about Japanese politics, especially in the popular press, also stresses the peculiarities and utter uniqueness of the Japanese way of doing things. Yet the story told above about relations between bureaucrats and politicians in Britain and Japan reminds us that there are underlying commonalities in the politics of modern democracies. These include, with the singular exception of the United States, prestigious and powerful bureaucratic institutions.

The alleged uniqueness of Japanese politics is less apparent than many people seem to think. It is magnified when Japan is compared with the United States, but that often has more to do with the distinctiveness of American political practices than Japanese ones. A powerful Congress, absence of a bureaucratic elite, and decentralization of education and many other governmental functions have set the United States apart from other advanced industrialized democratic countries, including Japan. Nonetheless, the view that Japanese politics is incomparably unique and that American practices constitute a universal norm is as popular among Japanese as it is among Americans.

Unique or not, politics in Japan is no more mysterious or enigmatic or resistant to systematic analysis than politics anywhere else. Once one gets inside Japanese institutions, the behavior of Japanese politicians and the dynamics of the Japanese political system reveal a particular logic. Politics in Japan makes sense in Japanese terms, and logical thinking can make sense of Japanese politics.

The Culture Issue

This book is about contemporary Japanese politics—about the struggles for power and control that take place within the opportunity structures created by the particular history and institutions of Japanese democracy. It emphasizes individual strategy, historical contingency, and institutional context. It is a book that I hope will leave the reader with a sense of the culture of Japanese politics. It is not a book that argues that culture explains Japanese politics.

Japan has a distinctive, sophisticated, complex culture that has evolved over the past nearly two millennia. It is one thing to appreciate Japanese culture and to recognize the cultural continuities that link Japanese who live today with Japanese who lived in the distant past. It is quite another to maintain that cultural analysis explains Japanese politics.

Culture does not explain why individuals make particular political choices. Japan in this century has experienced militarism and pacifism, authoritarianism and democracy. There was a two-party system in the 1920s, a coalition government for ten years after the war, one-party dominance for nearly forty years, and coalition government again in the 1990s. There have been times in Japan's modern political history marked by harmony and social peace, and periods where instability and conflict predominated. One of the standard Western-language works about Japanese politics in the 1930s was titled *Government by Assassination.*[7] Although Japanese place a high value on consensus building, the "spirit of harmony" *(wa no seishin),* and the avoidance of overt conflict, modern Japanese history is replete with intrigue, violence, and radical change. Culture cannot explain these variations unless one so devalues the concept that it stands for nothing more than whatever surfaces as the dominant pattern of social interaction at any particular point in time.

Sleeping on Money

Some Japanese observers, and many Japanese themselves, attribute to culture—to those values and patterns of social interaction that reach far back into history—behavior that is actually of quite recent vintage. Lifetime employment, for example, developed in Japan only after the First World War and became widely used by companies only after the Second. Labor-management cooperation and a low rate of strikes characterize the labor movement today. But if these harmonious patterns stem from culture, how does one explain the strife and violence and militancy that characterized Japanese labor-union dealings with management in the years following the end of the Pacific War? Clearly there is a different culture of labor-management relations today than there was in 1950, but culture fails to explain that difference. To say it does is only to say that culture explains culture and to engage in tautological, circular reasoning that goes nowhere.

Similarly, if there is one overpowering image of Japanese culture today, it is of the people as self-disciplined, orderly, frugal, and hard-working. Yet this image of Japan has far more shallow roots in Japanese "culture" than people sometimes realize. The historian Andrew Gordon offers a marvelous example.

Toward the end of the Meiji period, in 1908, a Japanese businessman named Sakutaro Kobayashi, at a company then called Tokyo Shibaura Denki, which later shortened its name to Toshiba, visited the United States. He returned to Japan impressed with the American work ethic and discouraged about Japan's economic prospects. For one thing, he was concerned about the lack of company loyalty in Japan and the stubbornness of Japanese workers. Young, well-educated workers, he wrote, would quit and move from factory to factory if they were not promoted rapidly. Elderly ones stubbornly refused to learn new things and relied only on past experience. "Teaching them anything is like trying to teach a cat to chant the nembutsu [Buddhist prayers]," he wrote.[8] American workers, Kobayashi discovered on his trip, followed rules, came to work on time, never loafed, and would every day seek to double their prior output. Americans also saved the money they made. "There is no such idiotic saying as that of the Edo artisan: 'Never sleep overnight on your money.' Everyone no matter what his income, works hard and tries to save."[9]

Americans now have the lowest savings rate of any industrialized country and Japanese are criticized for saving too much. To say that this is because their cultures changed is not to say very much. If American and Japanese cultures were different in 1998 than they were in 1908, the question is why and how did they change. And if "culture" can change so fundamentally in such a relatively short period of time, then how enduring is it?

What Culture?

Indeed, culture is constantly being redefined and reinterpreted in light of current realities, the observer's own prejudices, or in the service of political agendas. In popular discourse, culture is invariably treated in static terms, the essential something about a society that transcends time. America's culture is individualistic and Japan's is group-oriented, we are told.

How stable such perceptions are over time is another matter. Consider the following quote that reads as a rather typical assessment of Japan at the outset of its high-growth era in the late 1950s: "What is absolutely new about this society which is accomplishing such marvels is that in all its many aspects—even including idealism and religion—it is working toward the single goal of production. . . . Hence a growing tendency to reduce all virtues to the primordial ideal of conformity. . . . The nation is not individualistic in mentality. . . . [T]he enthusiasm of collective action in accomplishing stupendous tasks [is] so overwhelming, that in almost mystical abandon, other considerations are neither heeded nor missed."

The above quotation might read as a rather mainstream view of how culture has helped shape the modern Japanese economy, but it is not. It was written by a French author commenting not about Japan at all, but describing what he thought were the cultural features of the United States in the "roaring twenties."[10]

Giri Ninjō

Sometimes what people regard as being among even their most cherished cultural values are given short shrift when political interests are at stake. An incident told to me some years ago by Zentaro Kosaka, a longtime LDP Diet member who was foreign minister in the early 1960s, is a case in point. It concerns Prime Minister Tanaka's China policy. After President Nixon's unexpected opening of relations with China in 1972, the so-called "China shock," Prime Minister Tanaka decided to move quickly toward normalizing Japan's relations with Beijing. This upset the LDP's Taiwan lobby, which argued that Japan should not desert Taiwan, particularly since Chiang Kai-shek had not pressed Japan for reparations after the war and had taken a generally generous attitude toward his former enemy.

Kosaka, who was head of a special LDP committee on China policy at the time, asked Tanaka how he could contemplate deserting Taiwan and Chiang when Japanese attached such importance to values of *giri ninjō*, of obligation and human feeling. Tanaka replied instantly to Kosaka that "*giri ninjō* is important in relations among people, but the government has to consider what is in the best interests of the nation. We need to have relations with China. I'm going to recognize China." Culture did not stand in the way.

Cultural Pitfalls

An emphasis on culture can indeed get in the way of political analysis. Consider for example the following statement about practices in the Japanese Diet: "It is impossible to understand the reluctance of a parliamentary majority in democratic Japan to crush a minority unless one can see it as an extension of the attitude of the Japanese father toward the rest of the family, an attitude that stresses consensus and treats minority views cautiously."[11]

We shall leave aside the factual question of whether this is an accurate portrayal of the way the typical Japanese father treats the rest of his family. The point is that it is quite possible, and it is also important, to explain why the LDP, even when it had a solid majority of Diet seats, was reluctant to crush its opposition without introducing the culture of Japanese family life into the analysis.

The LDP made compromises with the opposition because it did not want to alienate voters or provoke the Socialists to resort to tactics that would paralyze the parliamentary process and make it difficult if not impossible for the government to pass any legislation. When the LDP was determined to get a particular piece of legislation through and willing to incur the political cost of doing so, it rammed it through *(kyōkō saiketsu)*. When Socialists were determined to prevent legislation from passing, they resorted to Diet boycotts and physically tried to prevent committee chairmen or the Speaker of the house from entering the Diet chamber. Fistfights were not an uncommon occurrence in the Japanese Diet in the 1960s; they do not occur any longer. A different culture prevails in the Diet today, but why that should be the case is what needs to be explained; to say that the culture changed does not explain anything.

The Civic Culture

Culture is defined in myriad ways.[12] While anthropologists agree that culture has something to do with social collectivities, political scientists have appropriated the term to characterize the aggregate of expressed "individual attitudes and orientations toward politics,"[13] mostly as measured by public-opinion surveys. Values and attitudes are important, but it is less confusing to refer to them as values and attitudes than as culture. Moreover, the causal relationship between attitudes and behavior is not unidirectional. Attitudes not only affect behavior; behavior also affects attitudes. Civic cultures, as has been pointed out by others, are made, not discovered.[14] The establishment of democratic institutions, for example, fosters behavior that can have a positive impact on people's belief in the legitimacy of their governmental institutions and their propensity to participate in politics. It can cause a change in values. The political reforms instituted in Japan during the postwar American Occupation had this impact. Institutional innovation created vested interests in the perpetuation of new institutions and their perpetuation over time affected attitudes and caused value change. There is an important reciprocal quality to the relationship between individual values and social behavior.

Values that do not change very much in the face of altered circumstances are probably too general to be of much use in explaining how individuals respond to these altered circumstances. Values that shift in response to changed circumstances cannot explain why those circumstances changed. The relationship between values and political behavior needs to be analyzed within specific contexts. Politics in Japan as elsewhere is a matter of people making choices. Those choices may be carried out in a style that accords with tradition-sanctioned patterns of behavior. But the choices themselves are not culturally determined.

The Uses of Language

Some years ago, during a lower-house election campaign, I stood on a street corner in Tokyo listening to a more than sixty-year-old six-time LDP incumbent give a short stump speech. The punch line of his speech was that getting elected to the lower house six times was like going to six years of elementary school. He had studied hard and he had learned a lot and he was ready to do more for his constituents. "Now," he implored his audience, "please graduate this elementary school student."

If an American politician who had spent six terms in the House of Representatives were to run an election campaign in which he said he felt like an elementary-school student ready to move on to junior high, voters would question his sanity. In Japan, however, this politician's plea—to a mostly elderly audience—to help him graduate elementary school amounted to an elaborate code language intended to remind them that he was still humble despite his success and had not forgotten who was responsible for allowing him to have such a distinguished career. (He subsequently won the election, "graduated," and went on to hold several important party and government posts.)

The strength of hierarchical arrangements in Japan and the expectation that one will be treated in a manner appropriate to one's status permits and encourages high-status individuals, such as the politician in this tale, to engage in public demonstrations of egalitarianism and humility more so than is often the case in other, less hierarchically ordered, societies. Company uniforms, communal eating and recreational facilities, and parking lots without special areas reserved for management are commonplace in Japanese corporations. In companies in the United States, there tends to be a greater use both of symbolic and material indicators of status precisely because status relationships are so ill defined.

Without knowledge of social structure and without an understanding of language and the ways in which language is employed to serve political ends, much about Japanese politics becomes exotic and enigmatic. A sensitivity to language and an understanding of Japanese social history does not, of itself, provide understanding of Japanese political life, but social scientists wielding even the most sophisticated methodological tools of their trade are not likely to discover much of significance without it. This is simply to say that knowledge of history and of language is necessary to get inside a society—to raise the curtain, as it were, on the stage of political action. "Cultural" knowledge in this sense is a prerequisite for understanding many aspects of Japan's political system, but it is not a substitute for it.

Politicians at the Center

The German political scientist Otto Kirchheimer, observing political party developments in the decade following the end of the Second World War, identified, and mostly lamented, the emergence of what he typed the "catch-all" party.[15] Kirchheimer argued that in postwar Europe, parties were losing their characteristic as the organizational weapon in the political sphere of large social movements such as labor—that they were no longer the agents of social integration and the propagators of distinctive political ideologies, as the greatest of them had been in the prewar period. He believed that parties more and more would endeavor to become broad-based people's parties. In order to do so, they would emphasize modern marketing techniques and downplay the importance of ideas and ideology in mobilizing people for political action. The implication was that catchall parties would become increasingly pragmatic and opportunistic and favor a kind of least-common-denominator appeal as a means to obtain support from as wide a range of voters as possible.

The trends that Kirchheimer identified have only grown stronger in subsequent years. Political parties have in a sense moved away from society, where they had represented particular social groups, to occupy a space between society and the state. From this intermediate strategic location, they design campaign strategies and policy proposals intended to draw the support of voters from across a wide political spectrum; they seek government policy outputs that enhance their ability to maintain and expand their catchall quality. Some writers recently have argued further that with extensive state financing of political parties, and the increased state oversight of parties and campaign practices that comes with it, political parties have gravitated ever closer to the state. This has enabled major parties in modern democratic systems to evolve a kind of "cartel" system in which they share the benefits of state support, lock other potential contenders out of the system, and become further removed from the voters who support them.[16]

The power of large, integrative interest groups has declined as the influence of narrow "special interests" has grown, as is discussed in the following chapter. Politicians cater to these special interests in order to obtain money and votes, but they do so as autonomous political entrepreneurs rather than as representatives of social groups seeking a political voice.[17] Rather than being the political representatives of large, powerful social forces, large, catchall parties try to represent all the "people." It is not surprising that they tend to make rather similar appeals to the people for electoral support. The difficulty involved in distinguishing the programs of Tony Blair's Labour Party from John Major's Conservative Party, for example, is indicative of this general phenomenon. The formation of a coalition government by the Liberal Democratic Party and the Japan Socialist Party also was possible because both parties claimed that they wanted to represent everyone.

The politicians' world, whether it be within the Washington, D.C. beltway or Tokyo's Nagata-chō, where the Diet is located, is to a considerable and increasing degree disassociated organizationally from the society to which it turns for electoral support. In popular perception, it is disassociated intellectually and emotionally as well. When Japanese refer to "*Nagata-chō no ronri,*" "the logic of Nagata-chō," and Americans talk about the way of thinking "inside the beltway," they are expressing the view that those who make their living there—including those in the media—see things differently from average people.

Politics as Business

Politicians in modern party democracies are political entrepreneurs, "a team of men seeking to control the governing apparatus by gaining office in a duly constituted election," as Anthony Downs put it.[18] Downs did not argue that politicians might not have multiple goals that they hoped to realize through political action. He posited a market theory of democracy to make a theoretical argument that politics in democracies could be analyzed in terms of the self-interested behavior of men seeking political power through election to public office. Downs's ideas have enjoyed a resurgence of popularity in recent years, not only because the political-science community has become infatuated with rational-choice theory, but because Downs's conception of a political marketplace is no longer only a theoretical construct but an all too evident empirical reality.

Modern democracies are political markets in a way and to a degree writers such as Kirchheimer and Downs had only an inkling forty years ago. Election campaigns have become an exercise in modern-marketing techniques. Politicians and political parties do not "represent" social groups; they try to sell their product—their policies, their leaders, their "brand name"—to enough people from enough groups to win elections. Politics is a profession and politicians are its professionals. Politicians and parties are situated outside of society in a sense busily trying to sell their product, and to manufacture a product that sells, to those inside it.

This does not necessarily mean that politicians and parties are not as responsive to the public, or that the system that gives them sustenance is less democratic than it was before the emergence of the catchall party and modern campaigning techniques. To the extent that politicians are determined to win elections and therefore to offer the electorate what they think will sell, the consumer, in this case the voter, is king just as much, or just as little, as he is in the economic marketplace.

The conceptual starting point for this analysis is that the voter is an object of political action by those who make politics their profession. This places voters in a reactive posture vis-à-vis politicians who hold public office. It is politicians who act and voters who react, not the other way around. Accordingly, politicians are at the center of the analysis in this book. They are there because politicians have become the focal point of modern democratic politics. This is as true in Japan as in every other mass-media-saturated, technologically advanced, affluent country in which political leaders are chosen through open and fair elections. This book then is an interpretative essay about contemporary Japanese politics that focuses on politicians and the institutions within which they operate.

The Appeal of Incrementalism

Throughout this book, I stress how the interplay of change and continuity in Japanese political development created resistance at all levels of the political system to anything more than cautious incremental policy adjustments. There has not been public support for radical departures in Japanese government policy, whether the issue relates to the economy or foreign policy. Nor has there been support for radical reform of Japan's basic economic and social organization. Some observers tend to emphasize the power of vested interests, bureaucratic intransigence, and corruption in preventing policy change. Their implicit assumption is that if these forces and pressures were not present, Japan would change. It would embrace massive deregulation, competitive labor markets, stringent enforcement of antitrust laws, and open markets, and would focus on the interests of consumers rather than producers. It would look more like the United States and less like Japan.

It is important not to let wishful thinking distort analysis of Japan's political and economic realities. There are powerful vested interests, there is bureaucratic intransigence, and there has been considerable political corruption. But resistance to radical change is anchored deep in Japanese society and its political institutions. Those leaders who have tried to make a case for drastic change have been notably unsuccessful in persuading many people to agree with them.

Japan's lifetime employment system is a case in point. In the late 1990s, the media both in Japan and in the United States paid excessive attention to evidence that was mostly anecdotal of the alleged crumbling of Japan's lifetime employment system. The argument that Japan must dispense with lifetime employment if it is to improve efficiency and be economically competitive in a global marketplace seemed to many to be self-evident.

Statistical data and careful academic analysis, however, suggest that the trend to working long years in one company in the 1990s was becoming stronger rather than weaker. There is an important story to be told, to be sure, about how lifetime employment is being modified by the introduction in some companies of more flexible wage and promotion policies and the forming of subsidiaries where lifetime employment rules do not apply. But on this issue, as one of Japan's leading labor economists has noted, there is a big gap between what people say is happening and what the data show.[19]

There is strong support among Japanese for the institutions that have brought postwar Japan economic growth with social stability and a fairly equitable distribution of income. No doubt Japanese confidence in these institutions has been shaken by the country's recent economic troubles. But there remains considerable resistance to dismantling institutions associated with the nation's postwar achievements no matter how much the argument is made that what were once associated with success are now, in Japan's mature economy, sources of weakness.

Japan in the 1990s has been characterized by a reluctance to part with past practices—by a kind of fear of flying into an unknown and potentially risky future. It also has been marked by public anger over the government's economic mismanagement and political corruption, and by a growing sense of alarm as Japan slid into its longest and deepest recession since the end of the Second World War. Political leaders reflected these conflicting sentiments, stressing the importance of radical reform while hesitating to adopt reformist policies. A curious combination of complacency and political turmoil comprised the two sides of Japanese politics in this decade.

The decade was ushered in by the bursting of the "bubble economy"— the sharp upward spike in real-estate and stock-market prices in the 1980s. At the beginning of the 1980s, the value of Japanese real estate was about equal to that of all the real estate in the United States; by the end of the decade, Japanese real estate was four times as expensive.[20] In the 1980s, Japan became the world's largest creditor nation, and the United States its biggest debtor. Nine of the ten largest banks in the world in 1988 were Japanese, and they had top credit ratings. Japanese business went on an investment binge. Purchases of Rockefeller Center, Hollywood movie studios, and prime real estate led to cries that Japan was buying up the United States. Investments in new factories in the United States and Southeast Asia and elsewhere gave rise to ominous warnings that Japan was out to dominate the world economy and was succeeding to the role long occupied by the Soviet Union as the greatest threat to U.S. national interests. Japanese leaders for their part boasted that they had devised a Japan Model of growth far superior to the model long championed by the economically troubled United States.

A few short years later, Japan found itself in serious economic trouble, and the United States was in the midst of an economic renaissance. Japan's real-estate values and its stock market—which saw the value of Japanese stocks increase eight times in the course of the 1980s—crashed in 1990 and 1991. By the end of the 1990s, fear that Japan was going to become the world's new economic hegemon had been replaced by warnings that Japan's weakness threatened to precipitate a world financial crisis. Dire predictions that Japanese economic problems would only grow worse unless government and industry embarked on a crash program of radical structural change were now as popular as forecasts of inevitable Japanese economic dominance were in the 1980s.

Japanese leaders themselves adopted the rhetoric of reform, but the rhetoric was far in excess of the reform policies they proposed. When the LDP government fell in 1993, a new coalition government led by Morihiro Hosokawa came to power on a platform of reform. But the only accomplishment it could claim for its reform agenda before it collapsed eight months later was a problematic revision of the electoral system.

The LDP was back in power less than a year after losing it, at first in coalition with its longtime antagonist, the Japan Socialist Party. In January 1996, after a year and a half with the Socialist Party chairman Tomiichi Murayama at the head of the coalition, the LDP's Ryutaro Hashimoto became prime minister. Hashimoto promised drastic reforms: to weaken the powers of the central government bureaucracy, strengthen local self-government, overhaul the education system, and deregulate the economy. But pressed by the Ministry of Finance to reduce the budget deficit and to restructure state finances to be better able to deal with Japan's rapidly aging population, the Hashimoto government's major reforms were to increase the consumption tax from 3 to 5 percent, terminate temporary income-tax cuts, and increase medical care and other user fees. It also sponsored a Fiscal Structure Reform Law that mandated annual decreases in the budget deficit and in the issuance of deficit financing government bonds and that consequently severely constrained macroeconomic policy. The result of these misguided policies was to abort Japan's economic recovery and further deepen its economic and financial problems. The policies also forced Hashimoto out of office in the aftermath of the LDP's disastrous performance in the July 1998 election for members of the upper house.

The public was cool to the reform rhetoric, furious about the consumption-tax increase, unnerved by Japan's growing economic problems, disillusioned by disclosures of corruption at the very center of the bureaucratic establishment, and unimpressed by the country's political leaders. The result, as we shall see later in these pages, was unprecedented volatility in voting behavior that in turn was reflected in rapid, bewildering changes in the party system. Parties appeared and disappeared with maddening rapidity. Some politicians grasped power only to lose it, while others whose careers seemed finished suddenly returned to prominence.

From 1989 to 1998, Japan had nine prime ministers; there had been only eleven over the previous thirty-four years. From 1955 to 1993, only one party, the LDP, was in power at the national level. Then during one year beginning in August 1993, every party in the Diet except for the Communists participated in one coalition government or another. The Socialist Party and the Sakigake, a small party of former LDP members, were part of the coalition that ousted the LDP from power in 1993, and part of the coalition that brought the LDP back to power less than a year later. Ichiro Ozawa, a major figure in the politics of this period, brought down the LDP in 1993 when he led his supporters out of the party. A year later, he engineered a merger of several parties to form the Shinshintō, or New Frontier Party, in an effort to create an essentially two-party system dominated by the NFP and the LDP. The NFP fragmented two years later, leaving Ozawa the head of a small new Liberal Party and still vowing to drive the LDP out of office and revolutionize Japanese politics. But in November 1998, as discussed in chapter 6, Ozawa and LDP president and prime minister Keizo Obuchi announced an agreement to form a LDP-Liberal coalition government. Ozawa and other former LDP members in the Liberal Party would now be joining forces with the party they had deserted a little more than five years earlier.

Opposition to the LDP now centered on the Democratic Party. This party came into existence just prior to the 1995 upper house election, when younger members of the Socialist Party and the Sakigake decided to band together to offer voters a new alternative to the LDP and New Frontier Party. After the NFP collapsed in January 1998, the Democrats welcomed into their ranks several of Ozawa's former colleagues. In 1999, as a result of these splits and mergers, there were five significant political parties in the

Japanese political system—the LDP and Liberal Party, the Democratic Party, the Komeito, and the Communist Party. The chart in appendix 1 illustrates the main lines of development of the party system from 1955 to 1999.

The purpose of this book is not to provide a political history of these and other political events, but to make sense out of them, and through them to explore important features of the Japanese political system. Some of these features have deep roots in Japanese political history; others are more recent innovations. Some institutions and procedures that are discussed are formally prescribed; others are more informal. Together they comprise a complex, dynamic, and changing political system.

Opportunities and perils alike await Japan in the twenty-first century. It remains to be seen whether political leaders will be able to arrive at policy decisions that will maximize opportunities and minimize risks or whether they will squander opportunities and instead compound the country's economic, social, and foreign-policy problems. What the government does will be determined in the context of Japan's democratic political institutions. The chapters that follow explore the structure of those institutions and the behavior of the people inside them.

Chapter One

The Politics of Complacency

Continuity and Change

In the late summer of 1993, the Liberal Democratic Party, Japan's governing party for thirty-eight years, suddenly found itself in the unfamiliar position of being in the political opposition. Power fell into the hands of a coalition that included every other party in the Diet, Japan's parliament, save the Communists. The toppling of the LDP from power seemed to offer new prospects for change. There was a charismatic leader in the person of Morihiro Hosokawa as the nation's prime minister and a palpable sense of excitement in the country as Japan seemed ready to turn to a new page in its political history.

The coalition collapsed in less than a year. The LDP returned to power in an alliance with the Japan Socialist Party and Sakigake, a small splinter party of former LDP members. The Socialist Party's chairman, Tomiichi Murayama, became prime minister. He remained prime minister for a year and a half, when the LDP's Ryutaro Hashimoto succeeded him as head of the LDP-JSP-Sakigake coalition government. The Socialists and Sakigake suffered devastating losses in lower-house elections in October 1996. They remained allies of the LDP, but withdrew from the cabinet. The LDP formed a single-party cabinet for the first time in more than three years.

In the course of these changes, parties opposed to the LDP, recently hailed as harbingers of a new politics in Japan, fragmented, reorganized, split, and merged again. It was virtually impossible to keep track of changing party names and party affiliations of Diet members. During a visit to Tokyo in April 1998, I was struck by the number of Diet members I met who had stopped indicating their party affiliation on their name cards. Some had changed parties five times in five years—for example from the LDP to the Shinseitō (Japan Renewal Party) to the Shinshintō (New Frontier Party) to the Minseitō (rendered in English as Good-Governance Party) to the Minshutō (Democratic Party). No doubt they had tired of printing new cards each time they changed their party label. More important, except for the LDP and the Communist Party, the only two parties keeping their names, party labels became virtually meaningless to the electorate.

The LDP's loss of power in 1993 was widely portrayed at the time as representing a dramatic rupture in Japanese politics. Overnight the party that for nearly four decades had monopolized political power at the national level was out of office. It was as though a great earthquake had shaken Japan's political world and had turned everything upside down. Stability had given way to uncertainty; predictability had been replaced by an unprecedented (at least in the living memories of most Japanese) volatility in political alignments. Hosokawa's coalition government seemed the immediate product of a sharp discontinuity in Japanese political history.

And yet, the political events in 1993 were not an abrupt break in Japan's political development. There was more continuity than met the eye. The collapse of LDP power was not caused by a sudden shift in Japanese voters' attitudes or in patterns of political support of powerful interest groups. It neither was preceded by nor did it precipitate social instability. Change in party power was accompanied by continuity in public policy.

When the LDP returned to power a year later, some observers concluded that nothing of lasting political importance had changed. After all, they argued, LDP Diet members remained bound to the special interests that had funded them in the past, and policy was once again in the hands of unelected bureaucrats.

LDP leaders themselves seemed to believe that they had got Japan back on its former political track. One by one, Diet members who had left the LDP to join one or another of the opposition parties began to return. In September 1997, these returnees made it possible for the LDP to recover the lower-house majority it had lost in 1993. With the opposition divided and seemingly unable to articulate a program the public found attractive, LDP leaders seemed confident that Japan had returned to a familiar system—a system in which the LDP was the natural party of government and the divided opposition was unable to convince the public it offered a credible alternative.

But the LDP's optimism was misplaced. Although it had regained power in 1994, the LDP could not put Japanese politics back on the same political track it had followed before Hosokawa became prime minister. The LDP's loss of control of the government to a seven-party coalition in the summer of 1993 was indeed the end of an era. The dynamics and the logic of the political system would be different in the future from what they were during the period of the so-called '55 system, the long era of LDP dominance that began in 1955 when the conservative parties came together to form the LDP and the right and left wings of the Socialist Party (which had formed separate parties in 1951) reunited.

In July 1998, the LDP's eyes were opened to Japan's new political realities. It had gone into a campaign for an upper-house election to be held that month, anticipating that it might win the sixty-eight seats needed to recover a majority that it had lost in 1989. If it succeeded, it would no longer need alliances with opposition parties in the upper house to pass legislation. Its recovery would be complete.

The election (discussed in greater detail in chapter 6) was a disaster for the LDP. The voting rate was fourteen points higher than in the previous upper-house election. Voters who had abstained before turned out to cast votes against the LDP. Instead of winning a majority, or obtaining the sixty-one seats that would have kept the LDP at its pre-election strength in the upper house, it won only forty-four seats. It was the LDP's worst performance ever in an upper-house election.

Prime Minister Hashimoto immediately resigned. The new LDP government of Prime Minister Obuchi seemed painfully aware that the public was now truly frightened by Japan's economic and financial problems, and furious with the LDP for failing to take adequate steps to deal with them. Obuchi brought former Prime Minister Miyazawa into the cabinet to be minister of finance, to spearhead a new effort to solve Japan's banking crisis and get the economy growing. This was the first time a former prime minister had returned to serve in another prime minister's cabinet since before the Second World War.[1] Suddenly the LDP was on the defensive, and the opposition parties were looking forward to a lower-house election, hoping to defeat the LDP there as well. Japan's political future was more uncertain than ever.

There are many dimensions to an explanation of why Japan found itself in this economic predicament and at this political impasse. This chapter tells the story of one of them. It is a story of how Japan's success in accomplishing its postwar goal of rapid economic development produced attitudes and political interests that sustained a politics of complacency through most of the 1990s. Precisely at a time when Japan needed policy change, its politics produced a consensus in favor of the status quo.

That consensus did not begin to unravel until near the end of the decade, making problems that might have been handled with relative ease if they had been confronted earlier all that more difficult and painful to solve. Throughout the 1990s, the public mood was cautious about change. There seemed to be a strong feeling that a period of fiscal austerity and low growth was the inevitable price to be paid for the excesses of the bubble economy. It was not until late in the 1990s, when it was no longer possible to deny that Japan's financial system was tottering on the brink of disaster and when all indicators made it painfully clear the economic situation was becoming worse rather than better, that this mood began to change. Government policy was no longer seen as squeezing excess out of the bubble but as squeezing life out of the economy.

Even then, there was a palpable resistance to fundamental structural change. There was, and there remains today, an ambivalence in the Japanese public mood. Most people are satisfied with their present circumstances, as we shall show later in this chapter, and averse to taking risks. But satisfaction with the present is combined with anxiety about the future. People wish things to remain as they are, and at the same time fear for the future if things do not change. The public mood is inherently contradictory: it favors change to the extent it helps retain the status quo. This chapter offers an interpretation of how politics evolved to create this situation.

The Progressive Challenge

The LDP's return to government in alliance with the Japan Socialist Party in 1994 spelled the definitive end to an era in which political competition pitted conservatives against progressives. This conservative-versus-progressive division was the defining feature of the '55 system. In 1960, Edwin O. Reischauer, then a professor of Japanese history and politics at Harvard University, published an article in *Foreign Affairs* entitled "The Broken Dialogue with Japan." The dialogue that Reischauer had in mind was not with the leaders in the LDP who held political power, but with the Socialists, intellectuals, college students, and public figures who were opposed to the LDP. These were "the would-be ideological pathfinders and the generation to which the future Japan belongs," Reischauer wrote, and their anti-Treaty actions were "a sign of a huge current of discontent with Japanese society—a frustration with present trends and a strong sense of alienation."[2]

The reason why the United States needed a dialogue with these anti-LDP elements, and presumably one reason why President Kennedy chose Reischauer to be the U.S. Ambassador to Japan, was that their voices were going to grow increasingly important in Japanese political life. "There is little prospect that their views will prevail in Japanese politics in the immediate future," Reischauer wrote, "but their victory at some future date seems not just possible but probable."[3] The Socialists and the Democratic Socialists "have a capacity for growth" and they "may prove to be the political wave of the future."[4]

The late 1950s and the 1960s were years of intense, bitter, sometimes violent ideological conflict in Japan. The sociologist Herbert Passin, surveying Japan's protest movements in 1962, opined that "this quality of all-out, uncompromising struggle is the most disturbing feature of the political climate of Japan today."[5] Japan was divided into two political camps advocating antithetical policies and ideologies. The LDP was committed to overturning the constitutional order imposed by the American Occupation. Its platform called for a sweeping revision of the constitution and it pressed vigorously if mostly unsuccessfully in the early postwar years to undo reforms sponsored by the American Occupation and to reintroduce features of the prewar political system. These efforts reached a peak in 1958 when Prime Minister Kishi attempted to expand powers of the police that had been curtailed by Occupation reforms. This provoked strikes and workshop rallies by some four million workers, protests from the press, and a Socialist boycott of the Diet. These activities amounted to the largest protest in postwar Japan up to that point and served as a "dress rehearsal" for anti–Security Treaty protests that would soon follow.[6]

As the LDP tried to push the political system back into more familiar and comfortable institutional and ideological patterns of the prewar period, the Socialists tried equally hard to pull it in the opposite direction. Marxism was the dominant ideology in the party and among Japanese intellectuals and college students, and also in the leadership of Japan's most powerful labor union federation as well. To be a college student in the 1960s in Japan was to be "progressive" in terms that French or Korean students would immediately understand. Marxism and a radical leftist political culture dominated Japanese intellectual life. The leftist camp included not only a large, militant student movement (the *zengakuren*), but also powerful citizens' movements against nuclear weapons and other mass movements linked to the Socialist or Communist parties.

Reischauer was not alone in believing that the progressives represented Japan's future. Prevailing Japanese opinion was much the same. In 1963, one of the LDP's then-popular young leaders published a much commented upon article in the journal *Chūō Kōron*. In it he argued that current economic and social trends, by spreading higher education among the masses and forcing wide-ranging changes in the occupational structure, were weakening LDP bases of support and would bring the Socialists to power within the decade.[7]

The LDP's support base was in the old middle classes of farmers, merchants, and the owners of, and workers in, family businesses and small manufacturing companies. The party was supported predominantly by middle-aged and older voters and by voters with relatively low educational levels. The Socialist Party was the party of choice for the modern sectors of Japanese society: organized blue-collar workers in Japan's large enterprises, the rapidly growing white-collar "salaryman" class, intellectuals and college students whose numbers had mushroomed thanks to the American Occupation's reform of Japan's higher-education system, and more generally the young, the urban, and the well-educated.[8] Given the rapid economic growth and concomitant social changes occurring in Japan, it seemed only a matter of time before power would shift from the tradition-bound conservatives to the modern progressive camp and change the face of Japanese politics.

The LDP Response

Predictions of the LDP's imminent demise proved premature. The LDP's determination to hold onto political power caused it to retreat from its revanchist program. It became a party committed to a policy of making cautious, incremental adjustments in the status quo as necessary to retain power. There were ideologues in the party to be sure, but the party leadership was not about to let ideology stand in the way of retaining control of the government. By the end of the 1970s, the LDP had successfully transformed itself from a traditional conservative party into a modern catchall party. It drew more support from all social strata than any other party, including industrial workers, who up until the early 1970s had supported the Socialists over the LDP.[9]

Partly because the society was so deeply divided over other issues, the LDP put great emphasis on the unifying themes of economic recovery, rapid industrial growth, and what amounted to a virtual ideology of "GNPism." The energies of this ideologically bifurcated society were mobilized in a most impressive manner to pursue a goal with which nearly everyone could agree: the century-long quest to "catch up with and overtake the West." As long as a consensus on the priority of growth prevailed, it provided guideposts to give direction to government policies and to measure the effectiveness of those policies.

The power of a consensus on growth to drive politics declined over time. It is not that Japanese no longer wanted their economy to be strong and to grow ever larger; rather, as double-digit growth rates sustained for more than a decade catapulted the Japanese economy into a new and higher orbit, it no longer was so evident what economic "success" meant, or what policies were most appropriate to attain it.

GNPism was an ideology that focused on aggregate national indicators of economic progress, on the *gross* national product. By the 1970s, however, Japan's emergence as an economic power, as well as environmental damage created by rapid industrialization, drew the public's attention not just to measures of overall national economic performance but to indicators of affluence as well. Arguments that affluence meant improved welfare services, cleaner air and water, better housing and urban infrastructure, and greater attention to consumer interests began to undermine the consensus on GNPism, even as it kept Japanese attention focused on economic issues. The growing salience of these so-called quality-of-life issues made the policy agenda far more complex than at the beginning of the '55 system.

From a Two-party to a Multiparty System

In the 1950s, Japanese politics was dominated by two parties, the LDP and the Japan Socialist Party. In the 1958 lower-house election, the first following the 1955 party mergers, the LDP won 58 percent and the Socialists 33 percent of the popular vote. The Communist Party obtained less than 3 percent, the remaining 6 percent of the vote going to an assortment of minor parties and independents aligned with the LDP. The competition between the LDP and the Socialists was not only over particular policy issues such as the U.S.-Japan Security Treaty, but also over basic values, a competition the sociologist Joji Watanuki characterized as Japan's "cultural politics."[10] The LDP represented conservatism and tradition; the JSP was the self-proclaimed voice of what was modern and progressive.

In subsequent decades, even as the basic conservative-progressive framework of the '55 system remained in place, within the opposition camp new parties emerged that tried to position themselves nearer the broad center of the Japanese political system. In 1986, the combined vote for the LDP and the JSP had declined to 66.6 percent, from the 91 percent they commanded in the 1958 election. Through the 1970s and the 1980s, there were five major parties—the LDP, the JSP, the Komeito, the Democratic Socialist Party, and the Japan Communist Party—and several other parties such as the New Liberal Club and the United Social Democratic League. The '55 system had shifted from a two-party to a multiparty format.

All opposition parties defined their goal to be to drive the LDP out of power, but social change gradually forced most of them to break away from the promise of fundamental, radical change made by the Socialist Party in the early years of the '55 system. By the late 1980s, opposition party leaders were trying to reassure the public they were as pragmatic as the LDP and would not change the nation's basic domestic and foreign policies if they came to power. This stance, while necessary to appeal to a public that did not favor basic policy change, presented the opposition parties with a serious problem of deciding what they did favor. Not surprisingly, they emphasized their commitment to bring about political reform, attacking the LDP not so much for the policies it pursued as for the way it behaved.

This shift in the opposition camp's political agenda was a response to the declining salience of conflicts that had been prevalent in postwar Japanese society. In the course of its rapid economic development, Japan had become a society remarkably free of wrenching social cleavages. Japan's postwar economic success and the emphasis that was placed on public policies that contributed to maintaining a relatively equitable distribution of income through the rapid-growth era[11] dramatically weakened perceptions of class differences. The overwhelming majority of Japanese thought of themselves as part of a large middle mass.[12] They became increasingly indifferent to class-based appeals.

Many observers in the fifties and sixties thought conflict between traditional and modern values would intensify and bring the progressives to power. But as Japanese developed their economy, they showed that "tradition" and "modern" were not antithetical but more compatible concepts than many people had assumed. Japan's "cultural politics" moderated and then virtually disappeared as Japan successfully modernized on its own terms.

By the 1980s Japan was rich, and Japanese levels of life-satisfaction were unusually high. The image of densely populated, highly urbanized metropolitan areas, constituting a mass society of alienated individuals disgruntled over high consumer prices and "rabbit hutch" housing, could hardly have been at greater variance with the realities of urban life in Japan. Japanese were more likely to compare the quality of their lives with what they knew in the past than with what they were told was the situation among middle-class people in the United States. Especially for Japanese old enough to remember what it meant to be poor, there was more to appreciate and to hold on to than to complain about. In a 1982 poll among residents in Tokyo, 83 percent of respondents expressed positive feeling about their city.[13] Even much later, with the economy in serious trouble, when asked what issues they were most concerned about, only 9.2 percent mentioned prices.[14] In a 1996 nationwide survey of ten thousand people twenty years of age and older, 72.8 percent indicated that they were completely or mostly satisfied with their lives. This was the highest level of satisfaction ever recorded in this poll—one conducted annually; the percentage in 1996 was higher even than that in 1988, when at the height of the bubble economy 64.6 percent of respondents said they were completely or mostly satisfied with their lives.[15]

This particular annual survey offers another interesting datum. Although life-satisfaction was as high or higher in the 1990s than in earlier years, pessimism about the future was greater than ever before. The percentage of respondents who said they expected their lives to be better in the future steadily declined from 1987 to 1997. In 1987, 21.8 percent of respondents said life would get better. A decade later (1997) this figure was 12.7 percent. Those who thought things would get worse increased from 14.2 percent to 21.8 percent over this period. In another poll taken in May 1998 that asked whether Japan was heading in a good or a bad direction, three out of four respondents (72.2 percent) said it was heading in a bad direction. This pessimism index was higher in 1998 than ever before, up from 55.5 percent just one year earlier.[16]

The Decline of Party Loyalties

Social changes over time had forced traditional antagonisms between mutually suspicious conservative and progressive camps to recede and pushed politics to converge at the center. These social changes benefited the LDP in the 1980s, but they also made possible its ouster from power a few years later. In the 1986 lower-house election, the LDP won a larger share of the popular vote than in any election over the preceding twenty years. However, this did not reflect newfound public enthusiasm for the LDP; rather, its success was largely the consequence of the failure of any of the opposition parties to convince voters that it offered an attractive alternative to continued LDP rule. The LDP had become a strong party of weak supporters, its victory in the 1986 election coming in the context of declining public identification with any political party.

A decline in political partisanship among Japanese voters affected all segments of society and it meant that voting patterns were potentially volatile. The upper-house election in 1989 illustrated that volatility in dramatic fashion. Public anger over a new 3 percent consumption tax and the popularity of Takako Doi, the new female chair of the Japan Socialist Party, resulted in the LDP losing its upper-house majority for the first time. Public opinion polls measured an 11 percent drop in LDP popularity compared with 1986 and a 12 percent increase in support for the JSP. The decline in LDP support was uniform across nearly all social strata. The highest percentage drop—15 points between 1986 and 1989—was among farmers, the traditional bedrock of LDP support.[17]

Dealignment continued to characterize the Japanese electorate as Japan entered the 1990s. The "non party supporting strata" (*mutōhasō*) now outnumbered those supporting all political parties taken together. In a 1995 *Jiji* wire-service poll, for example, only 23 percent of voters supported the LDP. Support for the JSP was but 8 percent. No other party gained as much as even 3 percent of public support. More than 55 percent of respondents said that they supported no party.[18]

In spring 1998, before the July upper-house election, the LDP's support rating hovered around 30 percent. Support for all other parties was in the single digits. A clear majority of voters continued to support no party. In a *Yomiuri Shimbun* April 1998 poll, 29.3 percent of respondents supported the LDP. No other party received as much as 5 percent support. Those who supported no party totaled 54.4 percent.[19] In an *Asahi Shimbun* poll taken a month later, the figures were similar: 31 percent support for the LDP, 5 percent for the Democrats, and less than that for the other parties.[20] A panel survey covering the period 1993–1996 found that only a quarter of the sample consistently identified with the same parties in this period.[21]

These figures indicated that more people identified with the LDP than with any other party. Indeed, the total percentage of people who supported all other parties together was lower than the percentage who said they supported the LDP. But the most significant figure was the more than 50 percent who identified with no party at all. In the 1998 upper-house election (see the final chapter of this book) these nonparty identifiers and the LDP's own "weak supporters" turned out to bring down the Hashimoto government.

Electoral Reform and Social Change

In 1994 the Diet passed legislation providing for a new electoral system. For many years Japan had a system in which members of the lower house were elected in multimember districts. The new system that came into force in December 1994 provided that three hundred lower-house members would be elected in single-member districts and another two hundred in eleven regional proportional-representation districts. It was adopted in the expectation that it would lead to the emergence of a two-party system in Japan.

The history of electoral reform and the particulars of this new system are discussed in chapter 4. The impact this reform has had on Japanese politics is a theme that threads its way throughout this book. Although the reform did not bring about the kinds of political changes its proponents said it would, the new electoral system changed the dynamics of the party system in important ways, and it changed the way social groups had been represented politically under the '55 system.

The old system of multimember districts in which each voter cast one ballot generated intraparty conflict when a party ran more than one candidate in a district. It also permitted small parties to survive since their candidates could win seats in some districts with as little as 15 percent of the vote, and sometimes even less. Interestingly, but not much appreciated in Japan, this electoral system reflected and represented Japan's particular type of political pluralism. Japan is a socially homogeneous country that has become an advanced industrialized democracy. Its occupational structure is characterized by differentiation and specialization. It has mass higher education and it is an urban society with a small but politically powerful agricultural sector. These features of modern society make for a system of political pluralism, but it is one that lacks the "primordial" social cleavages so common elsewhere.

Farmers, urban salarymen, owners of small businesses, medical doctors, and others have divergent interests and they organize to protect and advance those interests. Under the '55 system, given the LDP's umbrella-like character, the absence of strong racial, ethnic, religious, or regional cleavages, and strong Marxist influence and labor-union power in the JSP, most interest groups gravitated toward the LDP. Since LDP members ran against each other in multimember districts, however, they tended to look to different coalitions of interest groups for support as a way to compete against their party colleagues. This introduced an important element of competition within the structure of the LDP itself, giving rise to the policy tribe, or *zoku*, phenomenon discussed later in this chapter. Since this electoral system also enabled small parties to survive, it made it possible for interests that were not inside the LDP tent to find a political voice through one or another of the opposition parties.

The new electoral system created single-member districts and pressures for party consolidation. With the elimination of intraparty competition, the incentives for LDP candidates to align more with some interest groups than others became weaker. The new electoral system, however, rather than encouraging the development of a party system that reflected in a new manner Japan's political pluralism, instead compounded the problem of differentiating one party from another.

A party that simply claimed to be another pragmatic catchall party like the LDP was unlikely to generate mass support. Unlike the situation in Britain and elsewhere, where long-established parties of the left were able to retain the support of people who traditionally had supported them while they became more catchall-type parties, a new party could not draw on a bloc of loyal voters to support it out of habit if not conviction. If a new party talked like the LDP and walked like the LDP, then there seemed to be little reason for voters not to continue to support the LDP. On the other hand, if it called for a program of political action that the public did not support, it would be consigning itself to minority status. The '55 system had evolved from a two-party to a multiparty system. The introduction of a new electoral system precipitated the collapse of that party system, but its initial impact, as we shall see, was to generate pressures both for party consolidation *and* fragmentation. The resultant political turmoil to a considerable extent immobilized policy making.

Institutional Rigidities

Many political leaders, whether in the LDP or in the opposition, are adept at talking in cliché-ridden terms about the need for political reform, administrative reform, decentralization, and deregulation. As the 1990s unfolded, Japanese leaders argued that Japan faced a challenge as momentous and difficult as the challenges that confronted the nation at the time of the Meiji Restoration and in the aftermath of defeat in the Second World War. And yet, despite this rhetoric, the main lines of public debate about policy change were characterized by caution and indecisiveness. The public mood was characterized by ambivalence, the party system was in flux, a new electoral system left political leaders uncertain how best to cast their appeal to the voters, and the issues Japan faced were complex. Admittedly, some of the problems these factors produced were not unique to Japan. Kevin Phillips's comment in 1990 that American politics was "rudderless on a sea of compromise, caution and confusion"[22] was an apt characterization of the Japanese scene as well. But the fact that Japan's political problems might not be unique did not make them any less serious. Nor did it mean Japanese politics was not "rudderless" in a particular, Japanese way.

Economic growth and social and political changes had transformed Japanese society; now they would test the adaptability of Japanese institutions. Japan has a well-earned reputation for pragmatic adaptation to prevailing trends. Yet in the 1990s, Japanese government and business institutions appeared more inflexible than the image of an ever-adaptable and pragmatic Japan would suggest. In the private sector, some companies adjusted to the new global economy with impressive skill, but many others did not. In a book published in 1986, Ronald Dore lauded Japan's "flexible rigidities," arguing that Japanese institutions such as the system of lifetime employment, oligopolistic arrangements, union monopolies, an active government industrial policy, and so on had proven their ability to foster change and to adjust to new circumstances.[23] Only a few years later, these rigidities looked much less flexible. There seemed to be far more continuity than change.

Cautious Reformers

Why did institutional innovation fail to keep pace with the changing society these institutions were meant to serve? One reason was that arguments in favor of institutional reform were necessarily abstract and speculative, whereas the threat that change posed to those whose interests were served by maintaining existing institutions was immediate and concrete. Vigorous in opposing reform were both bureaucratic agencies anxious to prevent an erosion of their power and interest groups with stakes in the existing system.

The influence exerted by interest groups, bureaucrats, and other opponents of reform, however, was only partially responsible for creating a situation in which political leaders pursued policies of compromise and equivocation while paying deference to the principles of reform. Just as important was the ambivalent attitude of leaders themselves on the reform issue. American government officials proposed deregulated, open markets and permanent tax cuts as the way to restore Japan's economic health, but few political leaders in Japan shared this American enthusiasm for free-market reform and an unrestrained embrace of stimulative fiscal policy measures. Yet they offered no alternative program of their own, limiting themselves to incremental, cautious modifications of existing policy.

Political leaders might have been more aggressive in pursuing a reform agenda had they thought they would increase their public support by doing so. The most important factor inhibiting institutional innovation and structural reform was public skepticism that radical reform would improve the lives of ordinary Japanese. Although the press painted an increasingly bleak picture of Japan's economic condition in the 1990s, it was hard to find evidence that the Japanese public embraced the view that the nation was in economic crisis. Even late in 1998, with the public now deeply worried about deteriorating financial and economic conditions, there was little evidence of a groundswell of enthusiasm for fundamental change. The Japanese public wanted to see policies change to stabilize the financial system and get the economy growing again, but as suggested earlier there was no evidence that many people wished their leaders to perform radical surgery on the postwar system.

It is not difficult to understand why the public was caught in this conservative mindset. Japan's postwar political and social institutions were associated with half a century of social harmony and economic success in a land previously wracked by social conflict, controlled by a militarist government, and ruined by war. Success tends to make people risk-averse, and Japan's postwar "miracle" made many Japanese cautious about proposals for radical institutional innovations with unpredictable consequences. Thus in Japan in the 1990s there was a disconnect between public opinion that was risk-averse and the rhetoric of political leaders who argued for reform. The minority of political leaders who advocated fundamental, drastic political and economic changes were not reflecting public opinion, and their arguments seemed to make little headway in changing public opinion.

The LDP appeared to be the major beneficiary of this situation. Its leaders, too, voiced the importance of reform. Prime Minister Hashimoto came into office promising to reform everything from the bureaucracy to the educational system. His government, however, proceeded cautiously with implementing his reform program. It had to deal with a bureaucracy that resisted change. It needed to balance competing interests and avoid alienating any key constituency in its broad social base. And very few LDP leaders embraced wholeheartedly a free-market ideology in any case. The LDP was criticized by the media for taking only halfway measures, but as the decade drew to a close there was scant evidence that the public wanted enacted a much more vigorous reform program.

At its core, this LDP indecisiveness was a policy response to public ambivalence. One might argue that leadership means to educate and lead public opinion and not simply to follow it. But to lead means to know where you wish to go. It means having long-term goals. Japanese leaders, however, were still trying to accustom themselves to the reality that they no longer had to pursue the goal to catch up with the West that their Meiji forefathers had set out as the great national project a hundred years before. Many of the institutions of the postwar Japanese political economy structured to encourage rapid modernization were not necessarily suited to managing a mature economy. Changing these institutions however, was a political challenge more than a technical problem, and it would not be met until a new "post-catch up" consensus had been forged.

The Pillars of Policy Making

There were four crucial pillars supporting the '55 system. One was a pervasive public consensus in support of policies to achieve the catch-up-with-the-West goal. A second was the presence of large integrative interest groups with close links to political parties. The third was a bureaucracy of immense prestige and power. And the fourth was a system of one-party dominance. Just to list these features of the '55 system is to indicate how profoundly Japan changed in the 1990s. All of these pillars of policy making had either weakened or crumbled.

As Japan approached the end of the century, it was not clear what would replace these key elements of the policy-making system. There still was no public consensus on goals. Interest groups did not divide in any coherent fashion in terms of the political parties they supported or the broad economic policies they favored. The bureaucracy's prestige had never been lower or its power more threatened, and there was a dearth of other institutions capable of formulating policy. One-party dominance had ended and the party system was in a state of flux. The rest of this chapter traces the process that led to this state of affairs.

Collapse of the Postwar Consensus

Postwar parties, policies, and decision-making structures rested on a foundation of strong public support for rapid industrialization and "GNPism." Because this consensus existed, the Japanese government could implement policies that promoted high rates of savings and low interest rates on bank deposits, kept domestic consumer prices high by protecting Japanese markets against foreign competition while offering incentives to Japanese industry to expand market share in foreign markets, and encouraged cartels and restraints on "excessive competition." These policies were not adopted in the face of public opposition; they enjoyed widespread public support.

The overarching Japanese public consensus behind economic growth produced what Prime Minister Ikeda in 1960 called a "low posture" on foreign affairs and low spending on defense. Japanese focused their energies with single-minded concentration on growing the economy and on raising everyone's standard of living. The Japanese government determined to disprove the thesis that rapid economic growth necessarily aggravates income disparities. It adopted a steeply progressive income tax and designed an elaborate array of public subsidies, especially for farmers, and extensive public works programs that amounted to a huge incomes-transfer policy. The Japanese "miracle" was not that Japan grew rapidly, but that it grew rapidly while fostering social equality.

The public consensus on growth depoliticized a great deal of what in other countries are the most politically contentious issues of policy making in the economic sphere. As long as Japan pursued the goal of entering the ranks of the world's great economies, questions of priorities and specific approaches were treated largely as administrative rather than political matters. The bureaucratic agencies engaged in this policy making, especially the Ministry of Finance and International Trade and Industry, were expected to design policies that would make it possible for Japan to achieve its goal, and they were given great latitude to do so.

The public consensus on growth also defined the tasks of political leaders. These leaders played an important role in mediating relations between the bureaucracy and powerful interest groups and in resolving interministerial conflicts; they forced adjustments in spending on public works and in tax and other policies, thus insuring continued support for the LDP from important electoral constituencies; and they made changes in the overall policy agenda as necessary to keep Japan moving toward its target. Prime Minister Tanaka in the early 1970s laid out a blueprint to remodel the Japanese archipelago[24] and sponsored stringent antipollution legislation and a major expansion in state welfare services. He did so not to move away from the "catch up" public consensus but to sustain it. The overall direction of policy making in Japan's political economy was in the hands of political leaders, not professional bureaucrats.

In the 1990s, Japan's success in achieving its economic development goals confronted it with very different challenges. Yet no political leader seemed able to articulate a vision of the Japanese future that the public found compelling. Ozawa's vision of Japan as a "normal" country more like the United States or Britain was more popular with American journalists and public officials than with the Japanese public.[25] The idea of Japan as a "great civilian power" failed to capture the imagination of a public that was nervous about Japan abandoning its "low posture" in foreign policy to seek "greatness" once again, with or without military power.[26] The opposite notion, that Japan should be a "small and sparkling" environmentally conscious, postindustrial state that rejected involvement in great-power politics also failed to generate much interest.[27] Nor was there public enthusiasm for Japan finding its place in the sun as a leader of Asia and exponent of Asian values:[28] the suggestion brought forth too many unhappy memories of Japan's earlier attempt to lead Asia.

By the end of the 1990s, political and business leaders and the mass media were claiming that Japan had to emulate the American model to survive, but the public remained skeptical. No doubt many people were shocked by the resurgence of the U.S. economy, coming as it did just a few years after Japanese leaders had been disparaging the United States for having caught a malady more severe than the "British disease." But there was far less enthusiasm for the "American Dream" in the nineties than in the early postwar period when it was not just raw American economic power but American culture and way of life that Japanese found so fascinating and worthy of emulation. The Japanese public mood was to want things to change as little as possible, and no political leader had convinced people to think otherwise.

Japan Sinks

In the early 1970s, Sakyo Komatsu's science-fiction novel about how a massive earthquake literally sinks Japan—*Nihon Chinbotsu (Japan Sinks)*—became a runaway best-seller.[29] The expression *Nihon Chinbotsu* became a metaphor for all the perils that face Japan—economic, social, political, external and domestic, as well as the forces of nature. The idea that Japan would sink, doomed unless it changed fundamentally, exerts a powerful hold on the Japanese imagination, or at least on the imagination of Japanese opinion leaders. There has been a steady stream of popular books that are part of a "sinking discourse" *(chinbotsuron)* for the past quarter of a century.

Unlike Americans, who find common purpose in talking positively and optimistically about building bridges to the future, Japanese seem to tap the energy for change by ruminating about the dangers of falling behind, of failing to build that new bridge in time. Perhaps rhetoric about the perils that lie ahead if Japan does not change fundamentally is needed to build the kind of broad consensus that makes even incremental change possible. After all, even at the two previous major turning points in modern Japanese history, when no one doubted the nation faced a crisis, a consensus on what to do was not quickly forthcoming. Roughly a quarter of a century after Perry's "black ships," Meiji leaders put in place the basic policies to create a "rich nation and strong army" *(fukoku kyōhei)* to ward off Western imperialism and make Japan itself into a great imperial power. After the Second World War, Japan renounced its militarist past, but it was only because of the unique circumstance of its being under the authority of Occupation forces that were determined to impose democracy that many democratic reforms, including a new constitution, were adopted.

Only time will tell whether the wide divide between predictions of sure calamity if Japan does not dramatically change and the caution and skepticism about change that characterizes public opinion will give way to a new consensus. In any event, at the end of the 1990s, politicians faced an electorate that was worried about the future and anxious that the government adopt policies to deal with the country's economic problems, but that at the same time was risk-averse and skeptical about nearly all proposals for fundamental change.

From Interest Groups to Special Interests

Along with a powerful public consensus in support of the national goal of rapid economic growth, one of the hallmarks of the '55 system was the existence of large interest groups that exerted a strong influence over political parties and government and played an important role in setting the national policy agenda. Peak organizations representing big business, labor, and farmers were cohesive and powerful. During the period of rapid economic growth, roughly from 1955 to 1970, the nature of the demands they pressed on the government—whether with regard to industrial policy, the government-guaranteed rice price, or labor conditions—was national in scope. These organizations aggregated the interests of thousands of groups and millions of people into a limited set of coherent and competing policy demands. In so doing, they played a crucial role in defining the nation's policy agenda and in structuring political competition among the political parties.

As Japan moved closer to its catch-up goal, as the economy matured and the interests of business, labor, farmers, and other groups became more diverse, the earlier cohesion of peak organizations such as the big-business community's Keidanren, or labor's Sōhyō federation, or the farmers' agricultural cooperative association Nōkyō, weakened. It became increasingly difficult for any of them to speak with a single, clear voice on policy matters because their members had developed different and sometimes conflicting interests. Conflicting interests between workers in public-sector and private-sector enterprises, for example, weakened Sōhyō's ability to speak on behalf of organized labor and eventually led to the organization's demise. Internationally competitive high-technology companies in Keidanren took a different view of market liberalization issues than did industries that drew their profits from a protected domestic market. The farming community became divided: on one side were those, mostly part-time farmers, who insisted on maintenance of the food-control system and high government-guaranteed producer rice prices; on the other side were full-time farmers more supportive of policies that would provide financial assistance for farmers diverting land into other crops and encourage consolidation of small landholdings into more efficient, larger farms.[30]

The decline of cohesion and power of large, integrative interest groups is evident to a greater or lesser degree in all advanced "postindustrial" democracies. Industrialization encourages a pattern of interest aggregation among workers, farmers, and businessmen. Societies that are postindustrial, affluent, educated, media-saturated, and middle-class, where the majority of the labor force is employed in the service sector rather than in manufacturing, encourage a pattern of interest disaggregation, of a politics of "special interests" rather than interest-group politics. Through their political activities, large, integrative interest groups helped determine the overall policy agenda of parties and of government. The politics of the special interests encourages competition within as well as among political parties, as individual politicians energetically lobby on behalf of "their" special interests. At its worst, the politics of the special interests transforms the state into an arena for predatory activities of small groups seeking to satisfy private interests.

The shift from interest-group politics to the politics of the special interests does not necessarily mean a decline in the influence and power of social groups in the political system. In some ways, special interests are more powerful because they tend to pursue their goals through individual politicians who are dependent for their very political survival on the continuing support of these interests. It means the fragmentation of party activities. In industrial societies, interest groups provided cues to political leaders that helped define broad policy goals. The politics of the special interests, almost by definition, eschews concern with overarching issues in favor of "special" objectives.

This evolution in the representation of interests in economically advanced democracies became conspicuous in Japan from the late 1970s. The declining importance of national, peak organizations and the prevalence of a politics of special interests contributed in a major way to a status-quo politics of drift and complacency. Politicians occupied themselves serving the interests of narrow constituencies—leading to the *zoku* phenomenon discussed below. Political leaders and senior bureaucrats, under pressure to respond to specific demands in the allocation of government resources and not being pressed to redefine the overarching policy agenda, responded accordingly. The fragmentation of interests weakened one of the key pillars of policy making in the '55 system.

The Decline of Labor Militancy

Many of the most powerful interest groups in the '55 system emerged as a consequence of the democratic reforms imposed by the American Occupation, or—as was the case with labor—as a result of specific Occupation efforts to encourage interest-group formation. Occupation authorities had much more success than they bargained for in encouraging the organization of a vast array of groups that developed vested interests in their own perpetuation and set out to pressure the government to adopt policies that served their interests.

There had been the beginnings of a labor movement in prewar Japan—it reached a peak strength in 1935 of 420,000 members, or 6.9 percent of the nonagricultural workforce[31]—but the movement was suppressed and incorporated into the state structure during the Second World War. One of the earliest Occupation-period reforms was the removal of restrictions on the right of labor to organize. This spawned a large and, much to the chagrin of Occupation authorities, a Marxist-dominated, politicized labor movement.

The Occupation authorities' encouragement of labor-union organization, coming after years of political suppression, had an electrifying effect. On May Day 1946, labor unions in Japan, little more than eight months after the end of the war, had 2.7 million members in some seven thousand unions. By the end of that year, there were 4.5 million union members, and in May 1947 some twenty-two thousand unions.[32]

After encouraging labor to organize, however, the Occupation shifted policy in an attempt to eliminate Communist Party influence in the union movement and to prevent a planned general strike in 1947.[33] Subsequent actions by the Japanese government to prohibit strikes by public-sector union workers and other restrictions on labor-union activity[34] reduced the level of unionization. Nonetheless, from the 1950s through the 1970s, union membership was at 30 to 35 percent of the nonagricultural labor force.

Union membership has been on a steady decline ever since, much as in the United States. American labor-union membership peaked in 1960 when 37 percent of the nonagricultural, private-sector labor force was unionized. By 1997, U.S. private-sector unionization, after three decades of relentless decline, stood at 9.8 percent, the lowest rate since the beginning of the century (it was 9.3 percent in 1902); the total unionization rate, including the 6.7 million union members who work in federal, state, and local government, was only 14.5 percent.[35]

Labor-union membership in Japan reached its high point in 1975, at 34.4 percent of private- and public-sector workers in the nonagricultural labor force. In 1997, this had declined to 22.6 percent, the lowest unionization rate since the end of the war.[36] There were seventy thousand labor unions, with an average membership of only 171 people, organized almost entirely (99.4 percent) at the enterprise level.[37]

The Japanese labor movement was an important force in the politics of the '55 system. Its influence over the Socialist Party, through the Sōhyō federation, was so great that the party came to be referred to as Sōhyō's "political bureau." Sōhyō-led "spring struggles" to force the business community to agree to a general average level for annual wage increases were an integral, if increasingly ritualized, part of the politics of the '55 system. Sōhyō was committed to political struggle. Its leadership maintained that the interest of labor would be served only by bringing down the capitalist order, even as its constituent private-sector unions, organized almost entirely at the enterprise level, developed ever more cooperative relations with management. Many of these private-sector unions' national organizations eventually broke with Sōhyō's leadership, leaving it a federation almost entirely of public-sector unions. Its political influence withered, as did the political power of the Socialist Party that was dependent on its support. It disbanded in the late 1980s.

Sōhyō unions as well as unions in three other, smaller national federations were absorbed in a new peak organization of the labor movement called Rengō. With nearly eight million members, Rengō is one of the largest union federations in the world. Yet it is far from powerful. Through all the party splits and reorganizations, electoral-system change, and policy debates discussed in the pages of this book, Rengō played a decidedly secondary role. Rengō supports the Democratic Party, but unlike the influence its American counterpart exercises over its Democratic Party, Rengō is notable mostly for its lack of political power. In contrast to the '55 system, there is in Japan today no powerful national organization that speaks on behalf of organized labor.

The Decline of Nōkyō Power

Farmers enjoy a well-deserved reputation for political clout with the LDP. Although they comprise no more than 5 percent of the labor force, farmers exercise political influence far greater than their numbers might suggest. It is an influence that derives in no small measure from the policies of the American Occupation authorities. The Occupation's land-reform program eliminated tenancy and created a large population of owners of small farms.[38] These independent farmers organized them-selves in agricultural cooperatives, Nōkyō, that in addition to their eco-nomic function as the farmers' banker, wholesaler, and distributor of their products, used their electoral clout with the LDP to extract all sorts of benefits from the government.

A recent example of that power involved the *jusen*, financial institu-tions initially created in the 1970s to provide loans to individual home buyers that became a source of funding for the most speculative elements in the Japanese economy during the bubble years. With the collapse of the bubble, the *jusen* became insolvent, and local farmer cooperatives, which had invested heavily in them, faced huge losses. Although public opposition to the use of taxpayer money to rescue *jusen* investors was intense, the government decided to partially compensate the Nōkyō rather than risk incurring the wrath of members of one of the LDP's most important constituencies.

In spite of this demonstration of farmer clout, however, the political power of the federation of agricultural cooperatives is less today, and the economic interests of farmers more diverse, than was true earlier in the postwar period. Under the '55 system, the farmers' peak organization played an important role in structuring the national policy agenda, pri-marily by coordinating and leading the farmers' annual campaign for an increase in the government-guaranteed producer rice price. This issue dominated Nōkyo's political activities through the 1970s. As that issue declined in importance, however, the focus of agricultural politics shifted to more locally concentrated and competitive efforts to secure shares of the Ministry of Agriculture's project-specific subsidies.

The mainstay of farm income in the postwar years came from the sale of rice. After the end of the Second World War, the Japanese government retained the authority that it acquired during the war to set both the price paid to farmers for the rice they produced and the price charged to con-sumers for the rice sold to them through government-authorized dealers. Each year, Nōkyō would make the producer-price demands, replete with demonstrations around the Diet building and LDP headquarters. The producers' rice price doubled between 1960 and 1968 and doubled again between 1971 and 1977. A decade later, in 1987, the deficit created by the gap between the producers' and consumers' rice price amounted to ¥48.9

billion.[39] By contrast, the entire defense budget for that year was a lesser ¥35.2 billion.[40]

Rice *(kome)* became in the 1980s one of the notorious "three Ks" that produced huge government deficits (the others were the national railways *[kokutetsu]* and national medical insurance *[kenpō]*). The combination of burgeoning budget deficits, foreign pressure on Japan to liberalize its totally protected rice market, and changes in the agricultural labor market forced the government to move away from a policy of subsidized rice production even though that policy had been a key element in the LDP's strategy for obtaining support from Japan's rural voters.

As early as 1978, the Japanese government had started lowering the annual rate of increase in the producers' rice price to control the spiraling deficit in the special food-control account. As it did so, it increased the range of government subsidy programs to encourage farmers to diversify out of rice production. By 1980, as much as 60 percent of the Ministry of Agriculture's budget went to pay the cost of subsidies distributed through no fewer than 474 separate programs.[41]

In 1987, the Nakasone government, as part of a more general administrative reform program, cut the producers' rice price by 6 percent, the first reduction in thirty-one years in the price paid farmers for the rice they sold to the government. It was also the first time in twenty-five years that the price at which the government bought rice did not exceed the price at which it sold rice to the public. Farmers, incensed at the government and the LDP, made their feelings known at the 1989 upper-house election: the LDP lost its majority, as noted earlier. According to one poll, only 54 percent of farmers voted for LDP candidates in the 1989 election, compared with 77 percent in 1986.[42] The government's decision to cut the producers' rice price also made farmers furious with the Nōkyō leadership because of its failure to prevent the price reduction.

The government continued to move policy in the direction of decontrolling the domestic rice market. In November 1995, the food-control law was replaced by a law that permitted local cooperatives to sell directly to wholesalers and retailers, thereby enabling them to bypass Nōkyō. Furthermore, the new law allows individual farmers to market rice directly to consumers, making it possible to bypass not only Nōkyō but the local cooperatives as well. The rice market remains protected against foreign competition and the price of rice is several times the average international price. But with rice accounting for only 2.2 percent of household consumption expenditures, compared with nearly 15 percent in the 1950s, the rice-price issue does not loom large among consumer concerns. Nor does it enable Nōkyō leaders to mobilize farmers in a nationwide political campaign, as it once did. In 1955, three-quarters of Japanese farmers were either full-time farmers or part-time farmers who derived a major share of their income from farming. Today, three-quarters of Japanese farmers are part-time farmers who derive on average of less than 15 percent of their income from farming. The possession of a small farm in the 1990s—and nearly all Japanese farms are small, only about one hectare on average, compared with 114 hectares for an average American rice farm[43] —was important mostly for its asset value, and as a place where the elderly parents of farmers who spend most of their time away from their farm working in nonagricultural occupations could reside and lead socially useful lives.

These changes in consumption patterns and social structure, along with changes impelled by budget deficits and foreign pressure on Japan to liberalize its economy, seriously weakened the political power of Nōkyō. In the '55 system, the LDP's support for annual producer rice-price increases identified the party as a defender of the general interests of the agricultural community. Its relations with Nōkyō were important in structuring policy debate over agricultural policy. As Nōkyō's role in the political system has declined, farmers have retained political power, but that power is fragmented, where once it was impressively unified.

The Death of the Guilds

The decline in the power of traditional interest groups is evident also among professional organizations. This, too, is a universal phenomenon and not solely a Japanese one. The American sociologist Elliot A. Krauss has characterized the declining importance in the United States and in Western Europe of professional associations of medical doctors, lawyers, engineers, and teachers as a "death of the guilds."[44] A similar pattern of decline is evident in Japan.

The Japanese union of middle- and high-school teachers, Nikkyōso, was a politically powerful organization in the 1950s and 1960s. Dominated by a Marxist leadership, the teachers' union was militant in its opposition to the LDP and to the Ministry of Education. Union activists were a crucial element in the Socialist Party's support structure, especially in rural areas, where teachers ranked among the most respected and influential community leaders. The union's leadership fought the education ministry's censorship of textbooks, resisted the government's attempts to impose a national system of ranking teacher performance, opposed ethics education, the display of the national flag, and anything else that evoked echoes of the prewar education system.[45]

Compare this with the situation in the late 1990s. At Nikkyōso's national gathering on January 20, 1998, the minister of education sat on the dias with the union's leaders. In greeting the assembled teachers, he remarked, "I want to cooperate with you to bring about good education for our children." An *Asahi Shimbun* reporter observing this event noted that the sight of the union's leaders and the education minister sitting side by side and pledging cooperation was something unimaginable years ago, but now seemed perfectly natural.[46] The old battle lines between the teachers' union and the Ministry of Education had faded over fifty years of coexistence and growing recognition on the part of both teachers and ministry bureaucrats that the pressing issues confronting Japanese education did not involve a return to the past, but how to reform the system to prepare for the future. Nikkyōso's power among teachers had declined precipitously. At its peak in the mid-1960s, it represented more than 75 percent of all elementary, middle-school, and high-school teachers. In October 1996, the figure had plummeted to an all-time low of 33 percent.[47] Fearing its membership and power would continue to erode if it did not change course, in 1996 the union's leaders formally changed the union's line from confrontation with the Ministry of Education to one of cooperation.

The Japan Medical Association (JMA) offers another example, this one on the LDP side of the political spectrum, of the declining political influence of professional associations and of interest-group fragmentation in Japan. Among professional associations supportive of the LDP, one of the most powerful in the past was the JMA. It lobbied successfully for special tax benefits for doctors, opposed tightening legal restrictions on abortions, and opposed the introduction of the birth-control pill.[48] It retained the lucrative practice of dispensing prescriptions and fought to protect the economic interests of medical professionals as the Japanese government expanded its national medical-care system.

The political power of the Japan Medical Association has declined, much as the power of the American Medical Association has, and for similar reasons. National medical insurance in Japan and the passage of Medicaid and Medicare legislation in the United States increased the power of the state over the fees doctors and hospitals charge and led to more salaried medical professionals and fewer independently practicing physicians. Until the mid-1970s, most Japanese medical doctors ran their own clinics.[49] After 1976, salaried physicians became the majority. By 1982, physicians operating their own clinics and hospitals had declined to 39.1 percent. Three of five physicians were now salaried.

In the United States, the AMA's membership, which peaked at 73 percent in 1963, was less than 50 percent in 1990, the lowest since 1912.[50] In Japan, membership in the JMA was 74.5 percent of physicians in 1967, a percentage that declined to 56.7 percent in 1987. It has stabilized since then and in 1996 was 59.3 percent.[51] The majority of JMA members are clinic owners—now a minority of Japanese physicians.

The proliferation of interest groups concerned with health-care issues in the United States has produced countervailing power to the AMA. There are fewer such groups in Japan and they have less power than their American counterparts. There are, for example, no major private health-insurance companies, as in the United States, and the pharmaceutical companies, nurses, and other groups that are so influential in the United States (and elsewhere) play a much less important role in health-care policy making in Japan.[52]

Nonetheless, national health insurance in Japan has generated the formation of organizations that oppose many of the policies advocated by the JMA. The Federation of Health Insurance Societies, *Kenporen*, for example, is made up of more than eighteen hundred individual societies that cover employees in large firms. The employers' association Nikkeiren and labor's Rengō, Kenporen's main constituency groups, usually are united in their opposition to the JMA over fee increases and the issue of greater control over doctors.[53] These trends and developments changed the politics of health care in Japan. They made the JMA a less powerful interest group than it was in earlier years. They increased the number of interest groups concerned with health care and made the policy-making system far more complex and conflictual than it had been under the '55 system.

The Decline of the Zaikai

The Japanese business community organized itself after the Second World War into a number of powerful national organizations. Most important are four national economic organizations (the *keizai yon dantai*). Nikkeiren, the federation of employers' associations, is primarily concerned with labor-management issues. In the 1950s, it was known as "fighting Nikkeiren" because of its confrontations, during the so-called spring struggles and at other times, with the Sōhyō labor federation. The Japan Chamber of Commerce (*nihon shōkō kaigisho*) aggregates the interests of small- and medium-sized business firms. The Keizai Dōyūkai, the Japan Association of Corporate Executives, is mainly concerned with long-term issues of importance to the business community.

The most powerful peak organization of the Japanese business world is Keidanren, the federation of economic organizations. Keidanren's members include industrial and financial associations and the heads of Japan's most prestigious companies. The leaders of Keidanren traditionally have comprised the core of the *zaikai*, which literally means the "financial world" but is a term used more broadly to refer to the financial and industrial business community's power elite. In Japan's popular culture, in the fifties and sixties especially, the head of Keidanren, the "prime minister of the *zaikai*," and other *zaikai* leaders had the power to make and break prime ministers and to exert a commanding influence over economic policy. The image of *zaikai* power was doubtless exaggerated even then,[54] but the notion that the Japanese big-business community spoke with a single voice on many important issues was not.

As Japan approached the end of the twentieth century, the term *zaikai* was used less often and no longer evoked the image of a united, politically powerful leadership of the big-business community. Its meaning today is hardly distinguishable from terms such as *keizaikai*, the generic "business community." Keidanren itself is no longer the citadel, the "central command post" of the *zaikai*, but an umbrella organization for companies and industrial associations with diverse and sometimes conflicting interests.

Political power within the business community has fragmented. Industrial associations within Keidanren and individual companies pursue their own political goals. Until 1993, Keidanren every year would amass a huge fund from its constituent associations and corporate members to be used for contributions to political parties. It terminated its political funding activities that year, intensifying a trend among politicians to seek campaign financing from individual companies—mostly ones located in their own electoral districts. Business interests are far more fragmented than they were when Japan was in its "catch up" phase of economic development. There are differences, for example, in the political goals of companies that want protection against foreign competition and those that want removal of government regulations that raise the import (and domestic) cost of goods, commodities, and services they utilize in their own manufacturing processes. With Japan facing its worst economic and financial crisis in decades, the Japanese business establishment in the 1990s was unable to speak with a unified and authoritative voice about what the government should do to deal with these problems. Such disarray within the business community would have been inconceivable at the height of the '55 system. Economic development has profoundly changed the patterns of relations between business and government and it has weakened the unity of the business community. Fragmentation of business interests has reduced the political power of Keidanren and it has consigned the *zaikai* to the folklore of Japan's political past.

Interest Fragmentation and the Zoku

Interest groups in the '55 system performed two critical political roles. They were agencies of social integration and they provided a signaling device that alerted the LDP to the political demands of key social groups that it could factor into the government's policy decisions. The signals that "special interests" send to political leaders, however, do not concern the interests of broad-based social groups but only their own narrow demands.

The Japanese political system's response to this shift in the politics of interest representation was the formation of so-called *zoku,* policy tribes.[55] *Zoku* is a term that became widely used in the 1970s to refer to Diet members who had developed considerable expertise and practical experience about a particular area of government policy and enough seniority in the party to have influence on a continuing basis with the ministry responsible for that policy area. Over time, *zoku* have become increasingly specialized in their activities, concentrating not only on a specific ministry but on a narrow issue area within that ministry's purview. Thus there are politicians who are known as air-transportation *zoku* or telecommunications *zoku*. There is a fisheries *zoku*, a tobacco *zoku*, and even a sewage *zoku*. *Zoku* are the political agents of the special interests, intermediating between individuals and groups in civil society and the bureaucracy.

In Japanese popular discourse, interest-group politics and the behavior of the *zoku* are treated as nearly unmitigated evils. The press regularly attacks the party in power for responding to interest-group demands and for protecting vested interests. There is an underlying tone of moral condemnation of such political behavior, a strong sense that, small or large, groups that strive to serve particularistic interests rather than seek what is best for the general good are behaving in an unethical manner. Many years ago, the sociologist David Riesman observed that in Japan, "people refer to organizations as 'undemocratic' if there is no harmony or consensus. Thus, democracy and politics would seem to be antithetical."[56] The observation is still relevant. Much of the criticism of the behavior of Japanese politicians and political parties amounts to a kind of "anti-politics."[57]

The same Japanese commentators and newspaper editorial writers who complain bitterly of bureaucratic dominance of the policy process often are equally unrestrained in their attacks on the influence of interest groups. The normal push and pull of individuals and groups in civil society seeking to use their political influence to further their interests is treated as a somehow illegitimate exercise of political influence. Although there is a pervasive sense that ethical politicians should be above particularistic interests, the pervasive political reality is that what many politicians mostly do is serve particularistic interests. This gap between expressed norms and observable behavior creates a steady drumbeat of criticism and an exaggerated perception of Japanese politics as "backward." Political reformers, opposition party leaders, and the mass media critical of such behavior tend to embrace a vision of a kind of technocratic democracy where government is run by politicians who behave as bureaucrats are expected to behave, doing what is right for the general welfare and refusing to represent the particular interests of groups who support them.

Relations among interest groups, politician *zoku*, and the bureaucracy are regularly condemned as an invidious "iron triangle" that further demonstrates the backwardness of Japanese politics. Few Japanese observers seem aware that the term "iron triangle" is an American and not a Japanese invention. The term originated in the United States to characterize the close relations among interest groups, relevant congressional committees, and bureaucratic agencies. Japanese popular political commentary usually refers to one overarching iron triangle of business, the LDP, and the bureaucracy, seen as dominating Japanese politics. But policy making in Japan, more than in the United States, is characterized by the existence of disaggregated policy communities, of a multiplicity of iron triangles, as John Campbell and others have demonstrated.[58]

Incessant criticism of interest-group politics, the condemning of what in Japanese is referred to as *riken seiji*, the politics of the vested interests, complicates policy making in a particular way. Each instance of the state's award of particularistic benefits—a new bullet train here, a new highway there—is an occasion for media outrage over the politics of the special interests and criticism of the ruling party. Yet as party competition based on major differences over policy priorities and goals declined in the course of the evolution of the '55 system, the pressures on politicians to seek electoral support precisely through such special-interest politics increased.

In the early years of LDP rule, along with a public consensus on the importance of giving priority to rapid GNP growth, powerful interest groups, such as Nōkyō, Keidanren, Sōhyō, and the Japan Medical Association, exerted considerable influence over public policy. Japan in the 1990s was characterized by a public opinion that was uncertain and ambivalent about national goals. It also was characterized by the fragmentation and weakening of formerly large and powerful integrative and interest groups. The importance of peak organizations among business and labor declined, creating a more pluralistic system of interest representation. But in the context of a public nervous about fundamental change and anxious to hold onto what had been achieved and a political leadership unable to formulate new policies, the consequence of this decline has been reinforced support for the status quo.

Bureaucratic Power

If a strong public consensus on goals was one pillar supporting the policy-making system in postwar Japan and the existence of powerful interest groups that channeled public demands into decision-making processes another, a third pillar was Japan's administrative bureaucracy. For more than a century, Japan's elite bureaucrats have manned key positions of state authority and power. Recruited by competitive examination from among the best and the brightest graduates of Japan's most prestigious universities, especially from the University of Tokyo's law faculty, Japan's bureaucratic elite possessed high morale, a sense of mission, and a reputation for competence and integrity. They might have been haughty and arrogant, as exemplified by the prewar expression "bureaucrats exalted, common people despised" (*kanson minpi*), but the image of the Japanese bureaucrat was one of a man of ability and dedication who had forgone opportunities for material gain to serve the nation.

Events in the 1990s profoundly damaged the bureaucracy's reputation and weakened bureaucratic morale. Surely, few Japanese were surprised to learn that dealings between Ministry of Finance bureaucrats and bankers, or between Ministry of Health and Welfare bureaucrats and representatives of pharmaceutical companies, took place through a variety of informal contacts, from dinners in posh restaurants to rounds of golf at exclusive golf clubs. After all, informal relationships between bureaucrats and representatives of industries within their particular ministry's purview were a traditional and accepted practice.

Yet revelations in the 1990s that Japanese bureaucrats had abused these relationships for personal gain, engaging in conduct that was morally reprehensible if not illegal, shocked the public and produced a bout of bureaucrat bashing by the media and politicians that was unprecedented in Japan's modern history. The evidence that corruption in the bureaucracy was not limited to a few miscreants was overwhelming. A former administrative vice-minister, the highest position in the Japanese bureaucracy, in the health and welfare ministry was arrested for accepting bribes from an operator of nursing homes. Several bureaucrats suspected of receiving bribes committed suicide. Several finance ministry officials were forced to resign and scores more were disciplined for violating ministry guidelines about accepting gifts and entertainment from business. And this was just a small part of a seemingly endless exposé of corruption at the heart of the nation's professional elite bureaucracy. Newspaper reports of bureaucrats being entertained at a "no pan" restaurant, where waitresses wore short skirts and no underwear (the "pan" is for panties), symbolized how far bureaucratic behavior had strayed from the lofty ideal of the selfless professional who dedicated his life to serve the interests of the nation.

The finance ministry became a particular target of criticism, not only because of scandals involving MoF bureaucrats, but especially because of its policy failures. MoF was by far the most powerful ministry, with responsibilities that in the United States are divided among the Treasury Department, the Bureau of Management and Budget, the General Accounting Office, the Securities and Exchange Commission, and other agencies. MoF policies had encouraged a real-estate and stock-market bubble to develop in the late 1980s. Then the macroeconomic policies it adopted after the bubble burst, especially raising the consumption tax to 5 percent and rescinding cuts in income tax at the same time, effectively aborted Japan's economic recovery. Yet MoF bureaucrats insisted on the rightness of their policies and fiercely resisted any proposals to break up their ministry. After the LDP lost power in 1993, they were uncharacteristically open in publicly pushing their own policy preferences, as discussed in chapter 3.

By the late 1990s, it was difficult to find anyone in Japan who had anything good to say about the Japanese bureaucracy. Politicians, including those in the LDP, joined in the attack, in no small part because blaming bureaucrats was a convenient way for the LDP to avoid taking responsibility for the LDP government's performance. The role of the state in the Japanese economy, and the relationship between bureaucrats and politicians, was complex and dynamic, but as bureaucrat-bashing escalated, the notion that the bureaucracy virtually alone had responsibility for postwar Japan's economic performance, first for good and now for ill, became more and more a kind of uncontested assumption.

There are two theories of the structure of state/society, and politician/bureaucrat relations that are quite close to what has become the conventional public wisdom in Japan. One, which was initially inspired by Japanese Marxist analysis, is the theory that Japan is ruled by a triumvirate of the bureaucracy, the *zaikai*, and the LDP. The Marxist inspiration for this theory derives from the idea that the state is the superstructure representing the interests of the dominant or ruling class. Because the state, through its elected politicians and administrative bureaucracy, serves the interests of this ruling class, there is naturally a commonality of views among the three parts of the triad, whose relationship is marked by collusion.

In the 1950s and 1960s, this triad theory stressed the power of the *zaikai*, in keeping with the Marxist notion that state policies served the interests of Japan's monopoly capitalists. Later, this theory, shorn of its Marxist terminology, was embraced by American and non-Marxist Japanese writers as the theory of "Japan, Inc." In this version of the triad theory, the bureaucracy was the strongest leg in an essentially corporatist system in which the state and the business community colluded and conspired to pursue Japan's rapid industrialization.

A second theory emphasizes not a sharing of power by a triad of business, bureaucracy, and politicians, but the bureaucracy's dominance over politicians, the business community, and everyone else. According to this "capitalist developmental state" theory, bureaucrats in the ministries of finance and international trade and industry pursued a carefully constructed development strategy and used various instruments at their command, including control over foreign exchange and the flow of capital to the banking system, to compel compliance by the private sector. In this system, politicians reigned while bureaucrats ruled.[59] In this perspective, Japan is the quintessentially strong state and the Japanese political economy a form of state-sponsored capitalism in which the administrative bureaucracy, rather than putative political leaders, exercise political power.

The theory of the capitalist developmental state exaggerates both the extent and the uniqueness of the power of the Japanese state over the market and of bureaucrats over politicians. And it does so in part because its implicit comparative yardstick for measuring Japanese behavior is the United States. Yet Japan is closer to the norm among modern democracies, insofar as state involvement in the economy and bureaucratic power over decision making is concerned, than is the United States. Indeed, as measured by conventional indicators—the extent to which industry is nationalized or government spending as a share of GNP—the role of the Japanese state in the economy is less intrusive and less extensive than in any of the continental European countries.

It was perhaps inevitable that the academic controversies spawned by these state- and bureaucracy-centered theories of the Japanese political economy would produce their antithesis—that it is, after all, politicians who rule, and who adopt policies designed to win elections, which is to say that their policies are responsive to political demands coming from within civil society. In this rational-choice theory, politicians are the principals and bureaucrats their agents, carrying out the responsibilities entrusted to them by their political bosses. The bureaucracy may appear to exercise power because political leaders accord them considerable slack in policy making, so long as the policies they pursue serve the interests of the principals: the reality is that politicians are in charge; it is they who rule as well as reign, according to this principal-agent theory.[60]

This theory grossly underestimates bureaucratic power and exaggerates the extent to which the LDP can employ control-mechanisms to keep bureaucrats in line. It exaggerates the LDP's control over promotions within the bureaucracy and over the job opportunities available to bureaucrats when they leave the government. It overestimates the influence of elections on policy and the power of LDP backbenchers to influence the party leadership's policy decisions. Elections are rarely referenda on specific issues. Moreover, in Japan under the pre-1994 multimember district system, voters could vote against the LDP leadership by voting for an incumbent candidate from one of the factions not supportive of the current leadership, or by voting for an LDP newcomer instead of an incumbent, if one were running in the district. Voters' ability to make this kind of voting choice regularly produced the defeat of LDP incumbents, even as the LDP retained power.

Moreover, the exercise of strong party discipline in voting on legislation in the Diet made it possible for LDP incumbents to tell their constituents that they had disagreed with the leadership's decision on a particular issue, but in the end had no choice but to go along. They regularly promised their supporters that if reelected they would work to change the party's position.

Principal-agent theory has some merit perhaps for analyzing legislative-bureaucratic relations in the United States, where the theory was developed, but it does not travel well.[61] Japan's different institutional structures and historical experiences created a different logic of political action than that in the United States.[62] The theory "works" only if its proponents are determinedly oblivious to this reality.

The theory of politician dominance, as is the case with the theory of bureaucratic dominance, is curiously apolitical. Neither provides insights into what are intensely political relationships: between state and society, and between politicians and bureaucrats. The postwar Japanese political economy did not have a dominant or "strong" state that imposed its policies on the private sector. Nor was the state a neutral arbiter of the competing claims of social groups. It did less than command the economy and more than simply process private-sector demands.

In traditional American pluralist writings, the state is portrayed as a neutral processor of the competing demands of social groups, a kind of black box through which societal inputs are transformed into governmental policy outputs without any state-induced value added. This concept of the state is problematic in the American context and it is wholly inappropriate when applied to a country like Japan with a powerful tradition of an activist state. On the other hand, the assumption that an activist state is necessarily a strong state (that it has the power to impose its decisions regardless of the degree of support those decision have in civil society), and the implicit assumption that a strong state speaks with a single voice, are not supported by the extensive case-study research done over the past decade and more on Japan's political economy.

These studies have produced a long list of phrases to capture the particular quality of public/private relations in the making of state policy: "patterned pluralism,"[63] "governance by negotiation,"[64] "reciprocal consent,"[65] "negotiated polity,"[66] "network society,"[67] and "network state"[68] are some of them. All of these and other carefully researched studies of the Japanese political economy[69] describe essentially the same phenomenon of an activist state interacting with strong social institutions. Some studies put a greater emphasis on the role of the activist state; others accent the power of the private sector; but nearly all are highlighting what might be termed policy making in a refractive state.

A refractive state absorbs demands from society and it produces policies in response to them. But in reaching public-policy decisions, the managers of the state—its bureaucrats and political leaders—endeavor to bend and mold those demands to conform as much as possible to their own values, priorities, preferences, and organizational interests. Demands emanating from society in the refractive state are plural and competing. It is a system characterized by the existence of strong private-sector associations. The preferences of bureaucrats and politicians are plural as well. The state is not a unitary actor. Inter-and intraministerial rivalries are rife in the Japanese bureaucracy. So, too, are rivalries among politicians and between politicians and bureaucrats. It is a system of multiple strong-state institutions.

This is not a corporatist system. Power is disaggregated within the state and in society. Neither is it fully pluralistic. Some groups, labor most especially, have more limited access than in other pluralist systems. Other groups, consumers most importantly,[70] are poorly organized to press their demands. The process of arriving at policy decisions in a refractive state is necessarily messy and conflictive. The state exhibits "embedded autonomy,"[71] if that concept is understood to mean the state is "embedded" in society, exercising a degree of autonomy in decision making in the context of its responsiveness to social demands. It cannot simply impose its own policy preferences on society. Bargaining and compromise—in other words politics—are involved.

Politics is also what characterizes relations between bureaucrats and politicians. Bureaucrats are far more than "agents" of political leaders. They have political power. They control important information and policy expertise. Some LDP Diet members have extensive knowledge about particular policy areas, but politicians are necessarily generalists and need the support of specialists to formulate policy. Neither individual politicians nor the LDP has its own staff of policy experts. The bureaucracy has served in effect as the LDP's think tank. Moreover, career government officials man virtually all positions in the government administration. The only officials in the ministries who are not bureaucrats are the ministers themselves, plus one or two usually inconsequential parliamentary vice-ministers.[72] Bureaucrats are protected by strict civil-service laws against dismissal by political leaders, except for flagrant misconduct. They are an elite steeped in a tradition in which bureaucrats have the moral obligation to do what is in the national interest, and they are indefatigable in their efforts to convince the political leadership to follow their advice.

Politicians, too, have political power. Political leaders on innumerable occasions have imposed their policy demands on bureaucrats who wanted to pursue different courses of action. In chapter 3, we discuss the fiasco that resulted from the finance ministry's effort to get the Hosokawa administration to raise the consumption tax from 3 to 7 percent. Although MoF bureaucrats insisted that there could be no income-tax cut without a compensating increase in the consumption tax, in the end the Hosokawa government adopted income-tax cuts and rejected a consumption-tax increase. Bureaucrats have been frustrated time and again by political leaders who refused to pursue policies the bureaucracy insisted were essential and who insisted on pressing forward with policies the bureaucracy believed to be unwise.

Political leaders have the power to set goals. They make public—and international—commitments the government is then obligated to honor. The powers that the Japanese bureaucracy's economic ministries were able to exercise in the postwar period derived from the unambiguous nature of the conservative government's goals—a "low posture" on foreign affairs, a minimal defense establishment, rapid industrialization, generous pork-barrel outlays for rural areas, and so on. Japanese bureaucrats are not being disingenuous when they say that they desire and need strong political leadership. Strong political leadership defines the parameters of feasible government policy and gives bureaucrats the political opportunity to try to pursue their own preferences within those boundaries.

The unrelenting criticism of bureaucrats and demands for an end to bureaucratic control over policy making grew only stronger as Japan moved toward the end of the century. It was combined with equally intense criticism of the politics of the special interests and attacks on the LDP for being responsive to the demands of interest groups that gave it support. There was no new public consensus on what the nation's goals should be now that it had caught up with the West; there was great hesitation to push forward with economic reforms that carried unforeseeable risks.

The weakening of these three key pillars of policy making in the '55 system—a public consensus on goals, the existence of powerful integrative interest groups, and a strong bureaucracy with a clear sense of mission— produced a considerable degree of immobilism. And the collapse of one-party dominance, the fourth pillar of the '55 system, exacerbated it.

One-party Dominance

The LDP maintained a majority of seats in both houses of the Diet from 1955 until 1989, when it lost its majority in the upper house; in 1993, it then lost its majority in the lower house. For more than thirty years, the LDP's monopoly over governmental power at the national level was never seriously threatened. The stability of a system in which only one party ruled and opposition parties "opposed for opposition sake" provided a context for policy making that was characterized in particular by close relations between the ruling party and the administrative bureaucracy and with important interest groups.

Bureaucrats did not have to be concerned that policy directions might suddenly shift as the consequence of other parties coming to power. They were able to anticipate likely LDP reactions to their policy proposals and could back away from policy proposals that they concluded the LDP would reject. Bureaucrats had nothing to gain and potentially a great deal to lose by adopting a posture of openly challenging the LDP. Instead, they employed quiet persuasion, using their expertise and the close personal relationships they had developed with long-serving political leaders to convince the LDP to adopt particular policies. One-party dominance effectively deprived the opposition parties of the opportunity to utilize the bureaucracy's expertise. It also made unavailing to bureaucrats a strategy of promoting their own policy preferences by playing one party off against the other. The LDP was the only game in town insofar as political power was concerned, and the bureaucracy responded accordingly.

So, too, did major interest groups. They did not have to hedge their bets, as far as party support was concerned, because they did not worry about being disadvantaged by another party coming to power. They could concentrate their energies on developing close relationships with LDP members. The system of one-party dominance imparted a particular stability to relations between the LDP and interest groups.

LDP dominance was a main pillar of the postwar political system, but this pillar has crumbled. The LDP in the late 1990s had a majority in the lower house, but not in the upper house. It did so poorly in the 1998 upper-house elections that it had to be concerned whether it would be able to retain its lower-house majority the next time a general election was held, which at the latest would have to be before October 2000. It had to deal with a voting public that had no strong party loyalties and that had demonstrated a volatility and unpredictability in its voting behavior. The era of LDP dominance was irretrievably over.

The New Era

For nearly half a century, Japan's political system facilitated economic development and rapid social change. In so doing, it weakened the social cleavages that underwrote the '55 system, and the success Japan achieved in reaching its goal to catch up with the West economically weakened the main pillars of its policy-making system. The weakening of the four pillars of this system—a public consensus on growth, the existence of powerful integrative interest groups, a prestigious and high-morale bureaucracy, and one-party dominance—was a natural, unavoidable consequence of these developments.

The problem was not that these elements of the policy-making system were rendered obsolete by Japan's economic success and by the resolution of the political conflicts that dominated the early years of the '55 system. There is no reason to be nostalgic for the '55 system. The problem was that so little was done to innovate new approaches to policy making. Political leaders were unable to articulate new national goals or make a case for institutional reforms that the public found convincing. Fragmented special-interest politics made it difficult to aggregate social demands. Meanwhile, attacks on the bureaucracy were not coupled with the creation of other institutions capable of policy formulation. Japanese political parties and politicians do not have significant numbers of policy experts on their payroll, and think tanks and other institutions in civil society that play important roles in the public-policy process elsewhere are underdeveloped in Japan. Parties in opposition to the LDP attacked it for catering to vested interests, but the essential fuzziness of public opinion and the lack of sharply defined cleavages made it difficult for them to articulate policies that were both distinctive and appealing to large numbers of voters.

When Japan entered the 1990s, the cold war had ended, and the Japanese economy was reeling from the consequences of the bursting of its real-estate and stock-market bubble. The LDP had lost its upper-house majority in the 1989 election and politics within the party was dominated by corruption scandals and intense factional conflict. This made for a combustible combination, and in 1993 it exploded. The LDP lost power and a new period of tumultuous political change began. The following chapter tells the story of this beginning.

Chapter Two

The End of One-Party Dominance

Going to the Brink

The ouster of the LDP from government and its replacement by a seven-party coalition was at one and the same time the culmination of long-term trends, a response to relatively recent international and domestic developments, and a consequence of a fierce factional struggle within the LDP. No single factor caused the LDP to lose control of the government. Change was in the winds, but it shook Japan from a stable foundation of thirty-eight years of LDP dominance only because a particular historically contingent constellation of factors, ranging from the structural transformation of international politics to petty feuds among party bosses, surfaced in the summer of 1993.

Nonetheless, single-cause explanations of the events that drove the LDP into opposition and that brought every other party in the Diet, except for the Communists, into the government are popular. One explanation is that the LDP lost power because of a factional struggle. Another is that it was ousted from power because voters finally wanted to see a change after thirty-eight years of LDP rule. It is true enough that factions and voters had something to do with bringing change about, but neither alone, nor both together, "caused" it to take place. The story of the LDP's loss of power is an object lesson in the complexities involved in identifying causation with respect to political change.

A bitter factional struggle within the Takeshita faction, the largest faction in the LDP, triggered the sequence of events that led to the passage of a nonconfidence motion in Prime Minister Miyazawa in July 1993. This was followed by an election in which the LDP failed to return a majority, and the formation of a coalition government headed by Hosokawa. But to say that factional strife triggered the LDP's loss of power is not the same thing as to say that it caused it.

To argue that the split of the LDP was caused by factional strife begs another question: why did factional struggles cause the LDP to split in 1993 but not before? Bitter fights between and within factions were hardly new to LDP politics. The party had come to the brink of a split many times before. The LDP, after all, started out its existence as a loose confederation of factions that behaved much like parties. When factional bosses became unhappy with decisions—usually about the distribution of party and cabinet posts and the other spoils of political power—they threatened more than once to bolt the party, only to step back at the last minute. Why did they not step back in 1993?

The New Liberal Club: Boom and Bust

Before 1993, the only instance of an LDP "split" was in 1976, when five incumbent Diet members left the party. Yohei Kono, who was to succeed Prime Minister Miyazawa as LDP president in 1993, led this group of defectors, who then formed the New Liberal Club. Factional politics did not cause the split. Rather, Kono and his small band of allies saw an opportunity to build a new party with the support of voters angered by LDP corruption. Kakuei Tanaka had just been forced to resign as prime minister, brought down by an exposé in a leading monthly magazine of what were clearly unethical if not blatantly illegal business dealings with contractors and others wanting to secure government contracts.[1] His successor, Takeo Miki, had a clean image, but as long as he was part of the LDP structure, in the view of Kono and the others who moved out to form the NLC, he would not be able to do much in the way of reform.

Kono's New Liberal Club enjoyed a brief honeymoon, then languished, and after ten years collapsed. It won twenty-five seats in the 1976 lower-house election and reached its peak of thirty-one seats in the subsequent 1979 election. Its support steadily declined thereafter. As it did so, its leaders took to blaming each other for the party's troubles and became embroiled in a dispute whether the party should be conservative, progressive, or something in the middle. The NLC found it more and more difficult to raise money and to recruit attractive candidates or to articulate a policy program appealing to a large number of voters. Its lower-house membership was reduced to seventeen in the 1983 election, and to twelve in the election held in 1986. It thereupon dissolved, with Kono and most of its other members returning to the LDP.

The New Liberal Club's experience was treated by other LDP members as a cautionary tale of the perils of moving out from under the LDP umbrella. Kono himself had been warned by none other than Kakuei Tanaka that he was making a huge mistake in leaving the party. "Stay in the LDP and fight me here," Kono recalls Tanaka saying to him when he called on him to tell him that he was leaving the party. "You have a chance to succeed if you stay, but if you leave the LDP, after a few years you won't have either money or candidates or votes."[2] Tanaka of course was right, in no small part because he either lured into his own faction candidates that the New Liberal Club wanted to run or ran his own new candidates, sometimes without official LDP endorsement, in districts where NLC candidates were running, throwing his faction's formidable resources behind them.

The Ohira-Fukuda Feud

LDP unity was threatened again in 1980, in a manner that had many parallels with what would occur in 1993, except that the party did not split. The prime minister at the time was Masayoshi Ohira, the head of the same faction that Miyazawa subsequently was to lead. Ohira and his close political ally Tanaka had engineered something of a political coup toward the end of 1978. The prime minister at that time, Takeo Fukuda, in what was meant to be a political-reform gesture without substantive political consequences, had agreed to introduce a primary system into the LDP process for selecting a president. It was to be used for the first time when Fukuda's first term as party president expired in November 1978.

Fukuda ran for a second term, confident that the conference of LDP Diet members—the body with the formal authority to elect the party president—would choose him after the symbolic primary election had been concluded. But Fukuda underestimated Tanaka and his determination to put in place a government that was dependent on the support of his faction. Ohira was party secretary-general, and Tanaka's chief lieutenant, Noboru Takeshita, was head of the party's organization bureau. Together they mounted a vigorous campaign to turn out the vote for Ohira in the primary.

I have a vivid memory of a conversation with Takeshita, soon after the election, in which he described in colorful detail how he had directed the organization of the campaign in nearly every election district, getting Diet members of the Tanaka and Ohira factions to enroll the members of their support organizations in the party and out to vote. Fukuda treated the primary as a formality; the Tanaka faction used it as an opportunity to take over the party's leadership. Fukuda was beaten so badly in the primary that he withdrew from the presidential race even before a vote of party Diet members was taken. Ohira became party president and prime minister.

The incident effectively divided the party in two. Fukuda was intent on seeking revenge on Ohira and Tanaka and becoming prime minister once again. In October 1979, Ohira dissolved the house and held new elections, but when the Diet subsequently convened to elect the prime minister, the LDP could not agree on whom its candidate should be. The party was so badly divided that both Ohira and Fukuda stood for election in the lower house. Ohira won because he was able to secure the support of Kono's New Liberal Club and because the opposition parties decided not to vote for Fukuda. If they had done so, Japan would have had a coalition government in 1980.

The following May, the Socialist Party submitted a motion of nonconfidence in Prime Minister Ohira. Sixty-nine LDP Diet members in the Fukuda, Nakasone, and Miki factions absented themselves from the Diet chamber when the vote was taken. The motion passed, bringing down the Ohira government. It was the first time since the LDP had come to power that the Diet had passed a nonconfidence motion in the prime minister. It would be the only time such a motion would carry until Prime Minister Miyazawa met a similar fate in 1993.

Prime Minister Ohira decided he would not resign. Instead, he called for new elections, as is the prime minister's prerogative under article seven of the constitution. Miyazawa would do the same thirteen years later. The difference was that in 1993, LDP members who voted for the nonconfidence motion in Miyazawa left the party, whereas in 1980 LDP members whose abstention enabled the nonconfidence vote in Ohira to pass stayed in the party. If anything, the antagonism between pro- and anti-Ohira forces seemed to generate new energy in the LDP and provided a more interesting political story for the newspapers than did the competition, or lack of competition, between the LDP and opposition parties.

Then in the middle of the election campaign, Ohira died of a massive heart attack. Now the LDP's feuding faction leaders put their differences behind them. They traveled around the country together carrying a black-bordered portrait of their fallen leader in a solemn "mourning campaign" that they no doubt hoped would draw some sympathy votes to their party's candidates. They were not disappointed. The LDP secured more seats in the election, 296 compared with 248, than it had won in the previous race, held just eight months earlier, in October 1979.

Why did the LDP split in 1993 and not in 1980? If the argument is made that the LDP split because of a factional struggle, then a case has to be made that something had changed in the LDP's factional system that could explain the different outcomes. Much has changed in LDP factional politics, as will be noted later in this chapter, but those changes do not explain why a faction in the LDP decided to leave the party after voting for a nonconfidence motion in Prime Minister Miyazawa and why there was not a single defection among LDP members who abstained on the nonconfidence motion in Prime Minister Ohira. To explain why some LDP members decided to break out of the confines of the LDP after the Miyazawa vote, it is necessary to look beyond factional politics.

The Voters' Role

Were voters responsible for the LDP's loss of power? The casual observer of Japanese politics might assume that if the LDP lost power after holding it for nearly four decades, voters had something to do with it, but this was true only in an indirect sense. As a result of a lower-house election held in July 1993, after passage of the nonconfidence motion in Prime Minister Miyazawa, the LDP fell thirty-three seats short of winning a majority, thus giving other parties an opportunity to form a coalition government. The election's results are discussed in the following chapter: it suffices to note here that the results did not provide evidence that voters had turned strongly against the LDP. It remained the largest party in the Diet by far, and almost all incumbents running in the race who had won in the previous election as members of the LDP were successful again. The problem for the LDP was that enough of these successful incumbents had defected and were now elected on other party tickets to deny the LDP a majority. What was noteworthy about voter attitudes in this lower-house election, the first in which the LDP's majority was seriously threatened, was that voters seemed indifferent that thirty-eight years of LDP rule might come to an end. The voting rate was the lowest ever for a lower-house election. Indifference may have facilitated, but voting behavior did not drive, political change.

Once parties opposed to the LDP agreed to form a coalition government, however, voters became enthusiastic about the prospects for meaningful political change. Prime Minister Miyazawa's successor, Morihiro Hosokawa, became the most popular prime minister in Japanese history. One month after coming into office, his approval rating was 71 percent, higher than for any previous prime minister and considerably stronger than the earlier record of 62 percent set by Prime Minister Tanaka in August 1972.[3] Voters liked Hosokawa after he came to power, but they were not responsible for putting him there. He was the head of a party that did very well in the 1993 election, considering that it had no lower-house members when the election was called, but its total of thirty-six seats could hardly be considered a public mandate for leadership.

There is another, different, thesis that voters were responsible for the LDP's loss of power: that politicians who had bolted the LDP when the Miyazawa government fell did so in order to enhance their election prospects. This is a particularly important argument for devotees of rational-choice theory because it makes the actions of LDP defectors accord with the theory's assumption that politicians do what they do in order to get elected.[4]

The problem with this theory is that most of the incumbents who left the LDP had powerful constituency organizations and were in no danger of losing the election if they had stayed in the LDP. Some new candidates may have benefited from being aligned with a new party, but they were not the ones responsible for splitting the LDP. The veteran Diet members who left the LDP were not calculating that forming a new party would improve their reelection prospects. If they had any concern on this score it was that if their gambit failed and they did not come to power quickly, their reelection prospects would be harmed by being outside the LDP.

A Political Accident?

If factional struggle alone does not explain why the LDP lost power and if voters were not responsible for its loss of power, then the question arises whether the LDP's ouster from office was perhaps little more than a political accident of no long-term significance—a kind of errant blip on the screen of one-party dominance that would disappear in less than a year and do little to effect meaningful structural change in the Japanese political system. Some cynical observers, and some optimistic LDP members, believed this to be the case. In their view, the whole matter came down to the behavior of Ichiro Ozawa, an unconventional and domineering politician who violated the unspoken rules of the LDP factional game and caught everyone by surprise in the process.

The LDP's loss of power, however, was no accident. As important a player as Ozawa was in the events leading to the LDP's ouster, he alone was not responsible for it occurring. Ozawa was a charismatic leader, but charisma is in the eyes of the follower. The question remains why other LDP incumbent Diet members followed Ozawa out of the party, including not only the "Ozawa children," the first-termers who owed their election in 1990 in no small measure to the support proffered by then LDP Secretary-General Ozawa, but senior Diet members who were powerful in their own right.

To explain why the LDP lost power one must understand the tactics and strategies of political elites and the institutional framework that shaped their choices within a particular social, economic, and international environment. There are no shortcuts through this tangle. What happened in July 1993 was the consequence of interactions among politicians trying to seize or to hold onto power within a particular complex structure of opportunities and constraints. We will proceed from the general to the specific, from a consideration of the changing political environment to the gritty details of factional struggle.

The Changing Domestic Context

As discussed in chapter 1, economic growth had ameliorated the division of Japanese society into conservative and progressive camps, leaving the great preponderance of Japanese believing that they were part of a great middle mass and satisfied to be there. That chapter also noted how the bursting of the bubble economy undermined to a considerable degree public confidence in the ability of the LDP-bureaucratic alliance to manage the economy effectively. It is tempting therefore to conclude that changing public attitudes about the state's management of the economy must have driven the political system toward change in 1993, or more broadly that political change was a response to deep structural changes and new tensions in the Japanese political economy. There is little evidence to support such a conclusion.

It is hardly fashionable to say that political change was not propelled by economic concerns, and it sounds particularly counterintuitive to argue that the economy was not the major factor in the calculations of Japanese politicians in the early 1990s. After all, the economy was clearly in trouble, whereas just a few years earlier it seemed to many people, foreigners and Japanese alike, that Japan was an unstoppable economic machine on the road to dominating the world economy. Now, in the aftermath of the bursting of the economic bubble and the collapse in real-estate values, the banking system became burdened with a mountain of bad debt, and economic growth ground to a virtual halt. Government finances were badly out of balance and the situation was growing only worse as efforts to jump-start the economy by pumping government money into public works exacerbated the budget deficit without generating much in the way of new growth.

The public reaction to these economic developments, however, was conservative and cautious, and so, too, was the reaction of politicians. The reality was that politicians, like the voters who elected them, were uneasy about Japan's economic situation and about the government's economic policies, and ambivalent about what to do in the face of the country's new and unexpected economic troubles. The government had waged a campaign throughout the 1980s to convince the public that long-term demographic changes required Japan to exercise stricter fiscal discipline and to increase the share of government revenues raised by indirect taxes, especially in the form of an unpopular consumption tax. Virtually everyone in Japan now knew that the country was well on the way to becoming "an aged society." There was grudging public support for the notion that economic policies had to be adjusted accordingly.

Most politicians in 1993 who decided to leave the LDP criticized the Miyazawa government for failing to bring about political reform, but they gave little attention to his economic policies. There were important exceptions: Ozawa argued that Japan needed to reform its overregulated, cartelized, and closed economy, and he supported raising the unpopular consumption tax from its then 3 percent level not to 5 percent as Miyazawa proposed but immediately to 10 percent; Hosokawa also favored economic reform, and when he became prime minister he set as one of his major goals greater economic deregulation and trade liberalization.

But these economic policy proposals were not an attempt to tap the anger of Japanese voters over the economy. The anger was missing, and so too was widespread public support for fundamental change in Japanese economic policies. Deregulation was not an issue forced onto the political agenda by an irate public, and there was at least as much opposition to deregulation among opposition parties as there was in the LDP. The Uruguay Round negotiations, which included the politically controversial provision for the liberalization of Japanese rice imports, had entered their final stage under the Miyazawa government. His opponents did not argue that Japan should offer more than the government was prepared to concede to bring these negotiations to a successful conclusion. The Socialist Party wanted him to offer less, as noted in chapter 3. International pressure, especially from the United States, and the interests of globally competitive Japanese corporations, not Japanese public opinion, were driving these issues.

The economy impinged on politics in the early 1990s in the sense that voters were no longer convinced that the LDP and its bureaucratic allies were necessarily the best managers of the nation's economy; they also did not seem to expect that bringing another group of politicians into power would result in the adoption of drastically different basic economic policies than the LDP's. The assumption that not much would change, for better or for worse, in terms of economic policy, regardless of what parties came to power, was an important reason for the low voting rate in the 1993 election. Social forces did provide a context for political change in the 1990s, but they had surprisingly little to do with the economy. They had a lot to do with politics—that is, with public anger and a kind of elemental disgust with seemingly never ending and ever expanding corrupt political practices.

Corruption Politics

Political corruption is an old story in Japan. It was a source of repeated scandals in the prewar period. The need to eradicate political corruption was one of the rallying cries militarists used in the 1930s to justify their destruction of Japan's political party system. Every decade since the Second World War has seen at least one major corruption scandal and innumerable smaller ones. The Showa Denko scandal of the late 1940s was followed by a huge shipbuilding scandal in the 1950s. In the next decade, there were the so-called "black mist" scandals, and in the 1970s came the Lockheed scandal involving former Prime Minister Tanaka.[5] In the 1980s, and especially toward the latter part of the decade when an economic bubble produced excesses of all sorts, corruption grew more blatant and involved sums previously unimaginable.

On June 18, 1988, the *Asahi Shimbun* carried a story about corruption in the Kawasaki city government. According to the report, the city's vice-mayor had, in 1984, purchased thirty thousand shares of as yet unlisted stock in a company called Recruit Cosmos, the real-estate affiliate of the Recruit Corporation. Recruit was a young and enormously successful company that had started out as a publisher of job-placement magazines and rapidly extended its activities into other aspects of the burgeoning information industry. The purchase of Recruit stock by the vice-mayor was financed with a loan from Recruit's own financial affiliate, First Finance. When Recruit Cosmos went public in 1986, the vice-mayor sold his stock, paid off his loan to First Finance, and enjoyed a large profit. Two months before Recruit had offered him the opportunity to buy unlisted shares in the company, Recruit had announced its hope to take part in a "Kawasaki Technopia" urban-development project. The vice-mayor was the official in charge of the project.[6]

The Kawasaki story turned out to be the proverbial tip of a corruption iceberg. The scandal swept through the political world with lightning speed. Prime Minister Takeshita, former Prime Minister Nakasone, Finance Minister Miyazawa, the LDP's Secretary-General Abe, the chairman of the Democratic Socialist Party, and members of the Japan Socialist Party and the Komeito had all received unlisted shares in Recruit Cosmos, either in their own names or in the names of their personal secretaries. In addition, Recruit had given money to Abe, Miyazawa, Nakasone, and Takeshita in direct political contributions and through the purchase of hundred of thousands of dollars worth of tickets to fund-raising parties. Abe and Miyazawa, for example, each received more than a million dollars in these direct and indirect contributions from Recruit, in addition to the money they made on the stock transaction.

Recruit's founder and president, Hiromasa Ezoe, was an outsider to the Japanese business establishment, one of the nation's nouveau-riche business elite who used money to buy social acceptance, status, connections to people in power, and influence over government decisions that affected his business. Ezoe did not limit himself to currying favor with the political establishment. The offer to purchase unlisted shares in Recruit Cosmos, often with loans from First Finance, was extended to the president of the Nihon Keizai newspaper company, the vice president of the Yomiuri newspaper company, the chairman of NTT, Japan's telecommunications giant, a professor at Tokyo University, and the administrative vice-ministers of education and labor, to list just a few. Recruit was important not only in exposing extensive corruption in the political leadership, something the public had come to expect anyway, but in revealing that it existed among the highest levels of the professional bureaucracy as well. In all, more than two million shares in Recruit Cosmos stock were sold to 159 people from politics, the bureaucracy, the mass media, academia, and business.

The Recruit scandal resulted in the indictment of twelve individuals, but the legal process snared only two of the country's politicians. One was the chief cabinet secretary in the Nakasone government—indicted for having interceded with the Ministry of Labor to change the terms of a proposed law that would have adversely affected Recruit's job-placement magazine business;[7] the other was a member of the Komeito—indicted for having accepted money from Recruit in exchange for raising critical questions on the Diet floor about the Ministry of Labor's proposed legislation.[8] The prosecutor's office was unable to find evidence that other politicians helped Recruit by using the power of their official positions. Accepting money in return for a promise to be helpful is not bribery under Japanese law if the politician receiving money is not in a position of official responsibility relevant to the favor being asked of him.

This did not mean that politicians snared in the Recruit net escaped totally unscathed. Finance Minister Miyazawa, after contradicting himself in Diet testimony about what he did and did not know about his secretary's purchase of Recruit Cosmos shares, resigned as finance minister. Former Prime Minister Nakasone, who came under particularly strong criticism because the sale of Recruit Cosmos shares occurred during his tenure in office, made a gesture of taking responsibility for the incident by resigning from the LDP. He retained his Diet seat however, and two years later, in April 1991, after the furor over Recruit had quieted down, he returned to the LDP and in November of that year resumed his position as an LDP "supreme advisor."

The most important political casualty of the Recruit incident was Prime Minister Takeshita. Takeshita tried to ride out the Recruit storm. But his popularity, already battered by his decision to press on with the introduction of a 3 percent consumption tax, plummeted as the Recruit scandal widened, finally sinking into single digits. In April 1989, he told a session of the lower-house budget committee that an exhaustive search of his records showed that he had received a total of ¥151 million, roughly $1.5 million, from Recruit. Two weeks later, the *Asahi Shimbun* reported that in 1987, when he was running for the LDP presidency, Takeshita had borrowed an additional ¥50 million from Recruit in the name of his former secretary and long-time fund organizer. No longer able to withstand the storm of criticism against him, Takeshita resigned three days after the story broke. The former secretary in whose name the money had been borrowed committed suicide the following day.

Making unlisted stock available to Japan's political elite itself was not illegal; neither was Recruit's purchase of ¥80 million (roughly $800,000) worth of tickets to Takeshita fund-raising parties. Recruit's determination to exploit loopholes in the Japanese law regulating political contributions in order to give huge sums of money to politicians with whom it wanted to curry favor is somewhat parallel to business "soft money" contributions in the United States that are made to the Democratic and Republican national committees—monies that similarly skirt legal restrictions on campaign contributions. The amounts involved, however, were considerably larger in Japan than in the United States, and they went to individuals, not to parties. In Japan, as in the United States, the scandalous state of political funding and loopholes in the laws regulating political contributions led to demands for political reform. And again as in the United States, little was actually done in the way of reform other than to talk about it.

Recruit, however, generated public anger over political corruption that was far greater than in any previous corruption scandal. Many people seemed to be incensed particularly because so many powerful people made money through a stock deal. By the late 1980s, taking risks in Japan's new world of speculative investment was popular with housewives and others who were not afforded the opportunity to enjoy windfall profits on risk-free investments. The Recruit scandal seemed to give concrete expression to what many sensed was growing inequality and unfairness in Japanese society.

For years, Japanese had talked about having a "first rate economy and third rate politics" *(keizai ichiryū, seiji sanryū)*, usually with a shrug that suggested that simply was the way things were in Japan. As Japan emerged as one of the world's major economic powers, the belief that Japanese politics remained characterized by practices widely associated with underdeveloped countries became a source of anger and of embarrassment. The public became less willing to tolerate political corruption as an unfortunate and unpleasant but mostly unavoidable part of political life. Japanese were aware that the Recruit scandal and the image of Japanese politics as mired in "structural corruption" had become objects of attention and derision by foreigners. In a nation nearly obsessed with what the outside world thinks of it, the growing notoriety of Japan's "money politics" only contributed to fanning the flames of public outrage over political corruption. Angered by scandals that entailed enormous sums of money and that involved the most senior politicians in the country, the public demanded, and the mass media launched a campaign to bring about, fundamental political reform.

The demands for political reform quickly found expression within the LDP itself for two quite different reasons. One was that a considerable number of LDP Diet members, especially younger ones, shared the public's disgust with old-fashioned Japanese-style machine politics. Many younger LDP Diet members were the children of former members of the Diet; they came into national politics neither by way of local politics, as so many of their fathers had, nor after long careers in the government bureaucracy, the other main pathway to a political career in postwar Japan. As a rule they stayed out of politics until tapped to succeed their fathers. At best, their political experience prior to being elected to the Diet usually amounted to a few years spent working as a secretary in their father's Diet office or in the office of another Diet member. They brought different experiences and different values to politics than their fathers did.

Other younger politicians, though not the offspring of political families, also were dissimilar from earlier generations of LDP politicians. Those who were former bureaucrats had brief rather than long periods of service in the bureaucracy before entering politics. Many of those who came from local politics had little in common with the traditional professional partyman of Japanese political lore. Value-change had robbed most of these younger politicians of the enthusiasm for the kind of machine politics that older members of the LDP—like the Richard Daleys, Boss Tweeds, and Tammany Hall machine politicians in the United States—thought that politics was all about. They also were scared of finding themselves embroiled in scandal and possibly facing charges of criminal conduct. Seasoned LDP veterans may have believed they knew all the tricks of the trade of how to avoid being caught for illegal political activities, but many other politicians in the LDP read the news about Recruit and other scandals with a sense of dread as well as repugnance. By the time Japan entered the 1990s, demands for meaningful political reform were coming not only from the public and mass media but from within the LDP itself.

The other reason why demands for political reform surfaced in the LDP was that "reform" was an ideal weapon to use in a struggle for power within the party. As public criticism over corruption mounted and as factional disputes in the LDP and especially within the Takeshita faction became more heated, some of the LDP's most skilled political bosses suddenly became impassioned converts to the cause of political reform. It became nearly impossible to distinguish the true reformers from the opportunists who hoped to ride the political-reform issue into power. Factional power struggles and political reform became inextricably and hopelessly intertwined.

Beyond the Cold War

The LDP had maintained unity despite intense factional conflict during the cold war years because of the deep ideological and policy differences separating it from parties in the political opposition. The most important reason the LDP did not split in 1980 was that these differences made it impossible for a renegade wing of the LDP to find a common policy base to form a coalition with other parties. Although the gap between conservatives and progressives had narrowed over time, there were still serious divisions between them, especially over Japanese foreign and defense policies. As long as these foreign policy differences remained, it was inconceivable that LDP factional struggles, no matter how severe, would lead to a party split and to a coalition with the Socialist Party or the Komeito.

The end of the cold war dramatically changed this situation. With the dissolution of the Soviet Union and the end of a bipolar structure in international politics, the basic argument that the Socialist Party had long put forward for opposing the security treaty with the United States all but disappeared. There was no longer a danger that U.S. containment policy might involve Japan in a war. In a post–cold war world in which trade was emerging as a major source of tension in U.S.-Japan relations, the bilateral security treaty seemed to offer Japan assurance that its relationship with the United States would remain strong. The treaty also provided reassurance to other Asian nations that the United States would remain engaged in the region and that Japan would not augment its own military capabilities to an extent that would be seen as threatening by its neighbors.

The end of the cold war made it possible for ambitious LDP politicians such as Ozawa, Tsutomu Hata, and Masayoshi Takemura, three key
protagonists in the events that were soon to unfold, to look across the
parliamentary aisle and contemplate alliance with opposition parties,
including the Japan Socialist Party. For domestic Japanese politics, the
end of the cold war meant that the LDP's factional disputes would no
longer be contained within the boundaries of the LDP itself.

All this seems obvious in retrospect, but it was not so clear at the
time, especially to the old guard that ran the LDP. The party had survived crises in the past and party bosses were confident that it would do
so again this time. The latest demands for fundamental political reform,
they thought, were sure to blow over sooner or later, just as they had in
the past. Party leaders were not inclined to offer anything more than
minor gestures in response to demands that the LDP change its ways.
Apologies, promises of better behavior in the future, coupled perhaps
with some cosmetic reform of political-funding rules—such was the
formula that leaders of the LDP old guard believed would enable the
party to ride out this latest storm of criticism; there would be no fundamental change in the rules of the political game that had got them
elected and kept them in power. The LDP had been buffeted by scandal
so many times in the past, and through all of these scandals, the media
denounced the LDP and the voters returned it to power. The party
leaders could think of no reason why things should be any different in
the 1990s.

LDP leaders were dismissive of talk of a party split. The LDP had
faced that danger, too, in the past, and always it survived intact. Even if a
few politicians were to leave the LDP, as Kono and his small band of fol-
lowers did in 1976, surely few others would follow. Why would any rational politician give up the certainty of being in the party in power and of
getting a share of public-works spending and other government largesse
for his constituents and try instead to patch together a coalition with a
disparate group of parties, none of which had any national governmental
experience?

Thus when a group of LDP members led by Ozawa and Hata threatened in the summer of 1993 to support a nonconfidence motion against
Prime Minister Miyazawa and bolt the party, many of the seasoned veterans of LDP politics dismissed their threat as just one more bluff in a long
history of LDP internecine squabbles. They were not prepared for what
was to follow.

Factional Strife and Political Change

In the 1990s, as in previous decades, the major players on the stage of Japanese politics were LDP faction leaders. Although the LDP had developed over time a complex organizational structure with regard to policy formulation that was not entirely faction based, factions remained dominant when it came to the assignment of cabinet and key party posts and other matters related to the distribution of power.

Factional organization and the faction system itself had changed over time, however. There were fewer factions in the 1990s than in the 1960s, and they were larger and more complex organizations than they had been in earlier years. They were no longer dominated by one leader, as typically was the case when they first were formed.

The first generation of LDP leaders was made up mostly of politicians who had been at the head of their own political parties or quasi-party groups before the conservative party merger. They typically put their factions together man by man, providing financial and other support to each of their supporters in return for unwavering loyalty. These were prototypical *oyabun-kobun* arrangements in which the faction leader, the *oyabun,* or father figure, would look after each of his faithful, dependent *kobun* as his political children.

Later generations of faction leaders generally were not able to maintain the same intense personal bonds with faction members recruited by their predecessors. Moreover, the growing expense of professional political life, combined with changes in political-funding regulations, made it increasingly difficult for faction leaders alone to raise the huge amounts of money needed to fund the activities of their members. This gave rise gradually to a kind of collective leadership in which several senior faction members shared responsibilities for raising money and managing the faction's affairs.

For backbenchers in a faction, these developments created strong incentives to cultivate good relations, not just with the faction's putative boss but with other senior members of the collective leadership. The cost of political life also meant that faction members needed to raise a large part of their political funds on their own, usually from wealthy companies in their home districts. As a result of these trends, an individual faction member might be closer to one of the chief lieutenants of the faction than to the faction leader himself. And to the extent that a backbench member of the party depended primarily on his own organization rather than on his faction for his political funds, he could maintain an independence that would not have been possible in earlier years. Factions moved away from *oyabun-kobun* arrangements. They became organizations of individual political entrepreneurs banded together to divvy up the spoils of political power.

So while their internal structures had evolved, factions retained their critical importance in mediating the distribution of party and governmental power. And being able to operate effectively in the world of factional politics remained a necessary condition for political leadership. As factions became less cohesive, politics within them became at least as complicated and contentious as politics between them. In the LDP in the early 1990s, there were in effect factions within factions, plays within plays, that made the action on the stage of Japanese politics that much more complex and difficult to decipher. No faction exhibited these complexities more than the Takeshita faction, the largest and most powerful one in the LDP.

Leadership in the Takeshita Faction

The Takeshita faction was the successor to the one built by former Prime Minister Tanaka. When Tanaka became prime minister in July 1972, public-opinion polls ranked him the most popular prime minister in Japanese history. He had grandiose plans to "remodel the Japanese archipelago," largely by sponsoring massive public-works projects in Japan's underdeveloped regions along the Japan Sea, where Tanaka came from.

Tanaka was forced to resign in November 1974 under a barrage of accusations of corrupt dealings involving real-estate and construction companies that hoped to profit from these government projects. A few months later, he was arrested on suspicion of having accepted ¥500 million in bribes from the Lockheed Corporation. Indicted on August 16, 1976, he was convicted, a little more than seven years later, on October 12, 1983, in the Tokyo District Court, and sentenced to four years in jail. He appealed the court's decision. His final appeal to the supreme court was still pending when he died in December 1993.

The Lockheed scandal had a perverse impact on Japanese politics. It did not force Tanaka out of politics, but rather drove him into the dark recesses of LDP power, where as the self-styled "shadow shogun" *(yami shōgun)*,[9] he sought to control those who ostensibly controlled the party and the government. Over the next decade, until he was incapacitated by a stroke in 1985, Tanaka was the LDP's undisputed kingmaker. Anyone who wanted to become prime minister needed to have the support of the Tanaka faction. When Yasuhiro Nakasone became prime minister in 1982, the press chided him for being head of a "Tanakasone cabinet."

Tanaka never put forward a member of his own faction for the post of party president (and thus prime minister). He did not want to give an opportunity to someone in his own faction to usurp his own authority. His strategy was to leave the top position to someone from another faction, while exercising power over the prime minister and the party through control of the post of party secretary-general and choice cabinet positions.

The success of Tanaka's strategy fundamentally changed the LDP's factional system. Previously the LDP had been composed of mainstream factions and anti-mainstream factions: the former supported the prime minister and divided up among themselves cabinet and key party posts; the latter looked for opportunities to replace the prime minister with a candidate of their own. Tanaka was determined to replace this system with one in which his faction always would be in the mainstream. As his faction grew larger and more dominant, the factional system changed to what Japanese refer to as the "all mainstream faction" (*sōshuryūha*) system. It became impossible for anyone to become prime minister without the support of the Tanaka faction and without being willing to give that faction key party and cabinet posts in numbers proportional to the percentage of LDP Diet members that were in the faction. Since it was the largest faction, it received the most posts.

Eventually the faction was taken over by Takeshita, one of Tanaka's chief lieutenants. Takeshita had served in many cabinet and party posts, including a long stint as minister of finance in the cabinets of Prime Minister Nakasone. But what he wanted was to be prime minister. That was not possible as long as Tanaka remained in charge of the faction. Takeshita formed a "study group" within the faction, a move that Tanaka immediately recognized to be a challenge to his own power and that resulted in a bitter estrangement between the two men. After Tanaka's stroke, most faction members who were not already in the Takeshita study group joined it. It formally became a party faction in 1987. Reversing the strategy Tanaka had pursued over the previous decade, the Takeshita faction put forward its own leader as candidate for the party presidency and prime minister.

Takeshita became prime minister in December 1987. He lasted only a year and half in office, however, being forced out because of public anger over the introduction of the new 3 percent consumption tax and because of his involvement in the scandal surrounding the Recruit Corporation. The faction then returned to the former Tanaka strategy of recruiting prime ministers from other factions. It was the dominant power in three successive LDP cabinets, until the LDP was ousted from power in 1993.

One of the main ways the Takeshita faction exerted its power over these governments was by—as Tanaka had done—placing one of the faction's senior members in the post of party secretary-general—the most powerful post in the LDP. The secretary-general has final say on candidate nominations and is in charge of the party's funds, two sources of power that enable him both to do favors for and to punish party members. After Tanaka moved into his "shadow shogun" role, the secretary-general also took control of the composition of the prime minister's cabinet.

The secretary-general had played an important role in cabinet formation in the past, bargaining with faction leaders over how many posts they would receive, sometimes rejecting cabinet nominees put forward by the factions, and closely consulting with the prime minister on the final lineup. As the practice of proportional representation of factions in the "all mainstream" factional system became institutionalized and prime ministers were recruited who were politically weak, the Tanaka/Takeshita faction-appointed secretary-general's power over decisions as to who would enter the cabinet became all but final, leaving the prime minister to wait until the secretary-general, and the Takeshita faction, had put the new government together.

When Takeshita resigned as prime minister in 1989, his faction threw its support to Sosuke Uno, a Nakasone faction member whose tenure in office was cut short by a sex scandal. Revelations that Uno had an affair with a geisha might not in themselves have brought about his downfall—a liaison with a professional entertainer did not elicit much in the way of moral outrage—but public criticism of the shoddy and stingy way in which he allegedly treated her did. Uno was gone in two months. The Takeshita faction turned next to Toshiki Kaifu, a reform-minded member of the faction that had been founded by "clean" Miki and whose only previous cabinet appointment had been as education minister. The Takeshita faction sent Ozawa to occupy the critical position of party secretary-general in the new Kaifu administration.

Takeshita has private offices in the TBR office building, a short walk down a hill from the Diet members' office buildings in an area in Tokyo called Nagata-chō. In the Japanese language, "Nagata-chō politics" has much the same meaning that "inside the beltway" has in Washington politics. Unlike the spacious facilities provided for American congressmen and senators, each member of the Diet is allotted only a small, two-room office. Many of them therefore rent additional, and enormously expensive, space elsewhere in Nagata-chō; some of the most powerful of them are in the conveniently located TBR building.

Takeshita was elected to the Diet for the first time in 1958. When I first met him in 1968, he was already known within Japanese political circles as a "god of elections" (*senkyo no kamisama*) because of his mastery of the details of virtually every election district in the country. I interviewed him many times over the ensuing years, and on the morning of August 9, 1989, one day after Kaifu had been elected prime minister, I went to see him at his TBR office to ask about the new administration.

The newspapers were reporting who was likely to be in the Kaifu cabinet, but last-minute negotiations had held up a formal announcement of the new cabinet lineup. These negotiations involved an effort to bring at least one person into the cabinet who was not a Diet member, in the hope that this would help reinforce Kaifu's reformist image. Shortly after I sat down with Takeshita, the LDP's new secretary-general, Ozawa, telephoned to say that his efforts to bring a nonpolitician into the cabinet had been unsuccessful. Ayako Sono, a popular female novelist and social critic, had turned down an invitation to join the cabinet. Ozawa told Takeshita that Nobuo Matsunaga, a well-known career diplomat who was serving as ambassador to Washington at the time and who had been offered the post of foreign minister, also seemed unwilling to join the cabinet.

After summarizing for me the gist of his conversation with Ozawa, Takeshita mused that if the effort to recruit Matsunaga proved unavailing, an alternative would be to leave the current foreign minister, a senior member of the Abe faction, in the post. However, Takeshita already had agreed to move this politician into either the post of chairman of the LDP's executive board or chairman of the Political Affairs Research Council, which along with the secretary-general post comprise the party's top three positions. Leaving him as foreign minister would mean reconfiguring the entire factional distribution of party and cabinet posts.

Takeshita said in his phone conversation with Ozawa that he thought that one more effort should be made to convince Matsunaga to join the cabinet. He said that he would call the ambassador himself to see if he could persuade him to change his mind. The effort did not succeed. Perhaps because the Kaifu government looked too shaky, perhaps because Matsunaga recognized that the invitation to him to join the cabinet was intended to shore up Kaifu's reformist image and that it would not put much power over foreign policy in his hands, the foreign minister declined to accept the invitation to join the cabinet. In the end, another member of the Abe faction, Taro Nakayama, was appointed foreign minister.

The relationship between Takeshita and Ozawa in respect to formation of the Kaifu cabinet reflected some of the complexities of factional power. It was not entirely clear whether Ozawa was acting as Takeshita's lieutenant or whther Takeshita, the ostensible faction boss, was actually on the sidelines while Ozawa took charge of organizing the Kaifu government.

Even Japan's political journalists, thoroughly imbued with the culture of LDP factional politics, were puzzled by the power structure in the Takeshita faction. Following a long-established custom, Takeshita had given up chairmanship of his faction when he became prime minister. Then after being forced to step down as prime minister because of the Recruit scandal, he did not try to resume his former, formal, faction leadership role. Unable to place Takeshita, who now had no official position in a faction that he was widely credited as controlling, into any conventional category, the press resorted to referring to him as the "owner" (*o-na-*) of the faction, to distinguish him from the faction's new chairman, Shin Kanemaru.

From Recruit to Sagawa Kyūbin

The events that drove the LDP out of power in 1993 were triggered by the actions of Kanemaru, a classic political professional and party-machine boss who was more comfortable wheeling and dealing in teahouses and back rooms of the Japanese political world than he was sitting in cabinet meetings. The only cabinet positions he held in his long career were as minister of transportation and minister of construction. The control that these posts afforded over Japan's huge public-works budget more than made up for the greater prestige that attached to those who served as ministers of finance, or of international trade and industry, or foreign affairs. Kanemaru had a reputation for being the LDP's boss among bosses—the godfather, or as Japanese like to say, the "Don" (as in Don Correlone), of Japanese politics. When Miyazawa replaced Kaifu as prime minister in November 1991, Don Kanemaru became LDP vice president. Occupying that high political office, he was to give new depth to the meaning of "money politics" in Japan.

By the time Miyazawa became prime minister, the storm that had erupted over Recruit seemed to be subsiding. The new prime minister paid obligatory obeisance to the necessity to realize political reform, but he showed little inclination to change traditional LDP ways of doing things. Miyazawa, who was more interested in policy than politics, left party management in the hands of Kanemaru and the party's new secretary-general, Seiroku Kajiyama. Kajiyama, too, was an important Takeshita faction leader who later became a key figure in events leading to the collapse of the Miyazawa government.

In the late summer of 1992, less than a year after Miyazawa came to power, public outrage over political corruption was reignited, leading directly to the LDP's loss of power a year later. On August 22, 1992, the *Asahi Shimbun,* which had broken the Recruit story four years earlier, reported that Kanemaru had received ¥500 million from Tokyo Sagawa Kyubin, a large package-delivery company. Kanemaru's secretary at first denied the allegation, but a few days later, after the president of Sagawa Kyubin provided details to the prosecutor's office about his political-funding activities, Kanemaru publicly admitted that he had received the money and had not reported it as required under the political-funds regulation law. Kanemaru announced that he was resigning as vice president of the LDP and temporarily suspending his political activities. However, he did not resign his Diet seat, as some opposition party leaders were demanding, or his position as chairman of the Takeshita faction.

This did not put the matter to rest as Kanemaru clearly hoped it would. Demands that he testify before the Diet or resign his Diet seat continued to mount. The media focused its attention on Sagawa Kyubin, and as it did so it uncovered more and more unsavory information about Kanemaru that included ties to right-wing and gangster elements. A right-wing organization, possibly in an attempt to extort money from the Takeshita faction, though its motives are shrouded in mystery and Takeshita himself claims to have no idea what it was after,[10] sent its sound trucks out in the days preceding the LDP presidential election in 1987 saying that "we should support the able fund-raiser Takeshita for LDP president." This kind of support from a disreputable group was intended to result in criticism of Takeshita and undermine his drive for the LDP presidency. In Japanese, it is a tactic referred to as *homegoroshi,* "killing with praise."

Kanemaru set about the task of getting it to desist. He did so by asking the president of Sagawa Kyubin to intervene. Sagawa in turn went for help to the chairman of one of Japan's large underworld *yakuza* organizations. The sound trucks were turned off, and Kanemaru, grateful for the assistance, called on the yakuza boss directly to express his appreciation. This evidence of close LDP contact with gangsters and right-wing elements, something that many people suspect but about which little is known, brought down a further hail of criticism on Kanemaru and intensified even more the demands for fundamental political reform.

Kanemaru, however, thought that he could put his troubles behind him if he quickly resolved the matter of having violated the political-funds regulation law in not having reported Sagawa Kyubin's ¥500 million donation. He worked out an arrangement with the Tokyo district public prosecutor's office whereby he filed a statement admitting his guilt and accepting the penalties imposed by the authorities. He was never directly questioned by the prosecutor's office, and at the end of September he was fined ¥200,000, approximately $2,000, the maximum penalty provided for under the political-funds regulation law.

With the legal matter closed, Kanemaru announced that he was resuming his political activities. Now, however, the media and the political opposition were up in arms, not only about Kanemaru's relationship with Sagawa Kyubin but over the behavior of the public prosecutor's office as well. Kanemaru seemed so powerful that the public prosecutor would not even insist on directly questioning him in connection with the case. Kanemaru became the center of a media feeding frenzy. Realizing that the uproar over his activities was not about to subside, and perhaps hoping to forestall further investigations into his fund-raising activities, Kanemaru resigned his Diet seat and retreated to his home in Yamanashi Prefecture.

The Battle over Kanemaru's Successor

Kanemaru's resignation left the Takeshita faction without a chairman. This sparked a full-scale political battle that splintered the faction. By the time the issue was resolved, in December 1992, the group that lost the power struggle had broken off from the Takeshita faction to form a faction of its own. It was this group of Diet members that several months later brought down the government by voting with the opposition in favor a nonconfidence motion in Prime Minister Miyazawa.

The power struggle revolved around Ozawa, a favored disciple both of Kanemaru and Takeshita. Ozawa was the deputy chairman of the faction under Kanemaru, and he was one of Japan's most interesting, complex, and enigmatic leaders. Ozawa was outspoken on controversial public-policy issues. He was an ardent proponent of government deregulation. He also was a fervent supporter of the Ministry of Finance's position that Japan's consumption tax, then at 3 percent, should be raised. He derided Japan's passive foreign policy and minimalist defense policy, arguing that Japan had to act more like a normal country if it wanted to retain its alliance with the United States and be accepted and respected by the rest of the world.[11] None of these positions was popular, either among the Japanese public or within the LDP. It is a measure of Ozawa's political skill and the force of his personality that he was able to convince many who did not share his policy views that his kind of dynamic, no-nonsense leadership was nonetheless exactly what Japan now needed.

Ozawa seemed to revel in his power and to enjoy making others capitulate to it. These were aspects of his personality that later would undermine his efforts to build a party large enough to compete with the LDP. In a famous incident when he was secretary-general during the Kaifu administration, he insisted that each of the party leaders who aspired to succeed Kaifu, all of whom were considerably older than Ozawa, come to his office for an interview. Like schoolchildren heading off to take an entrance exam or applying for their first job—such were the terms in which the press reported it. While he was secretary-general, Ozawa also forced upon the LDP a decision to support jointly with the Komeito a candidate for governor of Tokyo to run against the long-time LDP-supported incumbent. The gambit failed, but the close ties that Ozawa forged with the top leadership of the Komeito in that 1991 governor's race later were to play an important role in making an Ozawa-Komeito alliance the center of power in the coalition government formed after the LDP's fall.

Ozawa knew how to manipulate the levers of political power as well as anyone in the party, but his was also one of the loudest voices calling for fundamental, radical political reform. Ozawa tapped into the mood of public exasperation over the seemingly never-ending parade of scandals, each one more outrageous than the one preceding. He succeeded in making a virtue out of his image as a politician adept at operating in the smoke-filled back rooms and luxurious geisha houses of the Japanese political world. As he called for a political "revolution," his implicit message was that he knew as well as anyone how corrupt Japanese politics had become, how much Japanese policy was hostage to deeply entrenched vested interests, and how nothing short of radical surgery could create a vibrant politics and make Japan into a normal country able to flourish in the new globalized economy and post–cold war world. Ozawa insisted that changing the electoral system was imperative. Japan must scuttle its system of multimember districts and replace it with one in which voters would be able to choose between two parties offering clear policy alternatives. Anything short of that would fail to attack Japan's political problems at their source. The succession struggle in the Takeshita faction that followed in the wake of Kanemaru's resignation became a fight between those who supported and those who opposed Ozawa and his reform ideas.

Factions in the LDP are informal institutions in the sense that they have no official standing in the formal party structure. As is the case with so many informal political institutions in Japan, they are organized in highly formal ways. The Takeshita faction had at the time an eight-member executive committee that had the formal responsibility to select the faction's chairman.[12] In October 1992, when scandal forced Kanemaru to resign, this executive committee became the site for the battle between Ozawa and the anti-Ozawa forces in the Takeshita faction.

The opposition to Ozawa was led by Kajiyama, a professional politician who had been active in prefectural-level politics before entering the Diet and who appears several times in these pages as one of the most consummate practitioners of machine politics, Japanese style. Kajiyama at the time harbored an intense dislike for Ozawa that seemed to derive from personal rivalry, resentment over Ozawa's haughty style, and personal pique that Ozawa did not wait until Kajiyama's return from an overseas trip to consult with him about how Kanemaru should deal with the Sagawa Kyubin scandal. It is impossible to decipher any ideological or policy content to Kajiyama's antipathy to Ozawa. Several years later, Kajiyama became part of a group of supposedly ideological conservatives in the LDP who favored an alliance with Ozawa. In 1992, however, Kajiya-ma led the forces in the Takeshita faction opposed to letting Ozawa or one of his associates occupy the post of faction chairman. Because he opposed Ozawa, he opposed what Ozawa was advocating in the way of political reform. The fight over succession to leadership of the Takeshita faction simultaneously became a battle over political reform—in particular over the question of whether the LDP should support a change in the electoral system.

Ozawa was an unusual politician not only in the ways already mentioned but in his preference to control politics from behind the scenes. He was one of the most vocal advocates of giving greater policy-making power to politicians and less to bureaucrats and was outspoken in his own policy views, but his only cabinet experience was as minister of home affairs. After he left the LDP he formed his own party, but he preferred control-ling others from his perch as party secretary-general and resisted becom-ing party president until forced to do so to avoid losing power altogether.

In the struggle for succession to Kanemaru's position as chairman of the Takeshita faction, Ozawa did not put himself forward as candidate but threw his support behind Hata, the finance minister in Miyazawa's cabi-net, a former minister of agriculture and a popular figure in the faction as well as among the public. Hata exhibited a modesty and a clean image that many people found attractive. He was a strong proponent of political reform, belonging to a group of people convinced that a single-member district system would right what was wrong with Japanese politics. Hata also wanted to be prime minister.

The candidate of the anti-Ozawa forces was Keizo Obuchi, a confi-dante of former Prime Minister Takeshita. Obuchi was a professional politician elected from the same Gumma prefecture district as former prime ministers Fukuda and Nakasone; he was a loyal faction man who lacked a public persona but had few enemies inside the faction. Takeshi-ta seemed to think Obuchi was the ideal compromise candidate and that an arrangement could be worked out whereby Obuchi would serve as chairman for a while and then be succeeded by Hata. Reminiscing sever-al years later about the breakup of his faction, Takeshita volunteered that he had lost control over events because he "had withdrawn somewhat from the front lines" and had not actively managed the faction's affairs. He also thought Hata would come around to support Obuchi in the end because "there would be a promise about the next thing," which in Takeshita's elliptical way of speaking meant promising Hata that he would succeed Obuchi.[13] Hata recalls that "a prestigious person" in the faction promised him that he would be next. "We are going to leave the future in your hands," he was told. "We're going to let you handle things so this time just be patient."[14] But Hata had already decided to follow Ozawa.

Ozawa saw himself as kingmaker, and Hata was the presumptive king of Ozawa's making. Hata knew he had little chance of being chosen the Takeshita faction's new chairman, since the makeup of the executive committee gave a clear majority to the anti-Ozawa forces. The alternative was not particularly attractive. If Hata stayed in the faction after losing out to Obuchi, he would not only fall behind Obuchi in the faction's leadership structure, but would also have to compete against Ryutaro Hashimoto, a powerful Takeshita faction member who had carefully distanced himself from this particular factional struggle. If Ozawa's thrust for power proved successful, on the other hand, Hata might find himself Japan's prime minister in an administration with a clear mandate to pursue electoral reform. Thus was the Hata-Ozawa alliance forged.

Ozawa and his two allies on the executive committee were not present when it met to make its decision on who should succeed Kanemaru as the faction's new chairman. Knowing the choice would be Obuchi, they boycotted the meeting. The committee then voted unanimously to make Obuchi chairman of the Takeshita faction, and the following day thirty-six Diet members left the Takeshita faction to form their own faction. Hata was the chairman of the new "Hata faction"; its boss was Ichiro Ozawa; and its mission was political, especially electoral, reform. Ozawa accused his opponents of being "defenders of the past" *(shuky{u}ha)* for opposing change in the electoral system[15]—a charge the press picked up and promoted.

The split in the Takeshita faction not only upset the factional balance in the LDP but led within months to a breaking-up of the party itself. The factional struggle had become framed as a struggle over the issue of electoral reform. If Ozawa won on that issue—that is, if the LDP supported the kind of reforms the Hata faction was proposing—Ozawa's victory would have meant a decisive political defeat for the Takeshita faction. If the LDP, on the other hand, rejected demands for electoral change, it seemed only a matter of time before Ozawa and Hata and their allies would conclude that they had no choice but to leave the party.[16] It was not possible at the time, however, to know that the split in the Takeshita faction had begun a process that within six months would cause the collapse of the

Miyazawa government and the exclusion of the LDP from power for the first time since its formation in 1955.

Prime Minister Miyazawa's Fall

When the LDP monolith cracked in the summer of 1993, the catalyst was once again Kanemaru. Perhaps stung by public criticism for the kid gloves it seemed to use in dealing with Kanemaru's violation of the political-funds regulation law, the public prosecutor's office decided to continue and expand its investigation into Kanemaru's finances after he resigned from the Diet.

On March 6, 1993, Kanemaru and his secretary were arrested and charged with income-tax evasion. At first, Kanemaru was charged with failing to declare ¥700 million in income for 1987 and 1989 and evading ¥400 million in income tax for these two years. A search of his office and homes, however, uncovered a veritable treasure trove of money. It included ¥2.2 billion (roughly $20 million) in bearer bonds issued by the Nippon Credit Bank, ¥1 billion in bearer bonds issued by the Industrial Bank of Japan, and nearly another ¥1 billion in cash, stocks, and gold bars. All together, the prosecutors unearthed more than ¥4.5 billion (the equivalent of more than $40 million) in hidden assets. When Kanemaru went on trial in July 1993, he was accused of failing to declare ¥1.8 billion in income; his secretary was indicted for not declaring another ¥700 million in income. Kanemaru apparently had secreted away a war chest of somewhere between $40 million and $60 million, an incredible sum even by Japan's "money politics" standards. There was now a public uproar and a media campaign for political reform that was not going to subside until some action was taken.

Prime Minister Miyazawa was swept up in the reform tide. In a speech before the Japan Chamber of Commerce shortly after Kanemaru's arrest, he promised to pass political-reform legislation during the current Diet session, including the adoption of a single-member constituency electoral system and greater restrictions on political contributions.[17] Later, in a widely reported TV-interview program, he once again promised that reform legislation would be passed before the current Diet session ended. Pressed by the interviewer on whether he really meant to say that legislation would pass, Miyazawa repeated his promise and added, "I'll definitely do it. Yes, in this Diet session. I don't lie."[18] Miyazawa had climbed far out on the limb of political reform, apparently failing to notice that Kajiyama and other key LDP leaders were busy sawing it off behind him.

Kajiyama and other Takeshita faction leaders were adamant in their opposition to political-reform legislation that would include revision of the electoral system, mostly because passage of such legislation would be a political victory for Ozawa. The issue of electoral reform had become hopelessly entangled in the LDP's factional power struggle. Kajiyama insisted that the Diet be closed without taking a vote on political-reform legislation and that debate be resumed in the next Diet session. Without the backing of his key party leaders, Prime Minister Miyazawa's hands seemed tied.

With the Diet session drawing to a close, and with no prospect of any reform legislation being passed, the opposition parties jointly submitted a motion of nonconfidence in Prime Minister Miyazawa. Usually such motions amounted to little more than grandstanding gestures by the opposition parties because the LDP had enough votes to defeat them. This time the situation was different. The Hata faction was threatening to vote in favor of the motion. Realizing that his government was about to fall, just two weeks before he was to host a G-7 summit in Tokyo, Miyazawa made a last-ditch effort to convince Hata to vote with the LDP against the nonconfidence motion.

It did not take much to work out an agreement with Hata. Hata's demands were very modest. He wanted Miyazawa to agree to extend the Diet session in order to have a full-scale debate on political reform. He did not ask that the LDP support any particular legislation, just that it act "sincerely" by extending the session and search for areas of compromise. Hata believed that all the parties now were of the view that some reform was necessary. He thought it might be possible to move toward a consensus on what that reform should be during the extended session. His desire to back away from the brink of a party split was evident in his willingness to have each of the parties bring proposals back from the extended Diet session to their party organizations for a final decision and to continue discussion in the next Diet. "Maybe the answer would be no. Okay, that's all right. After all, we need to follow democratic procedures. . . . The important thing is to make the effort. . . . In a democracy, in the end, the majority rules. It is possible that we could do our best and lose in the end. I can't say that things must be in a particular way."[19]

This no doubt was music to Miyazawa's ears. No champion of political reform, Miyazawa seems to have assumed all along that the way to deal with it was to talk it to death. Even though he promised in his tele-vision interview to pass political reform legislation in the current Diet session, he admitted later that he did not really believe it would pass. He expected the Diet would be extended, no decision would be reached, and deliberations would be carried over into the next Diet session.[20]

Miyazawa was not necessarily opposed to political reform; he simply was not particularly interested in it. He readily admits that he submitted a bill to change the electoral system into a simple single-member district system not because he either thought that it was a particularly good idea or believed that it stood much chance of being passed by the Diet, but because the reform mood of the time required that he do something. His rather indifferent attitude about political reform said something more basic and important and rather unusual about this veteran of LDP poli-tics: Miyazawa did not especially like politics. Despite a long career in public office and a position as head of a major LDP faction, at heart Miyazawa remained a technocrat, an MoF bureaucrat living in the politi-cal world. He was the first to admit that his instincts were still those of a government official who was uncomfortable with the personal power struggles that are so much a part of the rough-and-tumble of politics.[21] For the intellectual, policy-minded Miyazawa, political reform deflected attention away from the more weighty matters of state to which he want-ed to give his attention. He was well aware that the split in the Takeshita faction threatened his government's hold on power, but he did not think he could do much about it. After all, he once said to me, "my government was built on the Takeshita faction."[22]

Miyazawa had every reason to accept Hata's proposal that the Diet be extended, that the reform legislation be discussed, and that a final decision on electoral-system legislation be postponed until the next Diet was con-vened. He contacted the Speaker of the house and asked him to propose to the opposition parties that they withdraw their motion and agree to an extension of the Diet session.[23]

The Speaker sent out word on the morning of June 18—the last day of the regular Diet session and the day on which a vote on the nonconfi-dence motion was to be taken—that he wanted to meet with each of the party leaders to discuss an extension of the session. No one went to see him. According to Hata, "I called around, for example to the Socialist chairman Yamahana. 'Hata-san, Yamahana said, usually when we are asked to withdraw a nonconfidence motion that already has been submit-ted, the LDP's former secretary-general or its former chairman of the policy strategy committee, in any case prestigious people, would contact our party leaders one after another and ask for our help. This time there has been nothing.' For opposition parties to withdraw a nonconfidence motion they already had sent to the Speaker requires that they be told [by the LDP] that the Diet would be extended and the issues fully discussed. Otherwise they can't lower the fist they have already raised in the air. That was the view of the Socialists and other parties. But no one went from the LDP to say these things to them."[24]

Prime Minister Miyazawa made much the same point. "The Speaker of the lower house made his proposal but the LDP machinery did not move." Secretary-General Kajiyama could not openly oppose the proposed Diet extension since the idea for it was instigated by his own prime minister. But he sat on his hands.[25] Koichi Kato, then deputy secretary-general, was also adamant in his opposition to a Diet extension. If the Diet session were extended, it would be treated as a major victory for Ozawa and his band of reformers. Ozawa would use the momentum that such a victory would give him to work his way back into the center of power in the LDP. If Ozawa succeeded, Kato argued, he would become another Kakuei Tanaka, setting politics back, rather than reforming it. "Just look at the way he runs the New Frontier Party," a party that Ozawa later formed. "It's as though it were his own faction, his own personal property."[26]

Kajiyama and other party leaders seem to have calculated that few in the Hata-Ozawa group who might vote for the nonconfidence motion actually would bolt the party if Miyazawa dissolved the house and called new elections. There was, after all, the precedent of the Ohira-Fukuda fight a decade earlier, when Fukuda forces brought down the Ohira government by abstaining on a nonconfidence motion and then stayed in the party to contest the ensuing election. Hata believes that the LDP leadership thought that only two or three LDP Diet members would leave the LDP with Hata and Ozawa.[27]

Ozawa, however, was as opposed to a Diet extension as was the LDP leadership. Ozawa had proved himself a risk taker, a gambler unafraid of doing things that other, more cautious politicians hesitated to do. Now he saw the opportunity to knock the LDP out of power and the chance for himself to become the power behind an anti-LDP coalition government. He was ready to take the risk and he seems to have worked behind the scenes to pull the rug out from under Hata's Diet extension proposal. The Komeito, probably with Ozawa's encouragement, was the first to oppose a

Diet extension. The Socialists and the DSP quickly followed suit. The Diet could not be extended.

Hata called Miyazawa on the phone shortly before the nonconfidence vote was taken. "I'm sorry, but this isn't anything personal. The ruling party had to extend the Diet; it had to do something to demonstrate its sincerity if the nonconfidence motion was to be withdrawn. You did your best but the party didn't move. Even if you blow your flute, the party isn't dancing. So that's all there is to it."[28]

On the evening of June 18, 1993, the lower house passed the nonconfidence motion in Prime Minister Miyazawa. All the members of the Hata faction voted for it except for one who abstained. The next day, Hata, Ozawa, and their supporters, forty-four LDP members in all, resigned from the LDP and formed a new party that they called the Shinseitō, the Japan Renewal Party. On the same day, a group of ten LDP Diet members who had voted with the LDP against the nonconfidence motion but who had been critical of the leadership for its refusal to move forward with electoral reform, announced they were breaking off to form a party of their own—the Sakigake, which they translated as the Harbinger Party. As a result of these defections, the LDP was more than thirty seats short of a majority in the lower house. Some of its most powerful and popular younger members were outside the party, hoping to form a coalition government that would end the LDP's thirty-eight-year reign. Miyazawa dissolved the lower house and the LDP went into an election campaign, its monopoly on governmental power seriously threatened for the first time in its history.

The LDP's loss of power was not inevitable, and no single factor caused it to occur. By the early 1990s, basic ideological differences between the parties were no longer salient, economic success could no longer be taken for granted, and the question of how to align Japan in a world divided into two antagonistic camps was no longer relevant. Factional power struggles dominated the political process as they had in the past, but the political environment within which they operated was characterized by greater public interest in political reform than ever before.

Factional conflict, personal ambition and petty personal grudges, media exposure of corruption, public demands for political reform, and dramatic changes in international politics that had brought the cold war to an end combined to create pressures that ultimately undermined the seemingly indestructible edifice of LDP power. But these pressures determined neither the timing nor the substantive content of the actual changes that were to drive the LDP out of office. Change was caused by individuals—the aggressive and risk-taking Ozawa, the ambitious and conciliatory Hata, the policy-minded Miyazawa, the politically street-smart Kajiyama, and others—operating within particular structures of opportunities and constraints, intent on retaining or gaining political power, and acting and reacting to events as they unfolded. Politically, anything was possible. And within a year from the time the Diet passed the July 1993 nonconfidence motion in Prime Minister Miyazawa, Japanese politics was to show that almost *everything* was possible, from an anti-LDP coalition government to a minority government that excluded both the LDP and the JSP, to the LDP's return to power hand in hand with the Japan Socialist Party.

Chapter Three

The Rise and Fall of
Coalition Government

Introduction

This chapter is an essay in two parts. The first is an inquiry into why a coalition government of seven parties that excluded the LDP, rather than a coalition government of fewer parties that would have included the LDP, was formed in August 1993. The second is an inquiry into why that coalition government collapsed eight months later. The focus of analysis is on the strategic actions of politicians, since the choices they made decided the composition of the government and its subsequent performance. But the focus is even more on the institutions within which those strategic choices were made. Analysis of how that context constrained behavior is key to explaining why the coalition gained and then lost power, and it provides a window on some of the enduring features of the Japanese political system.

Politicians operate within structures of opportunities and constraints that vary from country to country. Somewhat less obvious but equally important is that the opportunity structure that faces one politician in a particular political system may differ considerably from the structure of opportunities that influences the behavior of another politician in the same system. What might be suicidal behavior for one politician can be entirely rational behavior for another. A politician's own attributes, the number of times he has been elected for example, or whether or not he is a faction leader, are part of the definition of his opportunity structure. The point will become clear in the course of the discussion.

Strategic choices are made not only in the context of specific institutions; they are usually made in the pursuit of multiple goals. Getting elected, or reelected, is obviously an important goal for a politician. It goes without saying (although some political scientists spend an inordinate amount of time saying it) that it is not possible in a democracy to be a successful and powerful politician if one is not elected to office. Yet getting elected may not be all that important in determining strategic choices: it may not be that significant a problem. It is unlikely that Hosokawa, for example, or Ozawa, or any of the other key political actors in the events that followed the passage of the nonconfidence motion in Miyazawa, ever had to make a strategic choice based on its potential impact on their reelection prospects. Like many other incumbent Diet members, their support bases in their constituencies were so formidable that their own reelection prospects were never in doubt.

The idea, more generally, that politicians do what they do to get elected is suspect. Many incumbents in the U.S. Congress and in legislatures in other democratic countries probably have fewer concerns about their reelection prospects than public-choice theorists must assume to make their theory work. In any case, getting elected was only one among many factors that drove the decisions of Japanese politicians following the nonconfidence motion in Miyazawa, and the more powerful the politician, the less its importance.

The pursuit of multiple goals forces politicians to structure their choices; they must decide what goals are more important than others. In a world in which goals may be contradictory, pursuing one may make it difficult or impossible to realize another. Calculations of long-term interest may conflict with choices promising short-term benefits. In the real world of politics, it is not possible to identify a stable and universal hierarchy of strategic preferences (e.g., election first, governmental power second, policy change third, and so on).

The presumption that political leaders want to stay in power is one of those seemingly commonsense assumptions popular with rational-choice theorists that, in explaining why political leaders act as they do, is of more limited utility than such theorists assume.[1] Ideological commitment, a concern for how one will be treated by history, or a strategic calculation that giving up power now might bring greater power later—any of these considerations may overwhelm a desire to stay in power. Preferences vary, as do opportunity structures. At the least, that is the implication of the analysis of what happened to the first non-LDP government to rule Japan in almost half a century.

Incumbent Power

Following the fall of his government, Prime Minister Miyazawa dissolved the house and called for general elections to be held on July 18, 1993. The election results gave the LDP 223 seats. It was the largest party, but 33 seats short of a majority in the 511-member house. The LDP's defeat in the election was of a particular kind. The voters did not turn against its incumbent candidates. They simply failed to elect enough new LDP candidates to make up for the 45 LDP incumbents who ran against the LDP. The reelection rate for LDP incumbents and for LDP former members of the Diet running on the LDP ticket was 85 percent (178 incumbents and 18 former members out of 235 incumbent and former-member candidates).

LDP incumbents who left the party with Ozawa and Hata to form the Japan Renewal Party did even better than the incumbents who remained in the LDP. All but one of the JRP's 35 LDP incumbents won election. In addition, 20 new candidates were elected on the JRP ticket, making this new party the third largest party after the Socialists.

Although it remained the second largest party in the lower house, the Socialist Party was the only one to suffer an unambiguous defeat in the election. It was bereft of attractive leadership, beholden to public-sector unions, torn internally by personal and ideological feuds, and unable to break away from policy positions that had been devised in the context of domestic and international conditions that no longer existed. Its representation in the lower house was nearly halved, from 136 to 70. This party, which once was the major political voice of the labor movement and a popular party among urban salaried workers, now won only 1 of 43 seats at stake in Tokyo. Incumbent loyalty among Japanese voters was all that saved the JSP from an even worse fate: 64 of the 70 successful Socialist candidates were incumbents, and one of the nonincumbents was a former house member.

If the Socialists had done well in the election, they might have taken a leading role in the subsequent negotiations over the formation of a coalition government. The election results put the JSP in an anomalous position. The voters had responded to the opportunity to end LDP dominance by inflicting a defeat on the Socialist Party that was worse than any it had ever suffered before. Yet they left the JSP with enough seats to make it the second largest party in the Diet and to make its participation in government essential if non-LDP parties were to have enough members to constitute a majority. The Socialists were too weak to lead and too strong to be ignored.

The Komeito's Strategic Opportunity

The party with the next largest representation was the Komeito, whose fifty-two seats represented a modest increase over the forty-five seats it won in the preceding election and made it the fourth largest party in the house after the LDP, JSP, and the Japan Renewal Party. The split in the LDP and the opportunity it offered for other parties to try to hammer together a coalition government came at an opportune moment for the Komeito. The number of voters supporting the party had not increased for more than a decade. In the 1993 election, slightly more than 5.1 million voters voted for its candidates. This was more than a 100,000 fewer votes than the party's candidates obtained in the preceding lower-house election and a million fewer than in the 1976 election, when the Komeito's popularity was at its zenith.

Despite protestations that it was independent of Soka Gakkai, the religious organization that had created it in 1964, and a decision taken in 1970 to officially separate the Komeito from the Soka Gakkai,[2] the Komeito was unable significantly to expand its support beyond the Gakkai membership. The Soka Gakkai had experienced two decades of spectacular growth in the postwar period, primarily among people in urban areas who had been left behind in Japan's race for double-digit GNP growth: nonunionized workers in small factories, marginal small-business people, shop clerks, bar hostesses—uprooted and unfortunate people who were promised health and wealth in this world in return for their faith. By the end of the 1960s, the Soka Gakkai had an estimated membership of some six and one-half million families, some 10 percent of the entire population.

However, as the Japanese economy matured and growth slowed, the frenetic pace of migration from rural areas to Tokyo and other metropolitan centers slackened, thereby reducing opportunities for the Soka Gakkai to expand its membership. Moreover, antipathy to the Soka Gakkai and to the Komeito was strong among the general public, and the Komeito's role as the political arm of the Gakkai made it a target of constant criticism.

Unlike many European countries, Japan did not have a tradition of denominational political parties. Its only modern experience with the involvement of organized religion in politics occurred in the prewar period, when the state, as part of its drive for total national mobilization, made Shinto the officially sanctioned religion of the country. The constitution adopted after the Second World War provides for the separation of church and state and specifically bars the state from providing support for religious organizations and observances. However, it does not prohibit religious organizations from endorsing candidates for public office or supporting the political parties to which those candidates belong. Many religious organizations support the LDP, but the Soka Gakkai was the only religious group to establish a party of its own. Support for the LDP by religious as well as many other kinds of organizations was compatible with its character as a party of inclusion; dependence of the Komeito on the Soka Gakkai defined it as an exclusionary party. Even though the Komeito has recruited candidates to run for the Diet who are not Soka Gakkai members to demonstrate its independence from the Gakkai, it remains essentially a party of Soka Gakkai supporters.

Soka Gakkai was founded as a lay organization of the Nichiren Shoshu branch of Japanese Buddhism. Over time, and especially in the aftermath of a bitter dispute between the Soka Gakkai and the main temple of the Nichiren Shoshu sect that led to a breaking of relations in 1991,[3] the Soka Gakkai increasingly became an organization devoted to propagating the ideas of its leader, Daisaku Ikeda. The Komeito, for its part, found itself in the position of having to defend itself against charges that Ikeda controlled the party. It also struggled to derail efforts by LDP politicians to force Ikeda to testify before the Diet on the Gakkai's political activities and to pass legislation that would increase the power of the state to force religious organizations to disclose details of their internal operations and finances. This bill, the Basic Law on the Separation of Church and State, was submitted in the aftermath of the March 1995 gassing attack in the Tokyo subway system perpetuated by members of the Aum Shinrikyo, but it seemed aimed especially at the Soka Gakkai.

The effort to pass such legislation eventually was dropped by the LDP. Nearly the entire community of religious organizations in Japan, including those that supported the LDP, concerned that it would open the door to the possibility of a reassertion of state control over religion, mounted a vigorous campaign against it.[4] Nonetheless, the Komeito in 1993, when the results of the general election left the LDP without a majority, faced a difficult situation. It had a stable but no longer growing constituency and it was under incessant attack for its relationship with Soka Gakkai.

With fifty-two seats, control over a bloc of several million committed voters, and the financial support of the Soka Gakkai, the Komeito suddenly found itself in a position where its support had become indispensable for Ozawa and others who wanted to form a coalition government against the LDP. Moreover, Komeito leaders shared the conventional wisdom that a new electoral system of predominantly single-member districts would force Japanese political parties to consolidate into a two-party format,[5] and they saw an opportunity to increase the Komeito's power by forging an alliance with Ozawa to create a new unified party.

The Japan New Party Boom

Continuity, not change, was the most salient characteristic of the 1993 election. Incumbents won, whether from the LDP, the Japan Renewal Party or the Socialist Party. The same was true for the Sakigake, the small party formed by LDP defectors who, unlike those in the Ozawa faction, had voted against the nonconfidence motion and then broke with the party. Nine of the Sakigake's ten incumbents, and in all thirteen of its candidates, were elected.

The only party that could claim that the success of its candidates represented a sharp break with the essential continuity of Japanese voting behavior was the Nihon Shintō, the Japan New Party. Formed by Hosokawa barely a year earlier, the Japan New Party had in its first lower-house contest run fifty-seven candidates and captured thirty-five seats. The party's success made it inevitable that Hosokawa would play a pivotal role in the struggle over the composition of the new government. His party had enough lower-house members to give either the LDP or a coalition of non-LDP parties a majority. Moreover, since the Japan New Party's Hosokawa and Sakigake's Takemura were allies planning a merger of their two parties, an alliance with Hosokawa would inevitably bring the cooperation of the Sakigake as well. If Hosokawa joined forces with the LDP, the result would be a three party LDP, Japan New Party, Sakigake coalition in which the LDP would be dominant. If Ozawa could entice Hosokawa to ally with non-LDP parties in the Diet, those parties would not only have a lower-house majority. Hosokawa's participation would provide an image of reform and modernity that Ozawa and other LDP veterans who were now outside the LDP could not deliver, notwithstanding their claims to be stalwart advocates of political reform.

Hosokawa had been a Diet member in the LDP, but that was long ago and it had little impact on his image as a maverick and as a symbol of a new breed of Japanese politician. He was urbane, handsome, and an articulate spokesman for political reform. He came from a famous aristocratic and political family: his grandfather, Prince Fumimaro Konoe, had been the last prime minister before the outbreak of the Second World War.

Hosokawa had left a career as a reporter for the *Asahi Shimbun* to run for a seat in the lower house in 1969. He was unsuccessful in that election, but he won a seat in the upper house in 1971 and again in 1977. In all these elections, he ran as a candidate of the LDP. In 1983, after two terms and twelve years in the upper house, he was elected governor of Kumamoto prefecture, the predominantly rural prefecture in Kyushu that was his family's political base back into the Tokugawa period. A popular governor, Hosokawa was reelected in 1987. He resigned from office in 1991 in order to prepare for his reentry into national level politics.

Although Hosokawa's political base was in a rural part of the country, he had a distinctly modern outlook and was popular among voters in Tokyo and other urban centers. Hosokawa understood that if he were to be successful in an effort to break into the leadership ranks of politicians active at the national level, he would have to do it by tapping the support of this urban constituency. He sensed that public discontent with conservative politics-as-usual had reached a new level of intensity among Japan's educated urban middle class and he thought that it offered him an opportunity to build a political movement to challenge the established parties. In May 1992, he set out on what many believed was a quixotic journey to form his own political party.

Hosokawa's political ambitions could not be satisfied by following the well-trodden pathway to political power traveled by LDP members of the Diet. He had neither a faction of Diet members to support him nor the seniority derived from being elected repeatedly to the Diet needed to obtain positions of power in the party and the cabinet. Over time, the LDP had become an increasingly bureaucratized organization with clear rules regulating promotion within the ranks of its Diet contingent. Virtually no lower-house member with fewer than five election victories could hope to become a cabinet minister. Conversely, almost everyone with six such victories could expect to receive a ministerial or important party post. But they also could stay in office only a short time since room had to be made to give everyone with the requisite seniority an opportunity to serve.

Hosokawa could expect to receive a certain number of seniority "credits" for his two terms in the upper house and his eight years as governor. Even so, under normal circumstances, he would have to remain in the lower house a considerable amount of time before making his way into the leadership councils of the party. Gambling on the possibility that he might be able to jump the leadership queue would have been very risky for Hosokawa. Even then the chances that he would become a powerful figure in the party, given its factional structure, were poor. And he knew from his experience in the upper house how uninteresting and tedious life could be for an LDP backbencher. Given his ambitions and the particular constraints he faced, it made sense for him to pass up the opportunity to have a seat in the lower house as an LDP member and to opt instead to strike out on his own. When he decided to do so, however, he could hardly have foreseen that only a year later the LDP would split and he would be thrust into the political limelight.

Hosokawa first returned to national politics by winning a seat in the July 1992 upper-house election, along with three other candidates of his Japan New Party. After the passage of the nonconfidence motion in Miyazawa and the calling of new lower-house elections, he gave up his upper-house seat to run for the lower house. He and his new party scored an impressive victory. Almost all of the Japan New Party candidates who were elected were little known by the voters in the urban constituencies in which they ran; they were mostly young political novices drawn into politics by Hosokawa's charisma and by the prospect of being part of a major transformation of Japanese politics. They generally were poorly financed and had almost nothing in the way of a traditional campaign organization. They won by riding on Hosokawa's coattails. The voters who gave Japan New Party candidates the opportunity to serve in the lower house were casting their votes not so much for the individual candidates in their districts as they were voting for Hosokawa and for political change. As a result of the election, Hosokawa was in the lower house not as a second tier leader in the LDP but as the head of a party that in effect held the casting vote to determine the shape of a new coalition government. His gamble had paid off handsomely. Hosokawa, the maverick politician with a radical reform agenda of deregulation, decentralization, and electoral reform, was now the man of the hour.

Sakigake's Leverage

The other key player in the politics surrounding the formation of a coalition government after the July 1993 election was Masayoshi Takemura, the head of the Sakigake. With only thirteen members in the Diet, this party should have been too small to be a significant player in negotiations over the composition of a coalition government. But Sakigake was more important than its numbers indicated. For Hosokawa, alliance with the Sakigake increased his bargaining power because it gave him a bloc of lower-house votes that was close in number to what the Japan Renewal Party and the Komeito each commanded.

Hosokawa and Takemura, both former governors who championed a similar program of decentralization of governmental authority and political reform, had been discussing the possibility of forming a unified party well before the events of the summer of 1993 erupted. When I spoke with Hosokawa in early June 1993, for example, he said that he and Takemura were planning to announce the formation of a new party probably toward the end of the summer. He showed me a list of some fifteen names of LDP members whom he said would leave the LDP to join this new party.[6] The unexpected passage of the nonconfidence motion in Miyazawa upset their plans, forcing Takemura to make a decision about leaving the LDP before he and Hosokawa had finalized an agreement on forming a new party. Although that party merger never took place and Hosokawa and Takemura later became political adversaries rather than allies, they operated as a team in the negotiations over the formation of a coalition government in the days following the passage of the nonconfidence motion.

Takemura began his career in the Ministry of Home Affairs from where he was recruited by Prime Minister Tanaka to work on Tanaka's remodeling of the Japanese archipelago project. In the early 1970s he ran successfully for mayor in a small town in Shiga prefecture, an area near Kyoto that includes the popular tourist destination of Lake Biwa. Takemura later became governor of the prefecture and stayed in that office for twelve years. He was a popular and innovative local leader, who among other things led a successful drive to clean up Lake Biwa and make environmental protection an important political issue. Takemura left the governorship in 1986 to make a successful bid for a seat in the lower house on the LDP ticket.

Once in the Diet, Takemura found himself in the frustrating position of being an ambitious and experienced political leader whose lack of seniority within the LDP Diet contingent excluded him from positions of influence in party councils. He also was a radical on the issue of political reform in the LDP, meaning he not only paid lip service to the importance of political reform, something that nearly all LDP members found it expedient to do, but actively tried to get the party to reform its fund-raising practices and other behavior. In 1988, he formed a study group of first-term Diet members who although drawn from several different factions shared a common interest in political reform. Most of the members of this Utopia Political Study Group were young politicians who were outspoken in their criticism of money politics.[7] Like Yukio Hatoyama, the son of a former finance minister and the grandson of the LDP's first prime minister and later one of the leaders of the Democratic Party, they were mostly second- or third-generation politicians, well-known and popular in their districts. The Utopia Political Study Group played a significant role in raising the visibility of the political-reform issue. Among other things, its members publicly disclosed their political funding practices, providing detailed evidence how even many first-term Diet members spent in excess of a million dollars a year to fund their political activities. The LDP members that joined Takemura to form the Sakigake came from this study group.

As a result of the 1993 election, in other words, the major players in the politics of coalition making were Hosokawa and Takemura, Ozawa backed by the Komeito, and the leaders of the LDP. Given their numbers, the Socialists were an important factor in their calculations, but the JSP itself, decimated and dispirited by the election returns, was a rather passive participant in the events that led to the formation of a non-LDP coalition government. The Democratic Socialist Party, with only fifteen seats, was too small to be a major player in the bargaining over coalition formation, and the Communists, who won fifteen seats and maintained a stance of independence from all the other parties, were not a factor.

The LDP's Response

The initial LDP reaction to the election results was rather optimistic. Despite the fierce attacks on the party in the press, it had come out of the election with more than three times the number of seats as the next largest party. The parties that performed well in the election, the Japan Renewal Party, the Japan New Party, and Sakigake, were all led by former LDP members and were closer to the LDP in terms of basic policy orientations than they were to the Socialists or to the Soka Gakkai-backed Komeito. One could hardly claim that the election represented the voters' rejection of the LDP's basic policy stance. After all, those LDP members who ran on the Sakigake and Japan Renewal Party ticket did not claim that they left the party because they disagreed with its domestic or foreign policies but because they disagreed with its stance on political reform. LDP incumbents running either on the LDP ticket or as members of the Japan Renewal Party and Sakigake together garnered 271 seats, which meant there was hardly a net loss at all from the 275 seats the LDP had won in the preceding election.

LDP Secretary-General Kajiyama and others in the LDP leadership came out of the election with a dual goal. They wanted to patch together a coalition that would give the LDP the seats it needed to restore its majority and they were determined to isolate Ozawa and his supporters. It appeared that the question facing the party seemed to involve little more than to figure out how much it would have to horse trade with Hosokawa and Takemura in order to get them to join a government with the LDP. Seemingly convinced that the LDP was the permanent party of government, they acted on the assumption that the offer of a few choice cabinet posts and other payoffs would prove irresistible to Hosokawa and Takemura.

They were quickly awakened to Japan's new political realities, not at first by the actions of the leaders of the opposition parties but by a revolt within the LDP's own ranks. Secretary-General Kajiyama's attempt to keep the decision of who should succeed Miyazawa as party president in the hands of a small group of party leaders produced a hue and cry among party members, especially among younger LDP backbenchers, and a demand that the decision be made in an open convention of all the party members in the Diet. Kajiyama was forced to concede on this procedural point and agreed to convene a conference of LDP members of both houses of the Diet.[8] Whatever hopes he may have entertained that he would be able to control the convention were quickly dashed. One after another, party members rose to castigate the leadership and to demand that the party commit to meaningful political reform.

Most importantly, they rejected Michio Watanabe as candidate for party president. Watanabe was the leader of a large faction in the party and ran for party president with the backing of Kajiyama and other party leaders. He had held many important party and government posts, including Minister of International Trade and Industry, but his image was primarily that of an ideological conservative and political operator who followed the tried and true practices of traditional LDP factional politics. With the public clamoring for political reform, many Diet members in the LDP feared that making Watanabe party president would simply reinforce the LDP's image as being a party mired in the discredited practices of the past.

The political-reform issue had undermined factional solidarity in the LDP. As the vote for party president approached, factional discipline broke down. Yohei Kono, the same Kono who had left the LDP twenty years earlier to found the New Liberal Club, decided to challenge Watanabe for the party presidency. Kono enjoyed a public image as a liberal and reformer, a man of principle who was opposed to politics as practiced by the party bosses. Although he no longer enjoyed the kind of movie star popularity he had when he headed the NLC, he still was popular with the public, especially compared to the old guard in the LDP which had become so closely identified in the public mind with the party's corruption and arrogance of power. In that sense he was an ideal candidate for a party anxious to change its image as one opposed to political reform and wishing to avoid further defections and the continued erosion of its popular base of support. When the ballots were counted, there were 159 votes for Watanabe and 208 for Kono.

The LDP's decision to make Kono its new president, however, did not seem to convince many people, least of all those LDP members who had defected or Hosokawa, that the party had changed in any fundamental way. There was no indication that the LDP was prepared to make any drastic changes in its position on electoral reform or that it would reform practices it had developed to regulate appointments to cabinet and party posts or to raise and distribute money. The LDP acted on the implicit assumption that it could remain in power by buying the support of the leaders of one or more small parties. However, now that the key factors that had sustained one-party dominance—ideological division at home and a cold war abroad—were no longer operable, the choices available to the LDP's challengers were greater than before. They were playing for higher stakes than simply a few key cabinet positions in an LDP-dominated government. They were looking for a way to restructure the party system and to secure important positions in that restructured system for themselves. LDP leaders were slow to understand this new dynamic and shocked when they discovered that they were making no headway in their efforts to entice Hosokawa or the leaders of any of the other parties to join in a coalition with them.

The Politics of Coalition Formation

While LDP leaders were trying to get their bearings and devise a strategy for retaining power, Ozawa and his colleagues in the Japan Renewal Party were moving forward aggressively with their plans to create an anti-LDP multiparty coalition. Of all the players in the post-election politics of coalition building, Ozawa was in an especially strong position to assume a leadership role: he and virtually he alone exhibited no ambivalence whatsoever about his goal. That goal was to drive the LDP out of power and to mastermind the operations of a coalition government that would be committed to electoral reform.

Ozawa and Hata had burned their LDP bridges behind them. There was no going back. The same was true for other Japan Renewal Party members who had allied with Ozawa and helped bring down the Miyazawa government. Many of them were typical constituency-oriented politicians who had assiduously built their electoral machines by channeling public works spending and other government benefits to their supporters. Help in getting access to these benefits was a major reason why they had joined the Takeshita faction and had drawn close to Ozawa in the first place. Bolting the LDP had been a large gamble for these politicians inasmuch as their electoral strength derived from their ability to keep the subsidy pipe flowing into their constituencies. That they took this gamble was testimony to Ozawa's power and charisma, but they also believed Ozawa would succeed in making his supporters the nucleus of a new non-LDP government. Ozawa was determined to make their gamble pay off.

In tracing developments in the days following the July 1993 general election that led to the formation of a Hosokawa-led coalition government, it is tempting to impute brilliant strategic thinking to those politicians who succeeded in grasping control of political power. Hosokawa and Takemura in particular seem to have behaved in a manner that was calculated to maximize their position as holders of the casting vote over the composition of the coalition. They hesitated to align themselves with either the opposition or the LDP, forced those parties that wanted their support to accept their political-reform program, and ultimately maneuvered themselves into a position where Hosokawa became prime minister and Takemura obtained the important position of chief cabinet secretary.

The reality is that strategies were not coolly calculated to achieve well-defined goals but were improvised reactions to evolving developments. Both Hosokawa and Takemura went into the 1993 election with no expectation that they would join the government. Their strategy was to position themselves as a new opposition force and concentrate their energies on expanding the support base of the new, merged party they planned to form. For the first few days after the election, according to Takemura, neither he nor Hosokawa were sure what they should do.[9] Their unwillingness to take a position on the formation of a coalition government was not the consequence of a strategic decision but the product of confusion and indecision.

Uncertainty rather than clever strategic calculations led them to adopt a stance that in the end gave them the leverage to decide whether the LDP or Ozawa's Japan Renewal Party would be part of a new coalition government. Several days after the election, Hosokawa and Takemura announced that they would cooperate only with parties that agreed to support a hastily drafted program of political reform, the centerpiece of which was a proposal to replace the current multimember district electoral system with a mixed system of single-member districts and proportional representation. They did not close the door to anything insofar as their relations with other parties were concerned. This meant, by implication at least, that coalition with the LDP was a possibility, although Hosokawa later claimed that he never seriously entertained the possibility of forming a government with the LDP.[10] Although this stance resulted from uncertainty, especially on Takemura's part, about what their goal and strategy should be, its effect was to spark a competition between Ozawa and the LDP for Hosokawa's and Takemura's support.

The LDP's initial reaction to the Hosokawa-Takemura demand for adherence to its political-reform proposals was to try to negotiate the details of the proposed new electoral system with them. Hosokawa and Takemura, however, insisted on unqualified support for their reform proposals. They did so with the intention of demonstrating to the public that they represented a new political force in Japan that would not compromise on matters of principle. Other parties, anxious to seize the opportunity to grasp political power away from the LDP, quickly accepted the reform proposal in order to secure Hosokawa's and Takemura's support for an anti-LDP coalition government.

Meanwhile, as the LDP inched its way closer to the Hosokawa-Takemura position on political reform, Ozawa became increasingly fearful that Hosokawa's Japan New Party and Takemura's Sakigake would end up forging an agreement with the LDP. He responded not only by embracing their political-reform proposal as his own, but by unceremoniously dropping Hata as candidate for prime minister and throwing his party's support behind Hosokawa. Hata had nowhere to go at this point and no choice but to accept Ozawa's decision.

Hosokawa's indecision had driven Ozawa to take the initiative in proposing a Hosokawa government, something Takemura did not want and Hosokawa did not at first anticipate. Hosokawa himself maintains that he did not consider standing as a candidate for prime minister until asked to do so by Ozawa. "Anyway, we had more success in the election than we had imagined having. All we thought about was how to maintain this momentum and increase our seats. Every day, after the election was over, we met to talk about how we should not make easy compromises but push forward with our principles and policies into the coming upper-house election and the next lower-house one. So until Ozawa brought that proposal [to make Hosokawa prime minister] to us, neither Takemura nor I had thought about it at all."[11]

Hosokawa did not hesitate to accept the proposal as soon as Ozawa made it. After all, this was the scion of a famous and powerful political family, the grandson of a prime minister. He was a man who had made an unorthodox return to national politics as head of an urban party with not even a single lower-house member in it when elections were called in July 1993. He had formed the Japan New Party in the hope that somehow he would be able to break through the seniority- and tradition-encrusted system of LDP dominance and become an important player on the political stage. Now Ozawa was offering him the role of leading man, and Hosokawa grabbed for it. The alacrity of his response also was intended to forestall any possible negative reaction by Takemura. "I knew that Takemura would not be pleased," Hosokawa said later. Takemura was older, had a longer career in the lower house, and "he thought that he should be the one to be asked."[12]

Once the decision was made, Takemura had no choice but to support it, since the Sakigake did not have enough seats to alter the outcome of the struggle for control of the government. Other non-LDP parties also quickly fell in line. On August 6, 1993, Hosokawa became prime minister of a coalition government that included the Japan Renewal Party, the

Japan New Party, Sakigake, the Socialists, Komeito, Democratic Socialists, and the Social Democratic League. Takemura assumed the position
of chief cabinet secretary. Hata became deputy prime minister and foreign
minister. Ozawa stayed out of the cabinet, using his position as secretary-
general of the Japan Renewal Party to play his preferred role as the power
behind the throne. The chairman of each of the seven political parties
that comprised the coalition took portfolios in the cabinet.[13] Cabinet
posts were distributed to the parties in proportion to party strength, just
as they had been distributed to factions in proportion to their strength
when the LDP was in power. The JSP received six, the Japan Renewal
Party five, the Komeito four, and one post each went to the DSP,
Sakigake, and the SDL. Two cabinet posts were given to non-Diet
members. The power of Ozawa's Japan Renewal Party in the coalition was
reflected in its control over the most important cabinet posts, including
ministers of finance, international trade and industry, foreign affairs,
defense, and agriculture.

Thus, Hosokawa came to power as head of a motley coalition of
reformers, political opportunists, socialists, pacifists, internationalists, and
others. The potential for conflict within the coalition was obvious from
the beginning. There were unresolved policy differences between the
Socialists and former LDP members who now were in the Japan Renewal Party. Many of the coalition's members were uneasy about alliance with
the Soka Gakkai–supported Komeito. And there was a deep animosity
between the two most important supporting players in the coalition that
had put Hosokawa in power, Ozawa and Takemura, who represented two
very different conceptions of political reform.

The Ozawa-Takemura Rivalry

Ozawa was a policy reformer. Changing the political process was important to him only to the extent that it facilitated policy change. He did not
evince any interest in reforming politics as an end in itself. His objective
was not to clean up politics and to strengthen democracy, but to make
Japan a "normal" country. Ozawa was a self-proclaimed revolutionary, and
as a revolutionary he was more interested in ends than in means. "So I'm
not arguing the usual simple-minded, 'Let's have a politics that doesn't
cost money' view. It's that very line of reasoning that's blocking the
progress of political reform."[14] "I never said," Ozawa emphasized in a

conversation in 1997, "that a single-member district system should be adopted to lessen the cost of politics." Electoral reform was needed to force voters to make hard choices between two parties standing for different policies. It was needed "to revolutionize the way Japanese people think."[15]

Takemura was not interested in a revolution, and he was at the other end of the political spectrum from Ozawa when it came to Japan's role in the world. Instead of Ozawa's "normal" country, Takemura wanted to see Japan as a "small and sparkling" country, a civilian power that was concerned about improving the environment and the welfare of its citizens. Takemura's vision was essentially of a Japan that recommitted itself to its peace constitution, democracy at home, and a role as a benign civilian power abroad.[16] He and the politicians closest to him wanted reforms that would clean up Japanese politics, make decision making processes more transparent, and make for a more open and modern political process.

For Ozawa, the primary purpose of electoral reform was to force parties to reorganize into a two-party format that would structure political competition around basic policy choices. For Takemura, a successful electoral reform would reduce the cost of elections and the role of personal campaign organizations. By having "party-centered" elections, there would be fewer opportunities to perpetuate the corrupt relationships that had developed between candidates and local business interests in their constituencies. Takemura and those who shared his outlook talked of the desirability of having a moderate, multiparty system with themselves representing a "third force" that would break out of the traditional framework of conservative-versus-progressive party competition.

Takemura saw Ozawa as representing precisely the old style of boss-dominated factional politics that he and his Sakigake colleagues wanted to eliminate. Months later, after Ozawa succeeded in forcing him out of the coalition, Takemura would play a critical role in forging an agreement between the Socialist Party and the LDP that would drive Ozawa out of power and bring about an LDP-Socialist-Sakigake coalition government.

Although voters who had cast their ballots in the July 1993 lower-house election could not have anticipated that the election would produce a Hosokawa-led coalition government, public-opinion polls indicated that they were pleased with the outcome. Public enthusiasm for what was in the personal experience of most Japanese the first non-LDP government ever could hardly have been greater. The Hosokawa government generated an excitement—a sense that Japan was on the threshold of a new and

positive era in its political history. The dragon of one-party dominance
had been slain, a charismatic, worldly, and unconventional politician had
become prime minister, political reform was in the wind, and all of this
was occurring without upsetting Japan's social stability or its key foreign
relationships. Politics finally seemed to be catching up with the society
that economic success had created.

The Hosokawa Coalition

Prime Minister Hosokawa came into office in August 1993 with a long
policy agenda. It included political reform, successful conclusion of the
Uruguay Round of trade liberalization negotiations, a wholesale reduction
in regulations constraining business activities, budgetary reform, and
strengthening Japan's ties with its Asian neighbors. While none of the
coalition parties publicly opposed any of these goals, they differed considerably on specifics. The exception was political reform. Hosokawa had
exacted a pledge from each of them to support the introduction of a new
electoral system of single-member districts and proportional representation. Fulfilling this commitment consumed the energies of the coalition
government for nearly five months, until the electoral-reform bill finally
passed the Diet near the end of January 1994.

It also kept the coalition united. The coalition parties could differentiate their common position from that of the LDP as long as the electoral-
reform issue was unresolved. Once the Diet passed legislation to change
the electoral system however, deep policy differences and intense personal
rivalries quickly exposed how fragile the unity of the coalition had been.
In April 1994, frustrated by his inability to govern effectively, and under
attack over allegations he had engaged in financial improprieties,
Hosokawa decided to resign.

"Kokutai Politics"

Why did Hosokawa lose power in spite of his personal popularity and the
coalition's success in passing political-reform legislation? The apparent
reason the anti-LDP coalition was unable to remain united was the
absence of agreement on any issue of importance other than electoral-system reform. This, however, only begs the question of why those who had

succeeded in ousting the LDP from power for the first time in nearly four decades did not try to retain power by downplaying their differences. Surely, they could have found some issues upon which they could agree and thus kept the coalition intact and in power until they could call a general election. Why would rational politicians throw away the power that was theirs knowing how difficult it would be to recover it if the LDP came back to control the government?

One important factor contributing to the coalition's collapse is that it came to power not only without an agreement on its goals other than passing political-reform legislation, but without an agreement on a process for deciding what its policies should be. For the previous thirty-eight years, policy had been processed through the Policy Affairs Research Council (PARC) and other organs within the LDP's institutional structure. With nearly all legislation being submitted to the Diet in the form of cabinet bills, the actual process of formulating and drafting legislation was characterized by close consultation and coordination between members of the LDP and bureaucrats in the relevant government ministries. The LDP might take positions of other parties into account in designing its legislative program, but these parties themselves entered the policy-making process only at a later stage, after legislation had been submitted to the Diet and the LDP needed to negotiate with them to facilitate passage of its legislation through the Diet.

During the LDP's thirty-eight-year reign, the Diet failed to establish itself as an important institution for these interparty negotiations. The Diet has a formal structure of standing committees and special committees that is comparable to the U.S. Congress's committee structure. However, these committees never developed a role in policy making that even began to approach the role played by congressional committees. The institution that most closely parallels the congressional committee structure in terms of its role in policy formulation was encased within the LDP itself, in its PARC and the PARC's array of committees.

Even though policy formulation was monopolized by the LDP and the bureaucracy, the LDP nevertheless had to negotiate with the opposition parties in order to facilitate the Diet's processing of the government's legislation. The logic of the '55 system of LDP dominance impelled both the LDP and the opposition parties to shield those negotiations from public view. Especially on issues where the Socialists and other parties felt compelled to make a public showing of their opposition to LDP policy, interparty relations became characterized by a pattern of private deal making rather than open compromise. The more the Socialists and other opposition parties resigned themselves to one-party dominance, the more interparty negotiations over legislation became centered in private and opaque venues. The policy-making process came to emphasize covert consensus rather than open compromise since the opposition, overtly, was uncompromising in its opposition to the LDP. The role of Diet committees in this system was to serve as formal agencies confirming informal understandings reached elsewhere.

One of the most important committees in both the lower house and upper house is the House Management Committee, *gi'in un'ei iinkai*, or *gi'un*. This committee is responsible for determining the distribution of committee seats to parties, the schedule for debate over bills, and many other matters relating to Diet procedures. It is roughly comparable to the rules committee in the U.S. House of Representatives, although on paper the *gi'un* has even more power than the rules committee commands.[17]

Power in the *gi'un*, as in other Diet committees, rests with its directors *(riji)*. Because the *gi'un* directors include representatives from all the major parties, from the LDP to the Socialists to the Communists, it proved virtually impossible to keep understandings reached among the *gi'un* directors confidential. Agreements that might be reached in private, between the LDP and the Socialist Party for example, were not possible in the transparent light of *gi'un* negotiations.

The result was that negotiations between the LDP and the opposition gravitated away from the *gi'un* and out of the Diet itself and into the privacy of informal meetings among party leaders serving on their respective parties' Diet-strategy committees, the *kokkai taisaku iinkai* (or *kokutai*). As the longest-serving chairman of the JSP's Diet-strategy committee put it, "In the Diet and in public meetings, you have to say what union leaders want to hear. In the privacy of the *kokutai* meetings, you can make realistic compromises."[18]

Over the years of LDP dominance, the *gi'un* became in effect the formal agency within the Diet for confirming informal agreements reached in discussions among leaders of the various party *kokutai*. If the *gi'un* was the arena for overt negotiations, the *kokutai* was where covert understandings were reached. Japan developed a pattern of interparty relations in the policy-making process that became known as *kokutai seiji*, "*kokutai* politics."

The *kokutai* is not an institution within the Diet structure. It is a committee within a party, and each party has one. The *kokutai* chairman is invariably a veteran politician and an important leader in his party. In the case of the LDP, *kokutai* chairman is a key post, usually occupied by someone with cabinet experience who is regarded as one of the party's leadership elite. In the Socialist Party, the *kokutai* chairman usually has been more important than the chairman of the party's policy-affairs committee, the ostensible center for policy making in the party, since the *kokutai* chairman is directly engaged in negotiations with the LDP over the government's legislation.

The role of the *kokutai* is not to negotiate the substance of policy, but to arrive at understandings about how to advance the parliamentary process. More than policy expertise, a successful *kokutai* chairman needs to have the ability to arrange political deals. Although former bureaucrats have accounted for more than a quarter of the LDP's Diet contingent and tend to dominate the most important cabinet posts, no former bureaucrat, with one minor exception, has ever served as chairman of the LDP's *kokutai*.[19] Most *kokutai* chairmen have honed their skills at negotiating with their opposite numbers in town, city, and—especially—prefectural assemblies before they entered Diet politics. They are specialists at what Japanese refer to as "the art of the belly" *(haragei)*, the art of sensing what is needed to strike a deal.

Kokutai negotiations emphasize informality, privacy, implicit understandings, and a willingness to make gestures that enable the other side to save face or to maintain an ostensible posture of opposition while in fact facilitating the passage of legislation. It follows that they are conducted not in the public glare of committee rooms but out of public view, in private rooms in expensive restaurants and in the even more exclusive geisha houses in Akasaka and Shimbashi. Singing, drinking, eating, and a demonstration of informal intimacy are all part of the process of creating a mood conducive to compromise between the LDP and the opposition. It is alleged that so, too, are financial payoffs given in the form of year-end presents or monetary gifts to opposition party leaders traveling overseas.

Kokutai politics involves more than covert collusion between the LDP and the opposition parties. It also involves similar relationships between the LDP and senior bureaucrats who want to ensure that the LDP pushes their legislative program through the Diet. LDP *kokutai* members spend a great deal of time entertaining their counterparts in other parties and they are entertained in turn by senior government officials.

One lower-house member, a MITI bureaucrat before entering politics, who was appointed in 1992 to the LDP *kokutai*, recalls a meeting with veteran *kokutai* chairman Kajiyama. Presuming that the *kokutai* would provide a venue for policy making, he asked Kajiyama for advice on how he could best prepare himself for his new responsibilities. "Well, why don't you learn how to sing thirty songs," he says Kajiyama told him. It soon became apparent why. In a one-month period, he attended more than twenty geisha parties with opposition party leaders whom the LDP wanted to coopt and with bureaucrats who wanted to coopt the LDP.[20]

Creating a Policy-making Structure

The pivotal role of the LDP's PARC in policy formulation, the centrality of the *kokutai* in managing LDP-opposition party relations, and the Diet's failure to play a constructive role in the policy process meant that, with the LDP's loss of power, there was no institutional framework in place for making policy decisions. One of the difficult challenges facing the new Hosokawa coalition government was to create such a framework.

Of course, the preponderance of government decisions in Japan, as in the United States and other complex political systems, is made by functionaries, not politicians. The shift from LDP dominance to coalition government had little impact on the bureaucracy's handling of the day-to-day business of the Japanese state. It did, however, leave the government with the challenge of creating new mechanisms for setting policy goals, ordering priorities, and mediating and coordinating competing demands. Beyond political reform, there was no agreement within the coalition on a policy agenda, or on the overarching goals that could give direction to the bureaucracy.

The LDP's loss of power exposed and made worse basic institutional weaknesses in the Japanese policy-making system. The coalition made several different attempts to gain control over policy making by institutional innovation. As it turned out, those efforts contributed to the collapse of the Hosokawa government.

Hosokawa set out to create a new formal structure for formulating policy and for managing the legislative process.[21] Overall management of the coalition government's affairs would be exercised by a "Government and Government Parties Leadership Council." The council, however, was neither a formal governmental organ nor a formal part of the institutional structure of any of the parties. It never developed a significant role.[22]

Policy formulation was to be the responsibility of the Policy Board, an entity the coalition parties intended to be the equivalent of the LDP's Policy Affairs Research Council. A number of project teams, comparable to the *bukai*, sections in the PARC, were established under the Policy Board. But the Policy Board did not become an important policy-making institution.

There also was a Management Board. This was supposed to replace the Diet-strategy committees, the *kokutai*, as the institutional setting for managing interparty relations. Its mandate was limited to managing relations among parties in the coalition government. As far as relations between the government and the LDP was concerned, the new, formal, decision-making structure aimed to eliminate *kokutai* politics of the LDP era by shifting negotiations between the coalition and the LDP into the more transparent House Management Committee, the *gi'un*. This effort to move from consensus-oriented *kokutai* politics to something closer to a Westminister model (and closer to the system in the prewar Japanese Diet), proved unsuccessful. The LDP responded to the coalition parties' refusal to engage in covert consensus building by resorting to the same kinds of obstructionist tactics that the Socialist Party had used years earlier before the informal practices of *kokutai* politics became institutionalized.

The formal structure never took hold. Instead, policy making in the coalition as well as political relations among the coalition parties came to resemble politics as practiced within the LDP in the early years of its rule. In those days, before party organs such as the PARC and routinized procedures had become fully institutionalized, factions and faction bosses dominated all aspects of party life. Now the chairmen and the secretaries-general of the several parties in the coalition behaved in the same manner. Most important, Ozawa was able by the force of his personality, and because of his strategy of close alliance with the Komeito, to establish himself as the dominant figure in the coalition, exerting extraordinary power over its policies and its personnel decisions.

The "Ichi-Ichi Line"

Ozawa had the most extensive background among the coalition's top leadership in managing political power. He had been both a faction leader and secretary-general of the LDP. Neither Hosokawa nor Takemura had held important LDP positions. Although both had executive experience in government at the prefectural level, neither had prior experience with policy making at the senior-most levels of national politics. The leaders of the other coalition parties had no governmental experience before Hosokawa came to power.

Ozawa's style was far from the consensus-oriented, time-consuming consultative approach so common in large Japanese organizations. He had little patience for the painstaking process of working out policy positions with his coalition partners. He knew what he wanted to do and he was in a hurry to do it. As soon as the coalition government was formed, Ozawa moved to take control of its decision-making apparatus. He did so by forging an alliance with the Komeito.

Ozawa was determined to bring the disparate groups that had joined the Hosokawa coalition into a single party powerful enough to defeat the LDP in an essentially two-party race under a new electoral system. Cooperation with the Komeito was a key element in his strategy since the party's relationship with the Soka Gakkai meant the support of a large bloc of highly committed voters and access to huge financial resources. The Komeito's leaders, as noted earlier, also assumed the new electoral system would push Japan in the direction of a two-party system. Although the Komeito had long embraced a vaguely left-of-center line on foreign policy, the need to form an alliance with Ozawa, the political leader who dominated the coalition and who had taken charge of the effort to forge a union among parties opposed to the LDP, overcame whatever qualms the party's leaders had about his foreign-policy positions. Ozawa's emphasis on alliance with the Komeito produced what the Japanese press dubbed the *ichi-ichi* line, the same Chinese character being used to write the *ichi* of *Ichi*ro Ozawa and Yu*ichi* Ichikawa, the chairman of the Komeito.

Ozawa was unrelenting in his determination to impose the *ichi-ichi* line on the coalition,[23] thereby alienating both the Socialists and the Sakigake. As relations between Ozawa and the Socialists, and between Ozawa and Takemura, deteriorated, Hosokawa found it increasingly difficult to maintain an equidistant position between Ozawa and the Komeito on one side and Takemura and the Socialists on the other. Tensions were contained as long as the coalition parties were united in their commitment to pass political-reform legislation. Once the electoral-reform bill passed the Diet in January 1994, coalition unity rapidly disintegrated and Hosokawa found himself more and more the captive of the *ichi-ichi* line.

Hosokawa's Predicament

Hosokawa had repulsed Ozawa's demand in December 1993 to remove Takemura from his cabinet post as chief cabinet secretary.[24] He tried to maintain his position by balancing the contending and increasingly antagonistic forces within his own coalition government. He had become prime minister even though he was the leader of only a small political party because he was someone both Ozawa and the Socialists could support. The coalition would hold together and he would remain in power only as long as he could retain the support of the feuding members of his government.

Hosokawa's decision to move closer to Ozawa even at the price of alienating Takemura and antagonizing the Socialists seemed puzzling to many observers at the time. The closer he drew to Ozawa, the more difficult it became for him to maintain any degree of unity within the coalition and the weaker his own position seemed to become. However, the price of coalition unity had become too high for Hosokawa. It meant not moving the government beyond electoral reform to adopt any of the policies that he had championed when he formed the Japan New Party and reentered national-level politics. Hosokawa was not modest in his ambitions. He wanted to be recorded in Japanese history not simply as a maverick who became prime minister, but as the prime minister who changed Japan— who restructured Japanese politics, improved relations with other East Asian countries, put U.S.-Japan relations on a new track, deregulated the economy, and set in place policies to deal with the long-term problems of an aging society.

On every one of these issues, he found himself blocked by the Socialist Party. It vetoed the national welfare-tax proposal discussed below, resisted efforts to decentralize the government and deregulate the economy, and complicated Hosokawa's efforts to undertake new foreign-policy initiatives, whether on matters of trade or security. Antagonizing the Socialists would undermine the unity of the coalition, but appeasing them would only make Hosokawa appear indecisive and prevent the government from accomplishing anything. As his frustration mounted, Hosokawa found himself pulled more and more into Ozawa's embrace even as it undermined the stability of the coalition that kept him in power.

The passage of time did little to soften Hosokawa's frustration with the Socialists. In a conversation in July 1997 he recalled with particular bitterness the troubles that the Socialists had caused him, whether it was over the Uruguay Round of GATT negotiations[25] or an increase in the consumption tax. And he claimed then, as he had done on earlier occasions, that the primary reason he resigned as prime minister was to trigger a restructuring of the coalition that would reduce the ability of the Socialist Party to obstruct the government from carrying out its program.

If Hosokawa had a particular cause, it was not electoral reform but deregulation and decentralization. For years, he railed against what he viewed as excessive power of central-government bureaucrats, power that he came to know all too well when, as Kumamoto's governor, he found himself stymied at every turn by bureaucratic regulations. He was a critic of bureaucratic power long before bashing the bureaucracy became popular in Japan.

During his first few months in office, before his government began crumbling around him, Hosokawa seemed thoroughly to relish being prime minister. He worked out of the same room in the prime minister's official residence, the *sōri kantei*,[26] where his grandfather had sat half a century earlier. The *kantei* was built in 1928 in the style of Frank Lloyd Wright's Tokyo Imperial Hotel, although it was not, as many people think, designed by him. The cultural legacy, for better or for worse, of prewar Japan was evident there in the prime minister's office, with its overstuffed chairs, their starched, white arm and head covers, and other nondescript furnishings. Prime Minister Hosokawa's espresso coffeemaker, conspicuously out of place in this tradition-laden setting, perched on a side table like an awkward visitor, a symbol of sorts of Hosokawa's desire to bring something new to this rather musty citadel of Japanese political power.

In an interview in that office late in January 1994, when the future of political-reform legislation being debated in the upper house hung in the balance, Hosokawa seemed oddly disinterested in the issue. He deflected questions about electoral reform with the comment that a deal would be struck and legislation would pass. He was not particularly interested in talking about details of a possible compromise or how the reform might affect political developments.

Confident that an electoral-system reform bill would be passed, Hosokawa wished to discuss what he considered far more important—his plans to reduce the power of what he viewed as an overly centralized and bureaucratically dominated government. Hosokawa had in mind an ambitious deregulation program. He enthusiastically explained that his program would invigorate the housing market by reducing the mass of regulations affecting housing construction, and that he was going to tackle excessive regulation of the distribution sector and reduce by more than half the ten thousand or so regulations that were constraining economic activity. In a conversation the preceding September, when he was visiting New York to address the UN General Assembly, Hosokawa remarked that he was determined to avoid what he saw as President Clinton's mistake of taking on too many controversial issues at once—health care, gays in the military, and so on. He was going to focus on electoral reform and, once that was done, turn his attention to deregulation and decentralization. With those accomplishments behind him, he would call an election and return as prime minister in a stronger position than the seven-party coalition government permitted.[27]

This was not to be. Personal antagonisms among the coalition's leaders made it difficult for them to agree on anything. Nor, as we have seen, were there institutionalized decision-making mechanisms that could restrain personal conflicts from dominating the policy process. Neither were conflicts only matters of personality. Deep policy differences divided the parties in the coalition, particularly with respect to Hosokawa's aspirations for deregulation. The Socialist Party in particular was resistant to dismantling the elaborate array of regulations that affected economic activity. More than a lack of enthusiasm for free-market ideology, the JSP's opposition to deregulation resulted from its dependence on public-sector labor unions in telecommunications, the postal service, and local-government offices threatened by deregulation and administrative reform. Without unified leadership, the coalition would be unable to overcome bureaucratic resistance to his reform program. As Hosokawa drew ever closer to Ozawa out of frustration over his inability to advance his policy agenda, the more antagonistic the Socialists became to whatever he tried to do.

The Consumption-Tax Conundrum

If these disputes alone were not sufficient to paralyze the coalition, circumstances forced Hosokawa to grapple with two contentious issues— they involved the Ministry of Finance and the United States—that he would have preferred to avoid. The need to deal with them forced him to shift his priorities and his policies. Hosokawa lost control of his policy agenda and then saw his popularity and finally his power slip from his grasp.

During the years of LDP dominance, Japanese bureaucrats preferred to operate as much as possible behind the scenes to line up political support for their policies. They were cautious about taking public positions that were at odds with the stated policy goals of the incumbent administration. They were adept at using politicians to sponsor policies that bureaucrats themselves had formulated, and unrelenting in their efforts to convince the political leadership of the rightness of their position. Japanese bureaucrats were careful to appear to be supporting the political leadership, rather than competing with it, understanding that maintaining such a public stance was a critical factor in preserving their own power.

The Ministry of Finance followed this strategy in its sustained effort to increase the proportion of state revenues obtained through indirect taxes and to reduce the state's dependence on corporate and personal income taxes. One form or another of a value-added tax was commonplace in Europe, but not in Japan. From the late 1970s onward, the finance ministry conducted an intensive campaign to change that situation.

Increasing longevity and a declining birth rate were profoundly changing Japan's demographic character. In 1970, little more than 10 percent of the population was over the age of sixty-five. Twenty years later, the figure was 14 percent, and projections were that it would rise to 26 percent by 2025. In 1975, there were nearly five people between the ages of twenty and sixty-four for every person over sixty-five. By 2020, this ratio would be only two to one. Japan was rapidly becoming the oldest nation in the world.

The finance ministry argued that, in an aging society, the state would have to tax people more at the point at which they spent money and rely less on taxing earnings if it were to avoid placing an excessive tax burden on working people and at the same time secure revenue needed to fund social welfare and the other programs that an older society would require.

In 1979, Prime Minister Ohira, who himself had been a high-ranking finance ministry official before entering elective politics, proposed the introduction of a European-style value-added tax in line with the position that was being advocated by the finance ministry. Greeted by a roar of public disapproval, Ohira withdrew his proposal almost as soon as he made it. The ministry went back to work on redesigning the new tax and emerged with a proposal to introduce a consumption tax.[28]

It took the LDP ten years from the time Ohira first raised the consumption-tax issue to get the Diet to pass legislation to create this tax. The issue proved costly to the political careers of each of the LDP prime ministers who tried to pursue it, from Ohira to Nakasone to Takeshita. A 3 percent consumption tax finally came into effect in April 1989 during the administration of Prime Minister Takeshita. Public anger over its introduction, coming on top of the Recruit scandal, forced Takeshita out of office.

Once the consumption tax had been introduced, the public seemed to become resigned to live with it, but it remained strongly opposed to the Ministry of Finance's demand for an early increase in its rate. Hosokawa no sooner came into office than he found himself caught between the contending pressures of a MoF-led campaign to increase the consumption tax, public opposition to a further hike in its rate, growing concerns in the business community that a consumption tax increase would only further dampen consumption demand, and intense pressure from the United States to take action to stimulate the Japanese economy in order to reduce trade tensions.

Without an effective system of decision making within the coalition, finance ministry officials were not able to operate mostly behind the scenes on this tax issue as they did when the LDP was in office. They sensed a political vacuum and they moved to fill it. Senior MoF officials, the administrative vice-minister in particular, were outspoken in insisting publicly that there could be no income-tax reduction without a consumption tax increase. This was a risky stance for MoF bureaucrats to take and they were later to pay a heavy price for it. Engaging openly in a political struggle over an increase in the consumption tax brought down a hail of criticism on the ministry. It later contributed directly to demands for basic reform of the ministry's structure and for a reduction in its power.

Finance ministry officials of course denied that they were trying to force any political decision on the government. They maintained that they simply were providing technical expertise to the political leadership. And their expert opinion was that an increase in the consumption tax was imperative and that the introduction of income-tax cuts without a compensating consumption-tax increase was unacceptable.

The Ministry of Finance found a powerful political ally in Ichiro Ozawa. Ozawa had not only been persuaded as many other politicians had been by the MoF's argument about the need for an increase in the consumption tax. Unlike other more cautious political leaders, he also wanted to move immediately to raise the tax rate from its current 3 percent level to 10 percent. He had advocated such a policy in his book *Blueprint for a New Japan* and now he worked closely with MoF officials to press the coalition government to approve a consumption-tax increase.

The last thing Hosokawa needed while his own position of power was so shaky was to be confronted by something as divisive as the consumption-tax-increase issue. Yet his resistance to a tax increase was steadily worn down by the intense lobbying of senior MoF officials and by the pressure exerted by Ozawa. In a conversation about a month after he left office, Hosokawa recalled how he was bombarded for days on end with arguments about the necessity of a consumption-tax increase by ministry technocrats. Lacking the expertise, or easy access to those with expertise, to counter these arguments, and irritated by what he saw as nothing more than obstructionist tactics by the Socialist Party—which had staked out a position of adamant opposition to a consumption-tax increase—Hosokawa himself became a reluctant convert to the ministry's line.[29]

Less than a week after the passage of political-reform legislation, Hosokawa called a press conference to announce that the government was going to adopt a new 7 percent "national welfare tax" to replace the 3 percent consumption tax. The press conference was held at one o'clock in the morning, having been delayed from one hour to the next because of Socialist Party resistance to the proposal. The "national welfare tax" was the same tax as the consumption tax, collected in the same manner and not limited to spending on programs related to social welfare. The finance ministry had rejected a proposal to sequester revenue from the new tax in a special account to fund social-welfare programs. Nonetheless, Hosokawa hoped that the rhetorical emphasis on social welfare in Japan's aging society would sweeten the pill enough for the Socialists to swallow.

It was not sweet enough, and within hours of making his middle-of-the-night announcement, Hosokawa was forced to beat a hasty and embarrassing retreat. The Socialists threatened to bolt the coalition unless he reversed his policy, and Takemura, whose position as chief cabinet secretary was to explain and defend the prime minister's policies, instead became a leading spokesman against this policy, remarking publicly about Hosokawa that "there's nothing like correcting your mistakes."[30]

This is what Hosokawa did. He announced that there would be a one-time ¥6 trillion reduction in personal income taxes in the following fiscal year budget and that the issue of increasing the consumption tax would be deferred to a later date. This represented a serious setback for everyone involved in the national welfare-tax debacle. It made Hosokawa look foolish, the Socialists irresponsible, and Takemura disloyal. It also brought down a barrage of criticism on Ozawa, who had led the drive to establish the 7 percent national welfare tax, and especially on the Ministry of Finance, not only for sponsoring such an unpopular policy but also for its aggressive political effort to impose its demands on the government.

Taxes and the Refractive State

The long saga of the Japanese government's handling of the consumption-tax issue indicates some of the complexities in Japan of bureaucrat-politician relations and of the political constraints on bureaucratic power. After Prime Minister Ohira was forced to back away from the initial proposal for a value-added tax in 1979, a full decade passed before a 3 percent consumption tax was introduced by Prime Minister Takeshita. Then, after Hosokawa came to power as head of a shaky seven-party coalition government, the MoF, working closely with Ozawa, managed to push the issue of increasing the consumption tax onto the political agenda and forced the prime minister to propose a policy that he did not favor.

However, the Ministry of Finance lacked the power to force the government to make its policy proposal law. Hosokawa's decision to withdraw the national welfare-tax proposal and move forward with income-tax cuts was a major defeat for MoF bureaucrats. In the end, they had to acquiesce to a large income-tax cut without a compensating consumption-tax increase, precisely the policy that they had insisted all along was unacceptable.

This was not the end of the story. In the autumn of 1994, about six months after Hosokawa's fall from power, a coalition government composed of the LDP, the Socialist Party, and the Sakigake, and led by Socialist Party chairman Murayama, got a bill through the Diet to increase the consumption tax from 3 to 5 percent. Although the Socialist Party had been in the forefront of opposition to the consumption tax, on this issue as on so many others, as we shall see in chapter 5, it did a complete about-face once its chairman became prime minister.

The consumption-tax increase was so politically controversial, however, and Japanese economic growth still so anemic, that the legislation the government submitted to increase the consumption tax provided for a delay of two and a half years in its actual implementation. It was scheduled to take effect on April 1, 1997. Politically this gave the Murayama administration some insulation against public anger over the tax increase since the tax itself would remain at 3 percent for longer than the Muraya-ma government was expected to remain in office.

Moreover, the legislation provided for a cabinet review of the decision before implementation in order that it would be in a position to recommend changes if necessary in light of current economic circumstances. The assumption in 1994 was that the Japanese economy was on the road to recovery and that it would have recovered sufficiently by the time the rate-hike kicked in to absorb a contraction in consumption demand. If this forecast proved wrong, the government would be in a position to postpone introducing the tax increase.

That cabinet meeting was held in June 1996. Murayama, as expected, was no longer prime minister, having been replaced by the LDP's Ryutaro Hashimoto—head of the LDP-JSP-Sakigake coalition government that took office in January of that year. The Hashimoto cabinet decided to go forward with the consumption-tax increase even though raising the tax, and terminating temporary income-tax cuts at the same time, posed potentially severe consequences for the economy. Whatever the economic risks of moving forward might be, for the political leadership they palled in comparison with the political risk of once again opening up this contentious issue. LDP leaders had paid a heavy political price to get the tax introduced in the first place and they had succeeded in getting the Diet to agree to the delayed introduction of an increase in its rate. To suspend that rate increase, even temporarily, would once again open up this issue with consequences that no one could foresee. And the MoF, convinced that the nation's long-term fiscal health depended not only on going forward with the scheduled increase in the tax rate but also on raising it once again as soon as possible, put enormous pressure on the cabinet not to back away from the decision.

Once the decision to go ahead with the increase was made, however, the consumption tax once again became the object of an intense political struggle. In the lower-house election campaign of fall 1996, Ichiro Ozawa, the politician who had pushed the hardest for a consumption-tax increase when he was the power behind the scenes of the Hosokawa government, now argued that the tax should be frozen at 3 percent until the end of the century in order to avoid further dampening consumption and aborting Japan's economic recovery. Ozawa's stunning about-face was interpreted by the media as little more than a ploy to garner public support for his party in the election. It produced the first major negative campaign in Japanese election history, with the LDP taking out full-page newspaper advertisements and producing political commercials for television attacking Ozawa for being inconsistent and irresponsible on the issue.

The Hashimoto government remained committed to maintaining the 5 percent consumption tax to the very end of its existence in July 1998, even though reducing its rate probably would have had a more powerful stimulative effect on the economy than the public-spending programs it proposed. Hashimoto and other LDP leaders refused to even consider the possibility of reducing the tax rate and they bristled at the suggestion, especially when it came from officials in the U.S. government, that they should consider doing just that.

The consumption-tax story seems to be never-ending, however. The LDP government headed by Keizo Obuchi that replaced the Hashimoto cabinet in July 1998, needing the support of opposition parties to pass its legislation through the upper house and hoping to draw none other than Ichiro Ozawa and his supporters into a coalition with the LDP, agreed to consider revising the consumption tax so that revenue derived from it would be earmarked for welfare-specific purposes. After having advocated an increase in the consumption tax to 10 percent in the early 1990s, Ozawa led the effort to get the Hosokawa government to propose a "national welfare tax" of 7 percent in 1994, called for a freezing of the tax rate at 3 percent in 1996, and now in 1998 was arguing that the tax should be temporarily suspended and then reintroduced later in stages. Ozawa backed away from demanding agreement to a reduction in the rate as a price for his participation in a coalition government, settling for a face-saving agreement in which the LDP agreed to review the consumption tax in all respects. Whatever uncertainties surrounded the future of the consumption tax, what was clear was that politics and politicians had once again wrested control over the issue away from the bureaucracy. The consumption-tax issue reveals as dramatically as any issue can the complexities of policy making in what in earlier pages I have referred to as Japan's refractive state.

The American Connection

The Hosokawa government's fiasco over tax reform—the early-hours press conference announcing the 7 percent national welfare tax, its retraction less than twenty-four hours later, the chief cabinet secretary's open criticism of his prime minister, and so on—caused relations between Ozawa's Japan Renewal Party and the Socialists and Sakigake to reach the breaking point, leaving the coalition in shambles. Hosokawa, unable to mend the rift, furious with Takemura for opposing him on the tax issue, and frustrated by the lack of policy cooperation by the Socialists, abandoned his attempt to maintain the support of all seven coalition parties and instead aligned himself with Ozawa and the Komeito. Ozawa intensified his campaign to bring most of the Diet members who were in the coalition into a single large party that he would control. Hosokawa now had to prepare for a summit meeting with President Clinton in a weaker position politically than at any time since coming to power..

President Clinton had come into office with a get-tough policy on Japanese trade relations. No longer would the United States accept vague Japanese promises of more open markets. Now it would insist on firm commitments and quantitative targets. The Clinton administration was determined to pursue a "results-oriented" trade policy toward Japan and to impose sanctions against Japan if tangible results the administration wanted to see did not materialize.

Prime Minister Miyazawa got a taste of this new hard line when he journeyed to Washington for a summit meeting with the new president in April 1993. Then at a joint news conference held after their meeting in which Clinton stressed the importance of "results," Miyazawa responded by saying that Japan was opposed to managed trade and would reject the kind of agreements the Clinton administration was demanding. It was an early sign that the United States and Japan were on a collision course over the American administration's "results-oriented" policy.

Clinton either did not understand or did not believe Miyazawa's message that Japan would stand firm against U.S. demands. His administration seemed convinced that a steady, forceful exercise of U.S. pressure on the Japanese government would work. When Prime Minister Hosokawa visited Washington in February 1994, he was confronted with even more-insistent demands than Miyazawa that Japan open its markets further and accept quantitative and other measures of foreign penetration as part of its trade agreements with the United States.

As he prepared to travel to Washington, however, Hosokawa was anxious to avoid a confrontation. He assumed that Clinton also wanted their meeting to be a success and that he would not want to weaken Hosokawa's standing back home. This was not only because both nations had more to lose than to gain from a confrontation that threatened a trade war. When he was in Tokyo for the G-7 summit in July 1993, Clinton had snubbed the LDP and made a point of indicating his sympathies for the views being expressed by Hosokawa and Hata and other non-LDP leaders about the importance of curtailing bureaucratic power and freeing the market from excessive state control.

Negotiations to avert a confrontation when the two leaders met continued up to the moment Hosokawa's plane landed in Washington. But those negotiations failed. For the first time in the postwar period, a summit meeting ended with an announcement that the two leaders were unable to reach any agreement on outstanding trade issues.

Clinton seemed to have been surprised by the collapse of the talks. He appears to have assumed, as other presidents have before him, that the Japanese would bend if pressure was applied long enough and hard enough.[31] Hosokawa, however, did not cave in to American demands; he returned to Japan with a new reputation as the prime minister who could say "no" to the United States.

The initial support Hosokawa gained back home by standing up to American pressure, however, rather quickly gave way to criticism that he was inept in managing important affairs of state. U.S.-Japan relations had deteriorated, tax reform had turned into a fiasco, a complex new electoral system that no one seemed to understand had been adopted, and the members of the coalition were busily attacking each other. Within two months of his disastrous late-night news conference announcing the national welfare tax and his unsuccessful visit to Washington, Hosokawa was no longer prime minister.

Upon his return from the United States, Hosokawa announced that he was going to replace his chief cabinet secretary Takemura and reorganize his cabinet. He quickly discovered that he would not be able to do that without seeing his entire coalition collapse. On March 2, he was forced to beat another humiliating retreat, announcing he had given up his attempt to reshuffle the cabinet. At the same time, he came under attack by the LDP and the Communist Party for allegedly having received money from Sagawa Kyubin. This was the same company that had been involved in the scandals surrounding Kanemaru that precipitated the breakup of the Takeshita faction and set in motion the chain of events that brought Hosokawa to power. Diet deliberations on the budget came to a virtual standstill as the LDP pressed Hosokawa to testify before the Diet about his dealings with Sagawa and other business firms. Hosokawa resigned as prime minister on April 28, 1994.

The Hosokawa Balance Sheet

There are many negative entries in the balance sheet of the Hosokawa government. Political reform amounted to little more than the adoption of a problematic new electoral system. Its one policy achievement was successful conclusion of the Uruguay Round of trade negotiations and the liberalization of the rice market. Later, reflecting on his eight months in office, Hosokawa said that, while the public viewed his government as a political-reform government, he himself liked to think of it as Japan's "rice-liberalization government."[32] It was a liberalization of an exceptionally slow and deliberate kind.[33] The Hosokawa government made virtually no progress with its program of deregulation and administrative reform, and its attempt to revise the tax system was a disaster. To say its policy accomplishments were modest would be to give it excessive praise.

There are some impressive entries on the other side of the ledger, however. The Hosokawa administration brought an end to the '55 system of LDP dominance and Socialist ritualistic opposition. It forced the reorganization of political parties and changed the mode of interaction among them. The Hosokawa administration's efforts to establish a new policy-making process were not entirely in vain, either. The LDP and the JSP learned from the Hosokawa government's mistakes and established a relatively effective system of interparty consultation, as discussed in chapter 5. Political processes became somewhat more transparent and the role of *kokutai* politics somewhat less important than before Hosokawa came to power.

Hosokawa's leadership style was new to Japanese politics. The public responded with enthusiasm to this unusual, aristocratic man-of-the-people. Hosokawa used normal everyday language when he spoke, avoiding the circumlocutions so common among Japanese political leaders. He stated his opinions frankly. He was accessible, through press conferences and public meetings. He succeeded in capturing the public imagination and he reached unprecedented levels of popularity.

That popularity extended to neighboring Asian countries. A number of Japanese prime ministers had made statements about Japan's wartime actions that they hoped would be taken as an apology by Koreans and Chinese. They uniformly failed. None managed to convey an impression that they were offering a sincere apology or indeed comprehended why other countries were demanding that Japan atone for actions that occurred so long ago. In the view of many LDP politicians, and in the public statements of some of them, Japan's actions were no worse than those committed by other armies.

Hosokawa was the first Japanese prime minister whose apologies were greeted in countries that had been victims of Japanese aggression as heartfelt and meaningful. His summit meeting in Seoul with South Korea President Kim Young Sam made him a popular figure there and contributed in a real, if intangible, way to improving Japan's difficult relations with its closest neighbor.

In the final analysis, however, the Hosokawa administration was a failure. The confrontational tactics of Ozawa and the Komeito's Ichikawa, the animosity between Ozawa and the Socialists, and the Takemura-Ozawa rivalry caused frictions in the coalition that Hosokawa was unable to manage. If Hosokawa had remained in office for even a few months longer, the subsequent course of Japanese political history almost surely would have been different. There probably would have been further defections from the LDP and there is no telling how voters would have responded if Hosokawa had been able to call a general election while he was prime minister. The opportunity to reorient Japanese politics was historic and it was fleeting, and the Hosokawa administration missed it. Politics subsequently did not return to what it had been under the '55 system, but there was less change and less reform, and greater public disinterest and cynicism about politics than would have been the case if his administration had been more successful.

Hosokawa's coalition government came into power with a commitment to legislate political reform and with agreement on no other policy. Once political-reform legislation had been adopted, the seven parties in the coalition could find no common policy goals to bind them together. They were unable to institutionalize a policy-making process that could take the place of the system that had been in effect for the previous four decades. Hosokawa was in a weak position politically because he had only a small party in the coalition and because he was caught between Ozawa and Takemura, two rivals with antithetical goals. Hosokawa's strength was his popularity with the public. As that popularity declined with his policy failures, especially over the national welfare tax, his position became increasingly untenable. A leadership and policy-making vacuum gave Ozawa the opportunity to grasp effective control over coalition management. As he pursued his *ichi-ichi* line, policy and personality differences with Takemura and with the Socialists reached the breaking point.

Moreover, the coalition's success in changing the electoral system contributed to its collapse. In a kind of classic instance of how institutional change can produce unintended consequences, the electoral reform engineered by the coalition parties set in motion a new political dynamic that strengthened the hand of the LDP at the same time that it sowed dissension within the coalition. Only the LDP was strong enough to contest all single-member districts. Only the LDP could benefit if two or more of the coalition parties ran candidates in those districts and thus divided the non-LDP vote. The irony of the situation was that the coalition parties would have had a far better chance of surviving and prospering under the old system than they did now under the new one.

Once legislation changing the electoral system had been passed, Ozawa, Hosokawa, Takemura, and other leaders in the coalition had to shift their strategies to respond to what they believed was the new system's irresistible pressures for party consolidation. This was bound to create friction, since the creation of a large, consolidated party made it inevitable that there would be an intense struggle for power and control over the new party. The major accomplishment of the Hosokawa government was to pass an electoral-system reform bill that helped pave the way for the LDP's return to power.

Chapter Four

The Politics of Electoral Reform

Pressures for Reform

The Hosokawa coalition government came into office having made a commitment to legislate electoral-system reform, and to do so within the year. The coalition parties had agreed that a new electoral system would include both single-member and proportional-representation districts. The first order of business for the Hosokawa administration was to design a reform proposal that would translate this promise of reform into concrete legislation.

It took the coalition more than five months to accomplish this goal. It took ten months more to prepare and pass legislation defining the district boundaries of the newly introduced single-member districts. As the coalition had promised, the legislation the Diet adopted in January 1994 provided for single-member districts and proportional representation. However, in the complex process of moving the legislation through the Diet, all political parties, with the exception of the Communists, wound up supporting an electoral system that was virtually identical to the one every party opposed to the LDP, and many LDP members as well, had rejected when a government commission had proposed it some three years earlier.

The decision to change the lower-house electoral system was arguably the most far-reaching political reform in Japan since those introduced during the U.S. Occupation after the Second World War. The new system introduced in 1994 replaced an electoral system that had been adopted at the time Japan adopted universal manhood suffrage in 1925 and that had been in effect ever since, with the exception of one election in the immediate postwar period.

Political reformers believed that abolishing the former electoral system and replacing it with a mixed system of single-member and proportional-representation districts would go a long way to make right what was wrong with the Japanese political system: it would create a more competitive party system, lead to an alternation of parties in power, reduce the cost of election campaigns, and make those campaigns focus more on important policy issues and less on local constituency interests. Other politicians who did not share an enthusiasm for electoral-system reform, and whose interests clearly were threatened by changing the system, nonetheless in the end went along with the reformers.

My primary concern in the discussion that follows is to explain why and how this reform came about. The focus is on three issues: why electoral reform was considered imperative in the first place; why a decision was made to adopt a mixed system of single-member and proportional-representation districts; and why a careful dissection of the process by which this decision was reached is useful for gaining an understanding of important features of the Japanese political system.

My purpose is not to assess the likely long-term consequences of Japan's electoral reform, although I will conclude with some observations on its short-term and mostly unintended consequences. Electoral-system change in Japan is a rather illuminating example of the perils of political engineering since, in the short term at least, its consequences were quite the opposite of what its proponents said the new system would accomplish.[1] It is clearly too early to say, however, what its impact is going to be over the long term. And it is too early for two rather different reasons.

One is the rather obvious reason that adjustments to changes in the rules of the game are made over time. How Japanese politicians and parties will organize their election campaigns ten years from now, assuming that the electoral system is not changed again in the interim, may be quite different from the way they organized those campaigns in the first election held under the new system—in 1996. There is bound to be a process of trial and error as politicians search for ways to manipulate the electoral system to their best advantage. It is true also that as incumbents who developed their campaign strategies and built their campaign organizations under an older system leave the scene, politicians less constrained by past practices may develop new and quite different strategies.

It is too early to say anything conclusive about the long-term impact of the new electoral system for another reason. Electoral systems, as the following discussion of the much maligned and now abolished Japanese "medium size election district" system shows, do not in and of themselves "cause" anything to happen in politics. Too many political reformers in Japan exaggerated the power of electoral-system change to serve as a kind of magic wand to correct all that was wrong with Japanese politics. Too many political scientists who supported their reform program viewed electoral systems as a powerful causative independent variable—they oversold the determinative effects of electoral systems.

Electoral-system specialists themselves, for the most part, have been rather cautious in claiming too much causation for electoral systems. That caution extends even to Maurice Duverger, the author of the so-called "Duverger's law," that a plurality system, of which single-member-district systems are a popular form, "tends to party dualism"—that is, to a two-party system. Writing many years after he propounded his dualism thesis (which he himself never referred to as a law), Duverger went to some pains to argue that "[a] particular electoral regime does not necessarily produce a particular party system; it merely exerts pressure in the direction of this system; it is a force which acts among several other forces, some of which tend in the opposite direction."[2] This is a fairly apt characterization of the short-term impact of electoral change in Japan. It has created pressures on parties to coalesce in order to compete in the single-member districts, and it has created pressures in the opposite direction as well; that is, for fragmentation among the very political forces that were endeavoring to coalesce.

One thing is quite clear: most party leaders and backbench members of the Diet who voted for electoral reform did not do so because they thought it would improve their own and their party's election prospects. Socialist Party leaders knew their party would be served best by retaining the existing system of multimember districts. The leaders of small parties (e.g., the Japan New Party and the Sakigake, the Democratic Socialist Party, and the Komeito) all understood the new system would put enormous pressures on them to disband their parties and merge into a larger party with uncertain consequences for their members. LDP Diet members for their part were not enthusiastic about having to revise election-campaign strategies to meet the demands of a new electoral system. Politicians in Japan changed the institution most directly affecting their election prospects because electoral reform was the culmination of a series of decisions taken by leaders of several political parties mostly for short-term, largely tactical, political reasons. Electoral reform in Japan offers a sobering lesson in how politics can drive politicians to sometimes do irrational things for perfectly sensible reasons.

Indicting the "Medium-size-Election-District System"

The electoral system Japan adopted in 1925 and abolished after the 1993 lower-house election is known in Japanese as a "medium-size-election-district system" *(chūsenkyokusei)*. This term focuses on what electoral-systems scholars refer to as "district magnitude," which simply means the number of candidates elected in an election district. The system was "medium-size" because fewer candidates were elected in each district than under the prefecture-wide "large-size-election-district system" Japan used from 1900 to 1920, and more than the "small-size-election-district system" *(shosenkyokusei)* used for two elections in the early 1920s.[3] Under the medium-size-election-district system, in principle each district sent three, four, or five members to the lower house.[4] In the 1993 election, candidates fought for 511 lower-house seats distributed among 129 election districts.

In English-language political-science writing about Japan, this system is often referred to as a single-entry, nontransferable-vote (SNTV) system. This terminology emphasizes the nature of the ballot; namely, that each voter is provided one ballot on which to write the name of his or her preferred candidate. The vote is single entry in that the voter can cast a ballot for only one candidate, even though several are elected to the Diet in the district. It is nontransferable in that there is no formula for transferring votes that are cast for one candidate to another.

This combination of multimember districts and single-entry ballots means that any party seeking a Diet majority (256 seats in a 511-member lower house) had to run multiple candidates in nearly all districts. In such a system, it made sense for candidates from the same party to target their campaigns at voters who supported their party rather than voters who did not. This led to intense intraparty battling among LDP candidates.

The combination of multimember districts and single-entry nontransferable votes not only generated pressures for intraparty conflict, however. It also made it possible for small parties, such as the Communist Party, the Komeito, and the Democratic Socialist Party, to survive. It was a system of imperfect proportional representation. A party whose candidate won 20 percent of the vote in a five-member district invariably would be elected. In districts where the distribution of the vote among multiple

LDP candidates was skewed in favor of one of them, parties with small shares of the popular vote could win seats.

A hypothetical example demonstrates the point: Suppose three LDP candidates together polled 60 percent of the total vote in a five-member district; that one of them, being enormously popular, alone received 42 percent; and that the other two each won 9 percent. Suppose further that candidates from four other parties won 10 percent of the vote apiece. In this imaginary district, the LDP's 60 percent would win it only one seat; the other parties' combined 40 percent would win them four, or 80 percent, of the district's seats. This example is unrealistic, but it demonstrates the advantages of this electoral system for small parties. They were reluctant to abolish a system that had enabled them to survive, and they adamantly opposed introduction of a simple "first past the post" system that seemed certain to destroy them. All of the parties in opposition to the LDP favored either retaining the single-entry ballot, multimember-district system or replacing it with a system of proportional representation.

In the real world of Japanese elections, it was not unusual for the LDP to lose seats in a district because it ran too many candidates. Where it might have won two seats if it ran two instead of three candidates, or one seat if it ran one instead of two, it ended up with none. Its candidates "fell down together"—*tomodaore,* in the widely used Japanese expression. Intraparty competition often left one LDP candidate in a district in the *jiten* position of being ranked highest among the losing candidates (e.g., fifth in a four-member district, sixth in a five-member district) because the distribution of the vote among the LDP's candidates left one of them with fewer votes than were obtained by the lowest-placed winner from another party. *Jiten* candidates usually would then spend the time until the next election strengthening their campaign machines and expanding their support in the district. Their success in the next election sometimes would put another incumbent LDP candidate in the *jiten* position.

This dynamic of the single-entry ballot, multimember-district system was responsible for producing considerable turnover among incumbents and new candidates during the long period of LDP dominance. Such a system had the advantage of infusing new blood into national politics when only one party was in power. Intraparty competition in elections in one-party-dominant Japan played a role in politics not unlike primaries in the American South during the long years of Democratic Party dominance.

Criticism of the medium-size-election-district system has a history almost as old as the system itself, and the belief that it was somehow responsible for Japan's political problems grew deeper with each successive political scandal. By the early 1990s, a consensus had emerged within the mass media and among business leaders, other public figures, and bureaucrats in the Ministry of Home Affairs who were election-system specialists.[5] It was that Japan's election system was primarily responsible for factionalism, money politics, the power of special interests, candidate-rather than party-oriented election campaigns, an emphasis on personality rather than policy in voting behavior, and LDP one-party dominance. If there was going to be meaningful political reform, there would have to be a radical change in the electoral system. Those politicians who were not in the forefront of the campaign for electoral reform got caught up in its wake. It became virtually impossible to be a proponent of "reform" and not be in favor of abolishing the medium-size-election-district system.

There were many reasons to doubt this system was the cause of Japan's political problems. There was even more reason to question whether abolishing it would eliminate those problems. Italy has had factionalism and corruption and the United States has enormously costly campaigns and intraparty competition in its primary-election system. Sweden and India and other countries have experienced long eras of one-party dominance. Yet not one of these countries had an electoral system even remotely similar to Japan's.

The issue of intraparty competition also was more complex than was generally recognized. A system of single-entry ballots and multimember districts does not necessarily cause intraparty competition. It would not do so for example in a system where a party running multiple candidates had an organization capable of orchestrating a fairly even division of the party vote among its candidates. Taiwan offers an example of such a system.

In the Taiwan system, where district magnitude—the number of representatives elected in each district—was greater than in Japan, the Kuomintang avoided intraparty competition that Japanese assumed was endemic to their system. The Kuomintang central party leadership controlled the campaigns of party candidates and effectively structured the vote among them. At least, this was the case in the past in Taiwan,[6] although the current situation in less certain.[7] In Japan, too, a highly centralized and well-disciplined party like the Communist Party or the Komeito, if it had enjoyed high enough levels of popular support to sustain more than one candidate in a district, in all likelihood would have been able to manage the campaign in a manner that avoided intraparty competition.

Whether or not there is intraparty competition, in other words, depends as much on the structure of the party as it does on the structure of the electoral system. There was intraparty competition among LDP candidates because the party itself did not control the campaigns of its candidates. Relations between candidates and the party organization was rather like a franchise system. The party offered a known name, financial support, and other assistance to its endorsed candidates, but each candidate was in effect an independent political entrepreneur with his own local organization and his own marketing strategies. Party endorsement was important, but LDP candidates controlled their own campaign organizations and competed for votes against other "franchised " LDP candidates in their districts.

A system like Japan's medium-size-election-district system causes intraparty competition under two related sets of conditions: when the party is unable to structure the vote among multiple candidates and when voter support for a particular party is high enough that the party can reasonably expect to elect more than one candidate in a district. There will not be intraparty competition in the absence of either of these conditions. There was no intraparty competition in those urban districts where the LDP, because of its limited public support, ran only one candidate. Intraparty competition in the Socialist Party disappeared not because the electoral system changed but because the party stopped running multiple candidates.

If, instead of abolishing the medium-size-election-district system, political reformers had insisted on redrawing boundaries to rectify district imbalances—thus reducing the Diet representation of rural districts (where the LDP was especially strong)—the LDP would have had to reduce substantially the number of districts in which it ran multiple candidates. If a one-man, one-vote principle had been imposed on that system, the LDP probably would have been forced to run only one candidate in a preponderance of districts. This, in turn, would have greatly reduced intraparty competition. A dynamic, moderately pluralistic party system might well have emerged as a result.

One of the most curious arguments political reformers advanced in support of their argument about the need to abolish the medium-size-election-district system was that it perpetuated one-party dominance. Japan needed to adopt a single-member-district system in order to create a situation in which there would be an alternation of parties in power, according to this view. This argument is curious in two respects.

First of all, the major theoretical argument in favor of plurality systems is not that they encourage alternation of power between parties but that they foster stable government by manufacturing single-party majorities. The stability of plurality systems is contrasted with what is alleged to be the cabinet instability produced by proportional-representation systems. When LDP leaders first proposed adoption of a single-member-district system back in 1955, they did so because they believed it would make it easier for them to consolidate their power, not because they thought that it would foster an alternation of power between the LDP and the Socialists. Yet reformers in the early 1990s wanted to introduce a single-member-district system not to reinforce one-party hegemony but to end it.

Second, the argument that the medium-size-election-district system perpetuated one-party dominance was odd because the political leaders outside of the LDP who made it had come to power under it. In his maiden Diet speech as prime minister, Hosokawa addressed the need for electoral-system reform. First he expressed the conventional view of the curent system's shortcomings: "Under the present medium-size-election-district system, it is impossible to avoid intraparty competition and that makes it inevitable that competition will be between candidates rather than a debate between parties over policies."[8] Hosokawa then proceeded to argue that "under the medium-size-election-district system, the power situation among parties has become rigid, causing a loss of political tension and exacerbating political corruption as well as the absence of policy debate."[9] It is mystifying why Hosokawa would emphasize rigidity and the loss of political tension. LDP one-party dominance had ended, leaving power in the hands of a seven-party coalition. And Hosokawa, the leader of a new and small party, was standing in front of the Diet, a new prime minister chosen by a lower house that had just been elected under this very system.

The political mood in Japan in the early 1990s was not conducive to rational arguments about the costs and benefits of the Japan's long-existing electoral system or proposals to modify rather than abolish it. Politicians, bureaucrats, businessmen, academics, and the mass media all joined in criticism of the system and in demanding that it be replaced with an entirely different one. By 1993, this popular mood had become so strong that it robbed the medium-size-election-district system of legitimacy and made electoral reform unavoidable. If it had not been replaced, at least temporarily, the electoral system would have continued to be blamed for Japan's political troubles, and reformers would have continued to champion electoral reform as a cure-all for Japan's political problems.

It became impossible to consider political reform without electoral reform. The claim that Japan could only achieve party-centered, policy-oriented, less-costly elections and develop a more competitive party system if it abolished the system of single-entry ballots and multimember districts was transformed from a debatable thesis into a commonly embraced assumption. Electoral reform had become synonymous with political reform. The voices of the "defenders of the past" were drowned out by a chorus shouting the need to change the electoral system.

The Origins of the Mixed System

Japan's political parties have shifted their positions on electoral reform over time. When the LDP came into existence in 1955, electoral-system reform was one of the most important planks in its platform. In 1993, however, its leaders refused to agree to change the electoral system that the party had wanted to abolish in 1955, even at the price of losing political power. The Socialists and other parties in opposition to the LDP had once fought fiercely to defeat LDP efforts to revise the electoral system, but in 1993 they formed a government committed to change the electoral system despite the LDP's opposition. Then in January 1994 the LDP and the governing coalition parties unanimously agreed to introduce a new system.

The Communist Party was the only party to maintain a consistent position on electoral-system reform. It favored either maintaining the medium-size-election-district system or replacing it with a national-list, proportional-representation system. It was the only party to vote against the compromise bill that the Diet passed late in January 1994 establishing a new electoral system.

For many years, the LDP advocated introduction of a simple "first past the post" system like that used to elect members of the House of Commons in Britain and the House of Representatives in the United States. The LDP anticipated that such a system would drive minor parties out of existence and that LDP candidates would win in the great majority of districts, perhaps garnering enough seats to secure the two-thirds majority needed to initiate the process of amending the constitution.[10] The Socialist Party and other opposition parties made precisely the same calculation. Their leaders argued that the medium-size-election-district system should be replaced by a system of proportional representation—in which voters would cast their ballots for parties rather than for individual candidates—or not be replaced at all.

In 1955, shortly after the LDP was established, Prime Minister Hatoyama attempted to get Diet approval of a bill to elect lower-house members through a system of single-member districts. Hatoyama's election-reform bill, which provided for 457 single-member and 20 two-member districts, drew district boundary lines in a manner intended to maximize reelection prospects of LDP incumbents and secure enough seats to obtain the two-thirds majority needed to initiate the constitutional amendment process. This attempt to gerrymander the districts to serve the LDP's interest created a new term in the Japanese political vocabulary—the "Hatomander."

On April 30, 1955, the Speaker of the lower house convened a plenary session to consider Hatoyama's election-reform bill. There was such intense opposition to the bill that it proved impossible to bring order in the chamber and the session adjourned almost immediately. The bill was sent back to committee to be revised. The revision consisted of removing the Hatomander by deleting the entire appendix to the bill that delineated the proposed system's district boundaries. Instead, the bill provided for creation of a special committee with authority to determine the division of districts. This was the origin of an approach followed in every subsequent consideration of election reform. The matter of defining district boundaries was put in the hands of a special commission, the recommendations of which were to be adopted by the Diet by means of a separate law. This approach was adopted with respect to the electoral-reform bill that passed the Diet in January 1994.

Stripped of its Hatomander, the LDP's electoral-reform bill was approved by the lower house over the strenuous objections of the opposition parties and sent to the upper house. At this point, however, the LDP had to make a choice whether to pursue electoral reform or to put its energies into getting Diet approval for another controversial bill that had been sent up from the lower house, and that was regarded by the LDP as a crucial element in its drive to reverse American Occupation–period reforms. This bill scrapped the American Occupation–imposed system of publicly elected school boards and returned full control over the school system to the Ministry of Education. Hatoyama decided that resolving the school board issue was more important than electoral reform. On June 2, 1955, with some five hundred police sent into the Diet chamber to maintain order, upper-house members passed the bill abolishing publicly elected school boards. No vote was taken on the electoral-reform legislation. The electoral system remained unchanged.[11]

The LDP continued to call for the introduction of a single-member-district system after Hatoyama's effort failed. In 1972, Prime Minister Tanaka once again attempted to introduce a bill to establish such a system, and once again the effort was rebuffed. The opposition parties remained as strongly opposed to a single-member-district system as they had been before. In addition, there was much less enthusiasm within the LDP for electoral reform than there had been when Hatoyama was prime minister.

Although constitutional revision remained an official party goal in the early 1970s, the LDP was no longer pursuing the issue with anything like the fervor it did in the late 1950s. The LDP had evolved from a party that had come into existence pledging to overturn key elements of the postwar political and economic order to become one that was claiming responsibility for Japan's postwar success. The public strongly supported retaining the postwar constitution and the institutions associated with this success story. Accordingly, there was little public appeal in the argument that Japan needed an electoral system that would give the LDP the two-thirds majority needed to revise a constitution the public opposed changing.

Moreover, while the LDP had been successful in returning majorities under the medium-size-election-district system, the Socialists had been losing strength as other parties in the opposition camp—the Democratic Socialists, Komeito, and a revitalized Communist Party—won seats in urban districts that previously had gone to Socialist Party candidates. This competition within the opposition camp helped the LDP retain its dominant position, even as its own share of the popular vote in Diet elections declined. LDP leaders were no longer enthusiastic about adopting a system that would encourage opposition parties to consolidate and confront the LDP with a single candidate in districts where the LDP currently won seats because of competition among the opposition parties.

One of the perceived advantages for the LDP of a single-member-district system when Hatoyama proposed it in 1955 was that it would eliminate the intraparty competition and centrifugal tendencies generated by the medium-size-election-district system. In a multimember district system, even if the LDP split, its two or three incumbents in a district might still stand a good chance of winning election under separate party labels. If two former LDP members ran as candidates of separate parties in a single-member district, however, the chances that they both would be defeated by a Socialist Party candidate would increase. Adopting a single-member-district system, therefore, could be expected to encourage LDP factions to work out their differences within the party. It would provide strong institutional incentives for unity in a party divided into powerful factions.

By 1972, the LDP had been in power seventeen years. The factional alliance had held together and the party had made considerable progress in building its organization. The likelihood that the electorate would vote it out of office seemed remote. Its incumbents had built campaign organizations that tended to be strongest in particular parts of their districts and among particular support groups. Intraparty conflict was limited by one LDP incumbent having his base of support in one part of the district and another having his in a different area. There was little support among LDP Diet members for tinkering with an election system under which they were successful and the LDP had secured a dominant position.

Over time, incumbents of other parties had developed an interest in retaining the medium-size-election-district system as well. Being incumbents meant that they had run successful election campaigns. Whatever alleged advantages one electoral system might have over another for their parties, no incumbent could be entirely sure what the consequences of the introduction of a new electoral system would be for his own reelection prospects. Success had made lower-house members of whatever political stripe conservatives on the issue of electoral reform.

The Electoral-System Advisory Council

In 1961, the Diet passed an Electoral-System Advisory Council *(senkyo seido shingikai)* law. Under this law, the prime minister was empowered to establish an advisory council to make recommendations concerning the electoral-system and political funding whenever he deemed it desirable to do so. During the first eleven years after passage of this law, the government convened seven successive advisory councils. The advisory councils made a number of recommendations concerning political funding and campaign practices and they considered a number of alternatives to the existing electoral system. They were unable, however, to reach agreement on electoral-system reform. When the term of the members of the seventh advisory council expired in December 1972, the government appointed no new council. The issue of electoral-system change disappeared from the political agenda, not to surface again until seventeen years later when leaders of the LDP, desperate to find ways to contain the political fallout from the Recruit scandal, once again took up the call for electoral-system reform.

In May 1989, a party political-reform committee that had been created the previous December presented a report to Prime Minister Takeshita calling for the adoption of a single-member-district system "in principle." The report suggested that the LDP should "consider adding a proportional-representation element to reflect minority opinion."[12] Though the proposal was tentative and vague, this was the first time that an official body in the LDP had proposed an electoral reform that provided for both single-member and proportional-representation districts.

With electoral-system reform back on the political agenda, Prime Minister Takeshita decided to convene a new electoral-system advisory council, the first since 1972. Takeshita was forced out of office before he was able to establish the council, but he had set a process in motion that led his short-lived successor as prime minister, Sosuke Uno, to establish the eighth Electoral-System Advisory Council in June 1989. Takeshita had proposed that the new council, unlike those in the past, not have politicians serve on it as "special delegates." This was intended to signal the LDP's seriousness about political reform since the presence of party representatives had been an important factor in preventing previous councils from mustering a majority in favor of any specific electoral-system reform.[13] The council could hardly be expected to keep political considerations out of its deliberations, however. Whatever it might recommend would become law only if passed by the Diet. Politics was never far from the minds of council members. In the end, the recommendations of the eighth advisory council were driven more by considerations of what would be politically acceptable than they were by an objective assessment of the merits of different electoral systems.[14]

Previous councils had been unable to produce a majority in favor of any single alternative to the medium-size-election-district system, but the report of the fifth advisory council in 1967 was the last to consider simply modifying it. The proposed modification was to replace the single-entry, nontransferable ballot with a double-entry, nontransferable one (in Japanese, *nimei seigen renki tōhyōsei*) that, its proponents argued, would reduce intraparty competition. Only one member of the fifth advisory council supported this proposal,[15] which subsequently disappeared from the council's list of possible reforms. When the seventh council concluded its deliberations in 1972, the one thing it could agree on was that modification of the existing system was not a viable option; it would have to be replaced by a totally different one.

The seventh advisory council's 1972 report considered four alternatives to the existing system: a single-member-district system, a prefecture-based, proportional-representation system, a system in which votes for candidates in single-member districts and for parties in proportional-representation districts would be linked in calculating the total distribution of seats, and a system of single-member and proportional-representation districts that would not involve any linkage in determining the distribution of seats. This last system was called a parallel system *(heiritsusei)* to distinguish it from a German-inspired linked system *(heiyōsei)*.

The eighth advisory council picked up in 1989 where the seventh had left off almost two decades earlier. It accepted without debate or qualification the conventional view that the medium-size-election-district system resulted in excessively expensive and candidate-centered rather than party-centered election campaigns, encouraged factionalism and corruption, discouraged a policy debate among parties, and prevented the emergence of a vibrant, competitive party system. It did not consider modification of the system and proceeded from the assumption that neither a simple single-member-district system nor one of purely proportional-representation districts stood any chance of being adopted by the Diet.

Having assumed rather than debated the merits of abolishing Japan's system of single-entry ballots and multimember districts, the council devoted most of its attention to considering different formulae for combining single-member and proportional-representation districts. The underlying political problem was that the LDP wanted a system that would give primacy to single-member districts and the Socialists and other opposition parties wanted one in which proportional representation would hold a commanding position. The LDP bias in favor of single-member districts derived from the party's "franchise" character. Its members had powerful personal bases of support and wanted a system in which voters would cast ballots for individuals in relatively small districts. Since the Socialist and Democratic Socialist parties depended heavily on the support of labor unions and the Komeito relied on the Soka Gakkai, these parties favored a system of relatively large districts in which voters would write the name of a party rather than an individual candidate on their ballot. It perhaps was inevitable that the advisory council, motivated primarily by a concern to find a compromise formula that all or most parties could accept, would try to steer a middle course between these two views.

The advisory council's 1991 recommendations called for a system in which three hundred members of the lower house would be elected in single-member districts and two hundred would be elected in eleven regional proportional-representation districts. Voters were to have two ballots. On one they would write the name of a candidate in their single-member district; on the other they would place the name of a party running a list of candidates in their proportional-representation district. Candidates running in the single-member districts could be included in their party's proportional-representation party list, thus making it possible for a candidate defeated in a single-member district to be elected through the party vote in the proportional-representation district. After two years of intense political conflict over the issue of electoral reform, the Diet in January 1994, as discussed later in this chapter, passed legislation that embraced the recommendations of this advisory council in almost every respect.

The eighth Electoral-System Advisory Council, having concluded its work, disbanded on June 27, 1991. Later that day, the LDP's Electoral-System Investigative Council and the Policy Affairs Research Council endorsed the government advisory council's recommendations for a new system of single-member districts and proportional representation and sent them to the LDP Executive Board for final approval. There was such strong opposition to the recommendations among members of the board, however, that its chairman, rather than putting the issue to a vote, simply declared the debate over, the meeting adjourned, and the recommendations approved. With opponents to electoral reform in the party furious and determined to prevent their party's leadership from ramming through legislation to change the electoral system, the fight over this issue moved into the Diet.

At this point Toshiki Kaifu was the prime minister. Kaifu, a member of the small faction that had been founded by former Prime Minister Miki, had been recruited by the Takeshita faction in August 1989 to become prime minister in the hope that his reputation as a liberal and reform-minded politician would help to muffle the public outcry against political corruption in the LDP. Kaifu and the LDP's new secretary-general, Ichiro Ozawa, were both ardent proponents of electoral reform. Both favored introducing a single-member-district system, Kaifu because he believed it would weaken factions and reduce corruption, and Ozawa because he was convinced it would produce a two-party system and force each party to take contrasting positions on major policy issues.

The legislation that Kaifu submitted to the Diet accepted the advisory council's recommendation for a mixed system of single-member districts and proportional representation, although it weighted the system more heavily in favor of single-member districts than the council had recommended. It kept the council's recommendation for 300 single-member district seats but provided for only 171 seats to be chosen through proportional representation instead of adopting the council's proposal for 200 proportional-representation seats. It also provided for a single, nationwide, proportional-representation district rather than the eleven regional districts called for in the advisory council's plan. Reducing the number of lower-house members elected through proportional representation made the legislation even less acceptable to the opposition parties than the advisory council's proposal.

Despite two years of work by the advisory council, an incessant media campaign for political reform, the railroading through the LDP's Executive Board of the decision to move forward with electoral reform, and repeated avowals by Kaifu to get legislation passed at all costs, the Diet scuttled his reform legislation with remarkable speed and with no attempt to save face, for Kaifu or for anyone else. The lower-house Special Committee on Political Reform met only six times to consider the reform package. All of the opposition party members who rose to interpolate the government at these sessions opposed adoption of the legislation. So too did nine of the thirteen LDP members who spoke. With no prospect that the committee would report out the legislation, the LDP chairman of the committee summarily declared that the bills were "discarded"—that they would, in American terms, die in committee. This spelled the end of Kaifu's political-reform efforts and hastened his departure as prime minister. He was replaced by Kiichi Miyazawa on November 5, 1991.

Reviving Hatoyama's Reform Proposal

Prime Minister Miyazawa could not avoid the political-reform issue, though he had no interest in putting it high on his administration's agenda, as was mentioned in chapter 2. How he dealt with it was largely determined by the LDP's new secretary-general, Seiroku Kajiyama, now one of the most powerful figures in the Takeshita faction, Ozawa having left to form his own faction.

Kajiyama and Miyazawa were contrasting figures in almost every respect. If Miyazawa was a prototype of the bureaucrat-turned-politician in the LDP, Kajiyama was the epitome of the pure party politician. He came to the Diet not from the bureaucracy but from a career in prefectural politics that culminated with his becoming Speaker of the Ibaragi prefectural assembly. As a key member of the Takeshita faction, he was a veteran of the LDP's political wars, and as LDP *kokutai* chairman, he was a skillful behind-the-scenes negotiator with opposition party leaders. Miyazawa left "politics" pretty much in Kajiyama's hands, and in Kajiyama's hands electoral reform became a political weapon to pursue the Takeshita faction's power struggle with Ozawa.

Since Ozawa and Hata claimed that their commitment to political reform was the reason they bolted the Takeshita faction, Ozawa's political opponents reasoned that any success the LDP might have in passing reform legislation would be interpreted as a victory for Ozawa and a defeat for Kajiyama and other Takeshita faction members. The last thing Kajiyama wanted to see was the drafting of an electoral-reform bill that might obtain a Diet majority and give Ozawa a political victory. Yet the Takeshita faction and the Miyazawa administration could not afford to appear indifferent or opposed to "political reform." So Kajiyama maneuvered to get the LDP to submit a political-reform plan he thought Ozawa would feel compelled to support and that was certain to be voted down by the opposition parties—who, it is to be remembered, had a majority of seats in the upper house.

Accordingly, the Miyazawa government scuttled entirely the recommendation of the advisory council for a mixed system and returned to the basic proposal Hatoyama had made in 1955 and that Ozawa and others had advocated: it submitted a bill to the Diet to create an entirely single-member-district system in the lower house with five hundred seats. Miyazawa, sensing the dangers to his government of getting entangled in the factional struggles that now dominated the LDP's political-reform agenda, tried to distance his government from the issue as much as possible. He had the proposal for a new single-member-district electoral system submitted to the Diet in the form of an LDP-member bill rather than stake the prestige of the government on it by submitting it as a cabinet bill, as Kaifu had done with his electoral-reform legislation.

The Socialists and the Komeito submitted their own legislative bill in response to the LDP's proposals. Doing so was intended as a tactical maneuver to show the public that they, too, were committed to political reform. Their joint proposal called for two hundred single-member districts and three hundred members elected in twelve regional proportional-representation districts. Intent on scoring a tactical victory against the LDP by posing as more sincere proponents of political reform, the Socialists and the Komeito seemed oblivious to the implications of their actions. They now had put themselves on record unequivocally as supporters of a mixed system in which voters would cast separate ballots for candidates in single-member districts and for parties in proportional-representation districts. In the future, they might argue about the balance between single-member districts and proportional representation, but they could not claim to be opposed to the principle of a mixed or "parallel" system. The die for an eventual compromise had been cast.

When the Diet met in January 1993, there were two political-reform proposals before it—the LDP single-member-district proposal and the opposition's mixed-system proposal weighted in favor of proportional representation. Neither of them followed the recommendations of the eighth advisory council. Both faced strong opposition even from within the parties that sponsored the legislation. Most important, both were submitted with the confident expectation that the Diet would defeat them.

With two competing bills in front of it, the Special Committee on Political Reform decided to suspend customary Diet procedures, procedures that are inflexible in the extreme. A cabinet minister, for example, being questioned in committee is required to limit his responses to directly answering the questions addressed to him. He is not supposed to raise other issues, or to ask a question in return; Diet proceedings allow for explanations, not for debate. Since these procedures are determined by custom rather than by law, however, changing them requires only a decision by the committee's members. The Special Committee decided to permit an open debate on electoral reform, an innovation in Diet management that was noted and applauded in several newspaper editorials.[16] It did not, however, produce an agreement on electoral reform. The debate was terminated abruptly and the bills died when the Diet passed a motion of nonconfidence in Prime Minister Miyazawa. Electoral reform had been abandoned once again.

The Hosokawa Reform

On July 23, 1993, five days after the lower-house general election that left the LDP without a majority of seats, Hosokawa and the Sakigake's Takemura held a joint press conference at which they called for abolishing the medium-size-election-district system within the calendar year and replacing it with a mixed system of 250 single-member districts and 250 seats elected in a nationwide proportional-representation district. They said that they would enter into negotiations over the formation of a coalition government only with parties that agreed to support this proposal, as noted in the preceding chapter. Every party except the LDP and the Communists quickly expressed support for it. Even the LDP's Executive Board, though not quite willing to support the specifics of the Hosokawa-Takemura proposal, adopted a resolution to accept in principle the creation of a mixed system. So now all the parties (except for the Communists) were agreed that there should be change in the electoral law to provide for a new mixed system of single-member districts and proportional representation.

Commenting on this near universal agreement to support an electoral system that was so widely rejected when the government's eighth Electoral-System Advisory Council proposed it three years earlier, the *Asahi Shimbun* concluded that "Nagata-chō is a strange place. Even though the government and opposition parties were bitterly divided for years over the electoral system, now all of a sudden eight parties, from the LDP to the JSP, are moving toward agreement." The *Mainichi Shimbun* voiced a similar view, saying it was shocking how the LDP simply turned around and accepted the mixed system when only weeks earlier it let a nonconfidence motion pass rather than extend the Diet session to consider establishing such a system.[17]

Hosokawa and Takemura had made support for their electoral-reform plan a condition for participation in a coalition government. They knew that if they did not have a binding agreement in advance, chances were slim that the coalition would be able to reach a consensus. Ozawa favored a simple single-member-district system, the Socialists a proportional-representation system. Hosokawa later said that he had not been enthusiastic about the mixed system himself and rather preferred retaining the medium-size-election-district system modified to give each voter two ballots, an idea that had been considered and rejected by earlier advisory councils, as noted above. He proposed the mixed system because it was the only one that could get the support of all the parties.[18] Other party leaders in the coalition agreed to support the mixed system since the alternative was to have no agreement at all on electoral-system reform. The survival of the Hosokawa coalition government now depended on its ability to get the Diet to approve a bill establishing a new, mixed, electoral system that no party found entirely satisfactory.

The Hosokawa cabinet submitted political-reform legislation to the lower house a little more than one month after coming to power. The reform package contained four bills providing for public subsidies to parties, new restrictions on political contributions, stiffer penalties for candidates whose senior campaign managers engaged in illegal campaign activities, and an electoral system that provided, as Hosokawa and Takemura had promised, for the election of 250 lower-house members in single-member districts and 250 in a nationwide proportional-representation district. The package also provided for the establishment of a commission of private citizens to determine district boundaries for the new electoral system.

Three weeks after the Hosokawa cabinet submitted its reform legislation, the LDP submitted a reform package of its own. Even the LDP's "defenders of the past" feared that a failure to join the electoral-system-reform bandwagon would lead to further declines in the LDP's popularity and to further Diet-member defections from its ranks. Just as the Socialist Party and the Komeito, anxious to avoid being criticized for opposing political reform, had submitted their own mixed-system electoral-reform proposal in response to the Miyazawa administration's single-member-district bill, now the LDP for the same reason submitted a bill to create a system of 300 single-member districts and 171 members chosen in prefectural proportional-representation districts.[19]

All of these maneuvers were undertaken essentially for tactical reasons. No party ever made a strategic decision that its interests would be served best by replacing the medium-size-election-district system with a mixed system of single-member and proportional-representation districts. The cumulative effect of these tactical decisions, however, was to bring the parties' formally stated positions on electoral reform close enough to make a compromise formula feasible. The drumbeat of public demands for "political reform" also made compromise politically unavoidable, even though there was no reason to believe that many voters understood the specifics of the various mixed-system proposals that were being fiercely contested by the politicians.[20]

There were party differences on what the balance should be between the number of members elected in single-member districts and through proportional representation, whether proportional representation should be calculated on a prefectural, regional, or national basis, and whether there should be a single or a double ballot. These differences were important, yet compared to the situation only a year earlier, when the LDP had been insisting on a single-member-district system and the Socialists and other parties were willing to support electoral reform only if it resulted in a system that was heavily weighted in favor of proportional representation, the parties now were in the same arena, putting forward various variants of the mixed-system formula. Hosokawa needed to have the Diet pass electoral-system-reform legislation to survive as prime minister; the Socialists needed to support him or else the coalition would collapse; and the LDP needed to change its antireform image. This set the stage for a compromise that none of the parties wanted or knew how to avoid.

After a month of inconclusive debate in the lower-house Special Committee on Political Reform, the coalition parties and the LDP agreed to enter into direct party-to-party negotiations to break the deadlock. This effectively took the issue out of the Diet and its committee structure and put it in the hands of Prime Minister Hosokawa and LDP president Kono. Hosokawa proposed a compromise formula of 274 single-member districts and 226 seats to be chosen through a regional proportional-representation system. In other words, he tried to make it more attractive to the LDP by raising the proportion of members elected in the single-member districts. Voters would have two separate ballots, one on which to write the name of a single-member-district candidate and the other on which to vote for a party in the regional proportional-representation district. The LDP continued to press for still further concessions, causing the Hosokawa-Kono negotiations to break down.

On November 18, 1993, the lower house met in plenary session to vote both on the government political-reform legislation, now revised to reflect the compromise formula Hosokawa had offered to Kono, and the political-reform bills that the LDP had submitted. A majority first defeated the LDP's bills. The house then voted on and passed the coalition's legislation. With legislation having been adopted by the lower house, the struggle over electoral reform now shifted to the upper house.

Upper-House Autonomy

American Occupation officials involved in designing Japan's postwar political system proposed that Japan should have a unicameral legislature, thereby eliminating any vestige of the House of Peers that existed under the Meiji Constitution. At the urging of Japanese political leaders, however, the decision was made to create a House of Councillors, half of its members to be elected every three years for six-year terms. Conservative Japanese political leaders hoped that this upper house would become a body of independent-minded legislators who would take a long-term view of the national interest and act as a brake on the more impetuous lower house.[21]

However, as the party system took root in the postwar period, the number of independents in the upper house rapidly declined. Upper-house members affiliated with political parties in roughly the same proportions on average as members in the lower house. As long as Diet members observed party discipline, the legislative function of the upper house appeared to be little more than to rubber-stamp decisions taken by the lower house.

In terms of parliamentary structure, however, the Japanese constitution provides opportunities for the upper house to exercise autonomy. A bill that is rejected by the upper house after being passed in the lower house becomes law only if it secures a two-thirds vote after being returned to the lower house. The same rule applies if the upper house fails to act on a bill within sixty days after receiving it from the lower house. The exceptions are budget bills, treaties, and selection of the prime minister; in these cases, the decision of the lower house prevails. Moreover, the parliamentary caucus system (discussed in chapter 5) gives upper-house members a certain degree of independence vis-à-vis their own parties' leadership. The relative absence in practice of upper-house autonomy in the legislative process was not so much a matter of parliamentary institutional structure as it was the consequence of there being a similar balance of power among parties in the two houses and a tradition of strong party discipline.

When the Hosokawa administration's electoral-reform bill came before the upper house, the balance of party forces was similar to what prevailed in the lower house, in the sense that the LDP was the single largest party and the parties supporting the Hosokawa coalition government controlled a majority. But the Socialist Party was in a relatively stronger position in the upper house than it was in the lower house. In the 1989 election, when the LDP lost its upper-house majority, the JSP won forty-six seats, compared with only twenty in the previous election in 1986. It won only twenty-two in the next 1992 upper-house election, but its total number of seats in 1993 was a combination of seats won in the two elections of 1989 and 1992. Many of the Socialists elected in the Doi boom in 1989 were critical of the party leadership that came to power after Doi resigned as party chair. They knew from the party's dismal showing in the 1992 election that their own chances of winning if they decided to run again when their term expired in 1995 were poor. Many of them had nothing to lose by defying the party leadership over the issue of electoral reform.

The upper-house Special Political Reform Committee voted out favorably the political-reform bills that had been passed by the lower house. But seventeen Socialists joined the LDP, the Communist Party, and some independents to vote against the legislation when the bill came to the floor of the upper house. Five LDP members crossed the aisle in the other direction to vote for the legislation.[22] With 118 in favor and 130 opposed, the upper house defeated the electoral-system-reform legislation that the lower house had passed.

The parties in the coalition government lacked the two-thirds majority in the lower-house needed to override the upper-house vote. Article 59 of the constitution, however, stipulates that the lower house may call for a joint conference committee of members of both houses in the event the upper-house decision on a bill differs from that of the lower house. If the conference produces agreement, the revised legislation becomes law if then passed by a simple majority in both houses. Prime Minister Hosokawa decided to invoke this constitutional provision—it was the first time it had been used in forty-three years—to convene a joint conference committee to resolve the differences between the two houses over electoral-system-reform legislation.[23]

The joint-committee provision in the constitution was modeled on the U.S. Congress, but Diet committees were not centers of legislative power and Diet members did not exercise the independence enjoyed by members of Congress. So while in theory the joint conference committee had the power to report out a compromise bill, in practice its members had no power whatsoever. In a familiar pattern in Japanese politics, Japanese political leaders retained the formal structure of the joint conference committee while setting up an informal second-track mechanism to negotiate an end to the stalemate over electoral reform.

The conference committee provided a formal cover for informal negotiations between the LDP and the coalition. Hosokawa and Kono, both of whom were anxious to come to an agreement, negotiated through the night to hammer out a compromise before the Diet session was scheduled to end. Announced at a joint press conference early on the morning of January 29, the agreement consisted of ten points, the most important of which was a proposal to create a new electoral system of three hundred seats in single-member districts and two hundred in eleven proportional-representation districts—exactly the formula the eighth Election-System Advisory Council had proposed in 1991.[24]

The joint conference committee convened for the final time on January 29, 1994, the last day of the Diet session, to rubber-stamp the Hosokawa-Kono proposal. There was not enough time left in the Diet session, however, to prepare new legislation based on their agreement. Rather than close the Diet without taking a vote and thereby risk the possibility that the compromise might unravel and the entire reform effort collapse, the committee by a vote of 17 to 3 voted out the original lower-house bill that had passed and the upper house had rejected, but now with the date of implementation stripped from the bill. The first order of business of the new Diet to convene on January 31 would be to amend this legislation to accord with the Hosokawa-Kono agreement. Both houses of the Diet passed the legislation later that same day. Seventeen upper-house Socialist members who had voted against the legislation when it first came up from the lower house and one upper-house LDP member voted against it. So did three LDP and six JSP lower-house members.[25] However, now that the LDP had shifted its position from opposition to the original bill to support for the bill reported out by the joint conference committee, the bill easily passed. It bears repeating that this was, legally speaking, the same bill the LDP previously opposed, but now it had no implementation date and there was a gentleman's agreement to amend it in the next Diet. This manipulation of formal processes to ratify informal agreements among party leaders elicited little comment in the Japanese mass media, probably because the Diet had performed in a manner consistent with expectations.

When the 129th Diet session opened on January 31, the coalition parties and the LDP convened an ad hoc Political-Reform Consultative Group to prepare legislation based on the Hosokawa-Kono agreement. The group made a few, mostly minor, changes to the informal agreement confirmed at the final session of the joint conference committee.[26] By the end of February, the group had completed its work and sent the draft legislation to the Special Political Reform Committee, the committee formally responsible for preparing legislation. This committee rubber-stamped the consultative group's decision and sent the legislation to the full house, which passed it the same day. With its passage by the upper house three days later, on March 4, 1994, the Diet completed its adoption of a new electoral system.

Drawing District Lines

An election could not be held under this new system, however, until the Diet passed separate legislation defining the boundaries of the new single-member districts. A commission responsible for drawing the single-member-district lines began deliberations on April 11, 1994.[27] The law that created the commission required that each prefecture first be allotted one district regardless of population size. In determining the boundaries of the other 253 districts (there are forty-seven prefectures) the law directed the commission to have district lines follow existing administrative divisions as closely as possible, to have no district cross prefectural lines, and to take into account geography, ease of transportation, and other factors. It also directed the commission to keep district imbalances—that is, the difference in the weight of the vote between the least- and the most-populated district—"in principle" to below two to one.

However, because every prefecture had to be awarded one district regardless of population, and because at the same time districts could not cross prefectural boundaries, it proved impossible for the commission to adhere to the "less than two to one" stipulation. The resulting overrepresentation of rural areas was the consequence of the technical difficulties of creating a "one man, one vote" district system and not the result of political interference in the work of the commission. Drawing the lines of the new single-member districts was handled entirely as an administrative chore, undertaken by experts in the Ministry of Home Affairs. No effort was made to repeat the history of the Hatomander.[28]

The commission concluded its work on June 2. The Diet adopted the bill defining new district lines in November, and the law came into effect a month later, on December 25, 1994. After this date, for the first time in Japan's political history, lower-house elections would be held under a mixed system of single-member and proportional-representation districts.

Japan's Mixed Electoral System

The new electoral system provides for a lower house of five hundred members, three hundred elected in single-member districts and two hundred in eleven regional proportional-representation districts. The largest proportional-representation district, Kinki (Osaka and surrounding prefectures) has thirty-three seats; the smallest, Shikoku, has seven. Each voter has two ballots, one on which to write the name of a candidate in the single-member district and the other for the name of a party in the regional proportional-representation district. Each party ranks its candidates on a party list. A threshold of 2 percent is needed for a party to win a seat in a proportional-representation district, but this is so low as to be meaningless. There is no likelihood that any party with fewer than 2 percent of the vote would win a seat in even the smallest proportional-representation district; nor of course does winning more than 2 percent of the vote guarantee that a party would win a seat. In the 1996 election, for example, the Socialists did not win a seat in the seven-member Shikoku district even though they polled 7.1 percent of the vote.

The system permits double candidacy in a single-member and proportional-representation district. If a candidate running in a single-member district who is on his party's proportional-representation list wins in the single-member district, his name is struck from the party list, allowing the candidates below him to move up the list. If he loses in the single-member district, he will be elected if he is ranked high enough on the party's proportional-representation list. A party may list several candidates running in single-member districts at the same position on its party list. The LDP might list six single-member-district candidates, for example, at the number three spot on its regional list. If two of these six are elected in their districts, their names are removed from the proportional-representation party list. The four defeated candidates are then ranked according to how small the percentage difference is between their vote and the vote of the winning candidate in their districts. If the party's percentage of the proportional-representation vote entitles it to, for example, a total of four seats, then in this case two of the candidates defeated in single-member districts (who are now ranked third and fourth on the list) would be elected. In the 1996 general election, the first one to be held under this system, there were eighty-four candidates defeated in single-member districts elected through their party's proportional-representation lists. There were seven single-member districts where three candidates who ran in the district were elected, one in the district itself and the other two on their party's lists. There was one Socialist candidate in Tokyo who did so poorly in his district race that he lost his ¥3 million deposit, yet he was elected to the Diet because he was ranked near the top of his party's list.

In Search of the "Modern Party"

Most advocates of electoral-system reform had favored introducing a simple "first past the post" system. The government's electoral-system advisory council's recommendation, and later the Hosokawa government's legislation, included a proportional-representation component as a concession to minor parties. The mixed system, however, was intended to give minor parties a voice without giving them power. It was adopted in the expectation that the system's dynamics would be driven by the single-member districts, and that one or another of two major parties would form a government.

Arguments about the supposed advantages of a single-member-district system have remained remarkably consistent in Japan for more than eighty years. In the early 1920s, the period known as Taisho Democracy, when modern party government began to take root in Japan, British practices were held up as the model of modern parliamentary democracy. The view then, and the one that prevailed in the discussion of electoral-system reform in the 1990s, essentially came down to the proposition that if Japan had the same electoral system as Britain, it would have pretty much the same party system as Britain.

This Japanese ideal model of the modern party, derived from British politics of the 1920s, is a model of mass-membership parties, a two-party system, sharply differentiated social bases of support for these two parties and thus fundamentally different policy orientations, voter loyalty to party rather than to candidate, and strong and centralized party organization. This model has become frozen in time in Japan, and it has led many people to believe with what only can be described as a kind of religious conviction that introduction of a single-member-district system would cause the advent of policy-oriented, party-controlled, inexpensive election campaigns and a two-party format.

The belief that single-member-district systems are characterized by debates over issues of high national purpose rather than by competition between politicians over the grubby details of how to get more roads, schools, and government subsidies of one kind or another into one's election district has been able to survive both empirical evidence to the contrary and elementary logic. As a general matter, the smaller the district, the greater is the tendency for candidates and voters to be concerned with local issues, other things being equal. For example, the U.S. House of Representatives—with single-member districts—is better known for pork-barrel politics than for sober consideration of how best to design policies to serve the broad national interest; it cannot be said that present-day voters in either the United States or Britain, the two cases of single-member-district systems that provide the referent point for Japanese thinking about this issue, are presented with clear alternative programs by the dominant parties in those countries.

Candidates that seek to obtain a majority of votes in single-member districts in societies characterized by the presence of a large middle class are bound to target their vote at this large and largely undifferentiated constituency. They aim their appeal at the so-called median voter, and they smooth the edges of their appeal so as to alienate as few potential supporters as possible. Modern catchall parties downplay any notion that they are offering zero-sum alternatives—that the victory of party A would necessarily mean rejection of the policies of party B—and emphasize their determination to be parties of all the people.

As might be expected, Japanese politicians seeking the support of as many voters as possible end up sounding very much like each other. Moreover, where they differ tends to depend more on the kind of constituency they are running in than the party they belong to. Elections take place in separate districts. They are rarely nationwide referenda on broad policy issues. In a country such as Japan (or the United States) where parties are loosely structured, what candidates say their policies are depends on what they think will get them elected in their particular districts.

Creating more disciplined, centrally controlled parties has been a long-term goal of Japanese political reformers.[29] Their emphasis on the need to eradicate constituency-service-oriented politics reflects not only a European model of what is (or was) modern, but a Japanese model of what is proper. It is a model of modern politics that is remarkably bureaucratic in conception. There is little room in this conception for "gutter politicians" *(dobuita seijika)* whose enthusiasm lies in doing things for voters in their constituencies. It is a view of modern democracy that almost exclusively emphasizes rational government administration and dismisses and condemns the messy and less efficient processes of bargaining and constituency service.

One of the strengths of the Japanese system, however, and one of its commonalities with the United States, is that politicians must themselves go out to convince voters to vote for them. This keeps them in touch with voter opinion and attentive to voter needs. The "rice-roots" quality of

Japanese democracy is its strength rather than its weakness. Grassroots or rice-roots politics no doubt provides rich soil for corrupt political behavior, but there are ways to penalize and control such behavior without creating more centralized, bureaucratically efficient political organizations. A political-reform program that implicitly rejects the idea that democracy is not about efficiency but about representation carries with it the danger that it will end up killing the patient of democratic governance in its enthusiasm for curing the disease of political corruption.

Although an image of Japanese politics as hopelessly corrupt is widespread, there is far less corruption now than there was in the past. Economic development and value change have reduced the effectiveness of traditional corrupt practices as well as the public's willingness to tolerate them. More stringent laws that are more vigorously enforced have also been important. Experience suggests that the way to reduce corruption is to pass and enforce laws that are targeted directly at corrupt practices rather than by changing the electoral system.

One of the political-reform bills the Diet passed in 1994 provided for the strengthening of the *renzasei* provision in the election law. Under this provision, a Diet candidate is legally responsible for illegal campaign activities by his supporters even if he has no direct knowledge of those specific activities. The 1994 revision widened the reach of *renzasei* to a far-wider circle of campaign supporters than in the past and stiffened penalties for violations. The courts now have the power to void a candidate's election victory and ban him from running for that office for five years if an immediate family member, his secretary, the head of his campaign organization, his treasurer, or someone without an official campaign organization title who is a close adviser is found guilty of a campaign violation.[30] By all accounts, this legal reform has had a constraining, indeed—according to some politicians critical of the reform—a chilling effect on campaign practices.

Less has changed as a result of electoral reform than reformers anticipated, for better and for worse. Elections are still constituency-service oriented and candidate dominated.[31] Major parties continue to be umbrella-type organizations for politicians whose views on important policy issues vary. There is no longer intraparty competition, but candidates continue to rely on their personal *kōenkai* rather than on party organization to organize their campaigns.

The distinction between *kōenkai* and local party branches, however, is becoming blurred as a result of the introduction of a new system of public party financing. The introduction of a public subsidy to parties was part of the political-reform legislation that the Diet adopted in 1994. It provides approximately $300 million per annum to Japan's political parties. These funds are supposed to be used to support parties and not individual candidate activities, but Diet members quickly found a way around this restriction. By becoming "chairman" of their party's local election district branch *(shibuchō),* they are legally qualified to use funds from the public subsidy. Since under the new electoral system there is no longer intraparty competition, there is no competition among Diet members of the same party for control of the election-district party branch. Party headquarters distribute part of the public subsidy to district branch chairmen who then in effect use the money to support their *kōenkai* activities. This practice is reducing the formerly sharp distinction between *kōenkai* and party organization. But it has not changed the reality that election campaigns are controlled by individual politicians operating with a party franchise.

A Two-Party System?

It is not at all clear whether Japanese party politics will evolve in the direction of a two-party system. There is no doubt that the single-member-district arrangement creates pressures toward party consolidation, although the first attempt at consolidation by the New Frontier Party proved to be disastrous, as discussed in chapter 5. In any event, a two-party system in which the parties offer sharply different policy programs is conceivable only if a new, deeply polarizing division erupts within Japanese society. Japan's amorphous middle class might become divided into antagonistic groupings as a result of adverse domestic economic change, especially if it produces large-scale unemployment. Relatively harmonious labor-management relations in Japan are not a cultural imperative: they emerged only after a period of bitter conflict between unions and management and were consolidated in the context of favorable economic conditions and an implicit social contract that traded job security for company loyalty. A decision by companies to engage in massive layoffs and unilaterally abrogate this postwar social contract might produce social unrest and result in the revival of a militant labor movement and the emergence of a polarized party system.

If relations between the United States and Japan were to deteriorate drastically, as a result of U.S. anger over Japanese economic policy or because Japan believed that the United States was failing to fulfill its treaty obligations on a matter of vital national security interest to Japan—involving China, for example, or North Korea—Japanese opinion might become bitterly divided on the issue of national security policy. A crisis in relations with the United States might generate a bipolar division in Japan between advocates of autonomous military power and supporters of a peace-at-any-price policy and a competition between political parties around this issue.

If such dire scenarios do not materialize and if the Japanese economy begins to recover, then it is conceivable that the new electoral system will reinforce the unity and the electoral strength of the LDP while leaving its opposition weak and divided. The LDP is far better positioned to win elections than a newly formed party that has fewer incumbents, little if any organization among locally elected officials, and no constituency in the habit of voting for it.

Even if, in other words, a predominantly two-party system evolves in Japan, it is not at all certain how these parties will try to distinguish themselves from each other or whether the new system will weaken or strengthen the LDP. The electoral system itself will neither cause a two-party system to develop nor will it necessarily cause parties to advocate basically different policies. Moreover, because of the proportional-representation component in the electoral system, some minor, and perhaps not so minor, parties also have an opportunity to obtain a far more strategically important position in the party system than Japanese political reformers anticipated. The Komeito in particular occupies a critical position in Japan's evolving party system, in effect commanding the casting vote in the upper house as a result of the 1998 election that is discussed in chapter 6.

More Reform?

The Japanese Diet changed the electoral system because Japanese leaders—in politics, business, and the media—were convinced that electoral-system reform was the key to political reform. They exaggerated the causal effects of electoral systems, believing that the "medium-size-election-district system" caused corruption and one-party dominance and that a single-member-district system, or something close to it, would produce policy-oriented, party-controlled, inexpensive election campaigns and an alternation of parties in power. They opted for a mixed system of single-member and proportional-representation districts not because the leaders of any party thought that this system was the most desirable but because all agreed that it was the only one they all could accept.

There now appears to be considerable unhappiness with the new electoral system among the very people who were most instrumental in pushing its adoption. There does not seem to be much energy, however, for again starting up the process of electoral reform. However, if the issue does arise, it is almost certain to revolve around four alternatives to the present system. Other options—quota systems, double ballots, and so on—do not fall within the historically constructed Japanese universe of electoral-system alternatives.

One option is a return to the former medium-size-election-district system. There is support within the Socialist Party and among some LDP politicians for a revival of this system, but not for the application of a strict "one man, one vote" apportionment in determining district lines. Attempts to revive a system that overrepresented rural areas would be opposed by the media and by public opinion, not to mention other parties, as simply an effort to return politics to the bad old days of the '55 system. So the possibility of reverting to this system does not seem very promising.

A second and even less likely possibility is modification of the current system to make it more like the one that operates in Germany. Such a modification, which appears to have considerable support in the Komeito, would strengthen the importance of the proportional-representation vote in determining the total distribution of seats. Such a reform would face intense opposition from single-member-district incumbents. It also is incompatible with the continuing dominant Japanese view that single-member-district systems are somehow superior to all others.

A third option is to eliminate proportional representation from the current system, leaving a smaller house, with members elected entirely in single-member districts. There is considerable support both within political circles and among opinion makers for such a reform. A proposal to reduce the size of the house plays well in the media, given the current popularity of the idea, discussed in the final chapter of this book, of moving Japan toward "small government." Yet proposals to reduce the number of candidates elected through proportional representation or to eliminate it entirely are opposed by the Komeito and the Communist Party and by LDP Diet members elected in the proportional-representation districts.

This leaves a fourth possibility, which is to modify the current system to eliminate so-called double candidacies; that is, the ability of parties to include their single-member-district candidates on their party lists. Judging from public opinion polls and media commentary, many Japanese apparently believe that it is somehow not right that a candidate rejected by voters in a district can be "rescued" by being included on his party's list. According to one poll taken shortly after the 1996 lower-house election, only 14 percent of respondents said that they thought introducing the "dual candidacy" provision was a good idea; 70 percent thought it had been a bad idea; 16 percent expressed no opinion.[32]

There is an important if little recognized merit of the double-candidacy provision, however. A single-member-district system is notoriously incumbent-friendly. It is difficult for newcomers to gain name recognition and build campaign organizations. Incumbents, on the other hand, are able to use their position to do favors for constituents and make their personal campaign organization even stronger. A "rescued" candidate who plans to run again in the single-member district in which that candidate was defeated, however, poses a threat to the reelection of the district incumbent, since the rescued candidate, too, is an incumbent with name recognition and a campaign organization. The double-candidacy provision increases the chance that there will be meaningful competition in the district, and it forces incumbents to give more attention to their constituents than might otherwise be the case. Eliminating the double-candidacy provision would have the predictable and entirely negative consequence of strengthening the reelection prospects of incumbents in single-member districts. Yet—if any changes at all are made in the present electoral system—this "reform" is the one most likely to be made.

It seems reasonable to assume that probably no major changes will be made in the Japanese electoral system for some years to come and that the impact of this system on political behavior and party organization will become clearer over time. But it will never be possible to identify the dimensions of this impact with any degree of certainty. Causation is complex. Much depends on many factors.

Economic recovery combined with a leadership struggle in parties opposed to it could produce a new era of LDP dominance. Economic catastrophe probably would drive the LDP out of power and spark another round of party fragmentation and reorganization. The absence of intraparty competition reduces the incentives for the existence of strong factional organizations, but factional power was ebbing even under the former electoral system. It probably would have continued to decline in importance even if the medium-size-election-district system had been retained.

The new system seems to have focused a great deal of voter attention on the personality of party leaders, but a relative increase in the importance attached by voters to party leaders compared with that attached to constituency candidates was occurring before the electoral system was changed. The success of Hosokawa's Japan New Party in the 1993 election held under the medium-size-election-district system offers a good example of this. Corrupt political practices are almost certain to continue to decline in importance, and the role of the Diet in policy making may increase. But the relationship of these changes to the electoral system is tangential at best.

Electoral reform was oversold as a means of solving Japan's political problems. In the process, a system that was closely identified with Japan's development as a modern democratic state was discarded and a system adopted that produces reductive pressures on the number of parties through its single-member districts and yet encourages the existence of small parties through its proportional-representation component. This complicates voter choice and makes the structuring of a new party system all that more difficult. The initial effect of this new system was to produce pressures for party consolidation *and* fragmentation. As the decade of the nineties drew to a close, and especially in the aftermath of the July 1998 upper-house election, the long-term impact of this electoral system on Japanese politics seemed more uncertain than ever.

Chapter Five

The LDP's Return to Power

Managing Coalition

This chapter seeks to provide answers to two important questions about Japanese politics in the mid-1990s. One question deals with the factors that caused Prime Minister Hata's coalition government—the government that briefly succeeded Prime Minister Hosokawa's—to lose power, resulting in the LDP's return to power in a coalition with the Socialist Party and with the Sakigake. The second question is about why the LDP was successful in managing its coalition relationship with the Socialist Party, whereas the conservatives who had left the LDP and formed a coalition with the Socialists were not.

The first question focuses our attention on the two months between the time Hosokawa resigned as prime minister in April 1994 and when the LDP forged its alliance with the Socialists. This period constitutes a critical moment in Japanese political history. It was not inevitable that the LDP come back power. If key political leaders had made different choices during these weeks, the LDP might have suffered further defections of its Diet members and the Japanese party system might have developed along very different lines. Analyzing why political leaders made the choices they did in this period is necessary for an understanding of why the LDP was able to come back to power, and why this happened so quickly. It also offers an opportunity to explore important features of Japan's political institutions.

Once back in power, the LDP was extraordinarily successful in managing its relationship with the Socialists. It kept Prime Minister Murayama, the chairman of the Socialist Party, as the titular head of an LDP-JSP-

Sakigake coalition government for a year and a half, nearly twice as long as the combined terms of Hosokawa and Hata. When Murayama resigned in January 1996, the coalition parties turned to Ryutaro Hashimoto, who had replaced Kono as LDP president in September 1995, to succeed him. Hashimoto had been MITI minister in the Murayama cabinet, and in that position his popularity soared with each confrontation he had with Mickey Kantor, the Clinton administration's trade representative, over U.S.-Japan trade disputes. The Socialists and the Sakigake remained in alliance with the LDP under Prime Minister Hashimoto until just prior to the July 1998 upper-house election.

Hashimoto was Japan's fifth prime minister in little more than three years—since the lower-house election that was held in July 1993. Government changed hands from one set of coalition partners to another during this period. New parties were formed and parties that had been successful in the 1993 such as Hosokawa's Japan New Party disappeared. New political alliances were forged and old ones were rent asunder. Politics in Nagata-chō were in turmoil, but at no time until October 1966 were Japanese voters given an opportunity to elect a new lower house.

When Hosokawa resigned in April 1993, the coalition parties that had supported him held together just long enough to elect the Japan Renewal Party's Hata to replace him. The lower house was not dissolved and a general election was not called. When, for reasons that are discussed below, Hata resigned after being in office for only two months, he decided not to dissolve the house and hold new elections. With a majority of seats in the lower house in their hands, the LDP, JSP, and the Sakigake then proceeded to make Murayama prime minister. The transfer of power from Murayama to Hashimoto in January 1996 also took place without a general election being held.

The history of this period, accordingly, is mostly a story of political intrigue and shifting political alliances among Japan's political leaders. The story is complex and most of the details are too inconsequential in terms of the long-term evolution of the Japanese political system to detain us here. Yet if one believes that politicians have an autonomy of choice, that history is not inevitable, then a recounting of the key decisions taken by Japan's political leaders during this period, and an analysis of why they made the choices they did make, are essential to account for the collapse of the coalition government and the return of the LDP to power.

Kaihashugi

An analysis of the political developments that led to the LDP's return to power puts in sharp relief the importance of a little understood institution called the *innai kaiha,* or parliamentary caucus. Nearly all candidates who are elected to either chamber of the Diet are members of political parties. Yet within the Diet itself, they organize themselves not in "parties" *(seitō)* but in *innai kaiha.* Each *kaiha,* which is organized separately in each house, registers by submitting its list of members and officers to the relevant house Speaker. For many politicians, to be sure, the differentiation of parties and *kaiha* amounts to a distinction without a difference since their *kaiha* and the party they belong to are one and the same. Lower-house members in the Communist Party, for example, are members of the Communist Party *kaiha* in the lower house. For others, however, the distinction between party and *kaiha* is crucial, as we shall see.

The importance of the *kaiha* system varies depending on the number of parties whose members are elected to the Diet. It is greatest when there are a large number of small parties, and when there are pressures for party reorganization, and least when the Diet is dominated by few parties and the party system is stable. For many years, political observers in Japan mostly ignored the *kaiha* system. It was an important institution with regard to the organization of the operations of the Diet, as is discussed below, but as long as Diet politics were dominated by the LDP and the JSP, the system did not have a major impact on the distribution of power among parties in the Diet or in influencing the evolution of the party system. However, in the aftermath of the collapse of LDP one-party dominance in 1993 and the adoption of a new electoral system, *kaiha* emerged as a critical factor in the strategies adopted by politicians seeking to restructure the party system.

The institution of the *kaiha* had an especially profound effect on the strategies employed by the coalition parties when they confronted the issue of finding a successor to Prime Minister Hosokawa in April 1994. Hata was elected to that post by the lower house on April 25. He received 274 votes, over the 207 given to the LDP's Kono. (The Communist Party leader received 15 votes). This 67-vote difference between Hata and Kono is to be compared with a difference of only 38 votes when Hosokawa won over Kono the preceding August. In other words, from the vote it appeared that the coalition under Hata was larger than it had been when Hosokawa was at the helm. Twenty-four hours after being elected, Hata became head of a minority government. Two months later, he and the parties that were in his government were out of power and the LDP and the Socialists were in. These changes took place within and were directly affected by the dynamics of the *kaiha* system.

Kaiha, as one author quite appropriately put it, are the foundation stone for the operations of the Japanese Diet.[1] The size of a *kaiha* to which a Diet member belongs determines how many positions on Diet committees that group of Diet members will hold, whether or not its members will be qualified to be selected to serve on the all-important directorates *(rijikai)* of standing committees, how much question time members of the group will be allotted to interpolate the government, and how much money it will receive for legislative expenses *(rippō jimuhi)*. Only *kaiha* with at least twenty members, for example, are permitted to submit Diet member bills; *kaiha* need to have at least fifty members to submit budget-related legislation.

Diet procedures including procedures for recording legislative votes in plenary session are based on the assumption that virtually all Diet members will organize themselves into *kaiha* and that the *kaiha* will exercise discipline over their members. Roll-call votes are rarely taken in the Japanese Diet. They are used when there is an election for a new prime minister and on votes on the government budget. Otherwise, a roll-call vote is used only when the Speaker decides to call for one or when more than one-fifth of the members of the house requests it. In practice, it is not taken even on critical legislation. No roll-call vote was taken when the Diet changed the electoral system in 1994 or when it passed a controversial bill to extend the leases on land occupied by U.S. military bases in Okinawa in 1997. In these two cases and on most other important legislation, members indicate their vote by standing *(kiritsu saiketsu)*. The votes of individual Diet members are not officially recorded. Usually, the only way those who were not in the chamber learn whether particular Diet members broke party discipline on the vote is if their names are mentioned in newspaper articles written by reporters covering the Diet session. On noncontroversial legislation, the Speaker will often simply declare passage of a bill by unanimous consent *(iginashi saiketsu)*.[2]

This voting system is widely accepted as appropriate because of the assumption, deeply embedded in the Diet's traditions, that each *kaiha* will decide its position on a bill before a vote is taken and will exercise discipline over its members on the vote. As long as the Speaker is informed about the decisions the *kaiha* have taken on a specific piece of legislation, the vote itself usually is little more than a formality.

Kaiha have a history almost as old as the Japanese Diet itself, which convened for the first time in 1890. In the first years of the Diet, when the suffrage was restricted and the party system was in an early stage of development, lower-house members formed informal groupings in order to facilitate negotiations among themselves over the parliamentary agenda and other matters and build support for particular policies.[3] The prototype of the *kaiha* system that exists today is believed to have emerged in the thirteenth Imperial Diet session that convened in November 1898. At that session, groups of Diet members established formal caucus organizations in the lower house, submitted the names of their members and officials to the Diet secretariat, and were assigned separate anterooms *(hikaeshitsu)* in the Diet building in which to consult and plan their legislative strategies.[4]

After the First World War and into the 1920s, political parties grew rapidly in strength. In 1918, the president of the Seiyukai became the first prime minister to be chosen because he was leader of the largest party in the lower house. Japan appeared to be on the threshold of an era of party government and to be evolving its own form of parliamentary democracy. The *kaiha*, which had first emerged in the absence of strong party organization, grew more important as the parties grew stronger. No longer groupings of independent Diet members, they had become the intraparliamentary organization of the political parties. *Kaiha* even became part of the organizational structure of the House of Peers at this time. In the forty-third Imperial Diet, convened in June 1920, separate anterooms were assigned to *kaiha* in the upper house.[5] The emergence of the *kaiha* in the House of Peers, a body that was supposed to be above party politics, was testimony to how powerful parties were becoming in this period, and it is indicative also of how pervasive the *kaiha* system had become.

Party government in prewar Japan was short-lived. Japan's transition to democracy was aborted in the 1930s by the military's takeover of political power. After the Second World War and adoption of a new constitution formally establishing the Diet as the "supreme organ of state power," however, political parties reemerged, and party government became firmly established. Along with the revival and strengthening of political parties, the *kaiha* system also reappeared, taking on more importance than ever before.

Despite its importance in the conduct of Diet affairs, there is nothing in the Diet Law, or in any other law, that relates directly to *kaiha*. The only reference to *kaiha* in the Diet Law is a provision that membership on standing committees and special committees in both houses shall be assigned to *kaiha* relative to their size.[6] *Kaiha* also are mentioned in the law regulating the distribution of legislative funds *(rippō jimuhi kōfuhō)*. This law provides that the Diet shall allocate a set sum for each Diet member, but that it shall disperse these funds to the *kaiha* and not to individual Diet members, except in cases where a Diet member is not a member of a *kaiha*.[7]

The organization and role of *kaiha* are regulated entirely by precedent and custom and not by law. That, however, does not make this informal institution any less important, nor does it mean that the rules regulating the *kaiha* are any less "formal" or exact than they are in the case of institutions defined by law. The Japanese political system abounds with informal institutions organized in highly formal ways that interact with legally established institutions.

Informal (that is not legally prescribed) arrangements, mechanisms, procedures, and organizations help to overcome the rigidities of formal procedures and the inadequacies of established institutions. Rather than change the existing formal structure, the tendency in Japan is to create informal institutions in order to "grease the wheels" of the political system. This has been an important source of flexibility and adaptability. It is a reason why the Japanese have not felt compelled to revise the constitution, and why many laws codified under entirely different circumstances as long ago as the Meiji period remain in effect today. A comprehensive institutional mapping of the Japanese political system must take into account both informal and formal institutions and the interactions among them.

What Japanese specialists on the Diet refer to as *kaihashugi,* "*kaiha*ism," the grounding of Diet operations in *kaiha* organization, has a profound effect on the behavior of politicians inside the Diet. Since opportunities for a Diet member to hold important positions on Diet committees, to submit legislation, question cabinet ministers, and so on are determined by the size of the *kaiha* to which he belongs, the *kaiha* system creates strong incentives for independents to join a *kaiha* and for members of minor parties to merge into a larger *kaiha*. Political parties also often face strong incentives to bring independents and minor parties into their *kaiha* or to form a "unified *kaiha*" *(tōitsu kaiha)* to increase the size of their Diet contingent and accordingly their power within the Diet structure.

This was true even under LDP one-party dominance. In 1989, to cite one example of how this system works in practice, a popular professional Japanese wrestler-turned-politician who goes by the name of Antonio Inoki won a seat in the upper house as the sole successful candidate of the Sports Peace Party *(Supōtsu Heiwatō)*. When he first entered the Diet, Inoki registered with the Speaker as a member of a five-member *kaiha* that included the successful candidate of another minor party and an elderly independent long identified with the peace movement.

However, Inoki was vigorously courted by the Democratic Socialist Party and urged to form a unified *kaiha* between his Sports Peace Party (of which he was the only Diet member) and the DSP. The DSP was anxious to draw Inoki into a unified *kaiha* because it had lost seats in the previous election and now had only nine members in the upper house. In the upper house, there is a world of difference between a *kaiha* of nine members and one of ten. A *kaiha* with ten or more members is entitled to a share of committee chairmanships and a position on the powerful directorate *(rijikai)* of the Diet Management Committee, and it is treated as a negotiating group *(kōshō dantai)* in the Diet. *Kaiha* with five to nine members are not permitted to ask questions in plenary sessions of the Diet except for ten minutes of question time when the prime minister gives his policy address.

The DSP succeeded in drawing Inoki into a unified *kaiha* that took the name *Minshatō-Supōtsu-Kokumin Rengō*, roughly the DSP-Sports-National Alliance.[8] So for all intents and purposes, the DSP and the Sports Peace Party were organizationally one party inside the Diet, even though they had no relationship outside of the Diet with respect to the voters who supported either of them.

A different case involving the DSP offers another illustration of the political effects of the *kaiha* system. In the 1986 lower-house election, the DSP won twenty-six seats and the Japan Communist Party won twenty-seven. According to lower-house precedent, members of the directorates of standing committees were to be drawn from among members in the lower house's four largest *kaiha*. The election results had relegated the DSP to the position of being the fifth largest *kaiha* in the house behind the JCP. Not wanting to lose its directorate posts, the DSP succeeded in convincing the small Social Democratic League *(Shaminren)* to form a unified *kaiha*. It thereby retained its fourth-place ranking and its position on the directorates of standing committees.[9]

Even in the case of parties that are large enough not to need to engage in *kaiha* coalition building, the *kaiha* system has a complicating impact on party organization. *Kaiha* are organized separately in each of the two houses of the Diet, as mentioned earlier. There is an LDP *kaiha* in the lower house and a different LDP *kaiha* in the upper house. (Neither is strictly speaking an "LDP" *kaiha*. The formal name in each house is the Liberal Democratic Party—Liberal National Congress *kaiha* [*Jiyū Minshutō–Jiyū Kokumin Kaigi*], the second half of the name providing a vehicle for conservative independents to ally with the LDP in the Diet without actually joining the party.) Since the *kaiha* are organized separately in each house, the LDP secretary-general, for example, who is always a member of the lower house, is the secretary-general of the lower-house LDP *kaiha*. However, there is an LDP upper-house member who serves as secretary-general of the LDP's upper-house *kaiha*. Upper-house *kaiha* have their own roster of officers, including in the case of the LDP a chairman and several vice chairmen, the above mentioned secretary-general and several vice secretaries-general, a chairman and vice chairmen of the Diet strategy committee, and a chairman and members of a policy-deliberation committee *(seisaku shingikai)*. This system has had the unintended effect of giving party members in the upper house some degree of autonomy, or at least some negotiating power, vis-à-vis their own party leadership. The upper-house secretary-general, in particular, is a powerful figure in the party. One of the reasons the upper house is not quite the carbon copy of the lower house that it is often portrayed to be is because of the structure of *kaiha* organization.

After the LDP lost power in 1993, *kaiha* became a much more prominent feature of Diet politics and an important factor in the strategies of political leaders looking to restructure the party system. With the proliferation of small parties that did not embrace widely differing ideologies and that were in agreement on basic policies, the formation of "unified *kaiha*" became much more common. And with the adoption of a new electoral system, the *kaiha* system became an integral element in efforts to build a large party that could mount an electoral challenge to the LDP.

Two of the features of this *kaiha* system, as these examples demonstrate, warrant emphasis. One is that parties regularly form coalitions within the Diet that are not linked to the activities of parties vis-à-vis the electorate. The other is that the creation of a unified *kaiha* is not the formation of an ad hoc policy coalition, but is the formal merging of the parliamentary organizations of political parties. Sometimes, as was the case with the examples given above of the DSP, the purpose is solely to strengthen a party's position with respect to the distribution of committee posts and other powers within the Diet. At other times, the purpose is to facilitate the actual merger of two or more political parties.

The Collapse of Coalition Unity

At the beginning of the Hosokawa administration, the seven parties that comprised the governing coalition clustered into three broad groupings. One included Ozawa's Japan Renewal Party and the Komeito. A second was dominated by the Japan Socialist Party, the largest party in the coalition. The third, led by Hosokawa and Takemura, was composed of a number of small parties that portrayed themselves as a "third force" in Japanese politics, distinct from traditional conservatives and progressives.

Relations between the Socialists and the Japan Renewal Party were strained from the beginning and became only more so over time. Ozawa sought to counter the power of the Socialist Party by forging an alliance with the Komeito, the so-called "*ichi-ichi* line" discussed earlier, and by confronting rather than seeking compromise with the JSP on such important policy issues as raising the consumption tax and permitting Japanese armed forces to participate in UN peacekeeping operations. By the time Hosokawa announced his resignation, relations between the Socialists and the Sakigake, on the one hand, and the Diet members aligned with Ozawa, Hosokawa, and the Komeito, on the other, had reached the breaking point.

Rather than try to paper over their differences and hold the coalition together, Ozawa decided to use the opportunity presented by the unexpectedly early demise of the Hosokawa administration to restructure the coalition. He tried to provoke a major split in the LDP and to divide the JSP at one and the same time, hoping thereby to set the stage for the formation of a party that would replace the LDP as the single largest and most powerful party in the country. He endeavored to do this by bringing most members of the coalition parties into a "unified *kaiha*" that was intended to be the nucleus for a new and powerful political party. And he urged LDP faction leader Michio Watanabe, who had been denied the LDP presidency in 1993 after the Miyazawa government collapsed, to leave the LDP and join forces with the coalition parties. Ozawa was ready to support Watanabe for prime minister if Watanabe could take his faction members out of the LDP with him.

Ozawa seems to have calculated that a major split in the LDP would precipitate a breaking up of the Socialist Party. Many Socialists were moderates and pragmatists who had little sympathy for the policy positions enunciated by their own party's left-wing leadership. They were pessimistic about their chances of getting reelected if they ran as Socialists in the single-member constituencies of the new electoral system. Ozawa's goal in trying to coax Watanabe to leave the LDP was to fracture both the LDP and the JSP and restructure the coalition so that it would be united under his leadership.

Shortly after Hosokawa resigned, Watanabe announced that he was considering leaving the LDP and standing as a candidate for prime minister. It was a curious tactic, leaving him with one foot in the LDP and the other outside, and creating the impression that he was not quite sure what he was prepared to do. Watanabe probably was torn between knowing that joining forces with Ozawa was his only hope to secure his long-coveted dream to become prime minister and sensing that few LDP members would follow him if he did in fact leave the party.

A few of Watanabe's staunchest supporters quit the LDP in the days immediately following this announcement, but Watanabe himself hesitated. His power over his own faction, not to mention in the LDP as a whole, was nowhere as strong as it had been in the past. Watanabe's reputation as an old-line conservative and traditional party boss made him an unappealing leader for LDP members who would have to justify their leaving the LDP ostensibly to forward the cause of political reform. Furthermore, the risks involved in leaving the LDP seemed even greater now than they did in July 1993 when the Miyazawa government fell. Not only had the Hosokawa government collapsed, leaving coalition unity problematic at best, but LDP politicians now needed to calculate how their party affiliation would affect their chances of getting elected in the single-member districts of the newly adopted electoral system. Watanabe was unable to persuade more than a handful of LDP members to join him in leaving the party. He was forced to make a humiliating retreat, announcing on April 19 that he was going to remain in the LDP.

The failure of Ozawa's gambit to reconstitute the coalition with Watanabe as prime minister finally gave Hata the opportunity to occupy the post that had been denied to him eight months earlier when Ozawa decided to support Hosokawa for prime minister. Hata had a reputation as a decent person, a clean politician, and someone who did not harbor resentments, even when he was passed over for the government's top position. This latter trait had earned him the unflattering sobriquet "Mister Spare," as in spare tire, always available if needed but rarely used.[10] Now there was a need to use the spare to keep the coalition on track because Hata was acceptable to the Socialists and other parties in the coalition. Even the Sakigake, which had left the coalition after Hosokawa resigned, agreed to vote for Hata for prime minister even though it decided that it would not join his government.

Although his strategy to split the LDP and JSP had been set back by Watanabe's decision to remain in the LDP, Ozawa continued to look for possible LDP defectors and to pressure the Socialist Party. Ozawa's approach to politics was the antithesis of the cautious, consensus-building style embraced by so many Japanese political leaders. He was uncompromising in negotiating with the Socialists over the policy platform of the new coalition government. He insisted that the Socialists agree to pass Uruguay Round–related legislation, support the U.S.-Japan security treaty, endorse participation by Japan's self-defense forces in UN peacekeeping operations, raise the consumption tax within the year, promote deregulation, and adopt a districting law in the current Diet session to permit an early election to be held under the new election system.[11] He did not shrink from confrontation with the Socialist Party's leadership, apparently having concluded that the JSP would stay in the coalition no matter what, in order to hold on to power. He also seemed confident that the JSP would split sooner or later and that most of its lower-house members would join his party because of their concern about getting elected under the new, predominantly single-member, constituency system.

At the final stage of the negotiations over the coalition's policy platform, Ozawa was quoted in the press as saying that "given the way things are, I can't help it if the Socialists leave the government. No matter how much I tell them to like me, if they are determined to dislike me, well then that is that."[12] Two days later, in a nationally televised interview, he all but dared the JSP to quit the coalition and form one with the LDP. The idea of an LDP-JSP coalition, he said, was totally out of step with current realities and would be suicidal for the Socialists. But "please, why don't you go ahead and try," he challenged them.[13] Two months later they did just that. For the moment, however, the Socialists swallowed their pride, supported Hata's candidacy for prime minister, and remained in the coalition.

The Kaishin Debacle

On the afternoon of April 25, 1994, only a few hours after Hata was elected prime minister, several parties in the coalition—the Japan Renewal Party, the Japan New Party, and the Democratic Socialist Party—announced their decision to merge their parliamentary members into a new unified *kaiha* that they named *Kaishin*, or Reformation. The Komeito did not join the new *kaiha*, but its leaders publicly welcomed its formation and indicated that they would merge with it eventually.

That hardly describes the reaction of the Socialist Party, however. Its chairman denounced the move, saying that "the formation suddenly of a new *kaiha* excluding the JSP right after selection of the prime minister and just before the formation of the cabinet is a violation of trust within the coalition government."[14] Later the same day, the Socialist Party, furious at the "act of betrayal" the new *kaiha* represented, decided to withdraw from the government. Hata had been elected prime minister with the support of more Diet members than Hosokawa had received only to wake up the following morning to find himself the head of a minority government.

Why did the Socialists react with such fury to the decision to form *Kaishin*? After all, relations between the JSP and the parties in this new *kaiha* were just as hostile before the group was formed as they were a few hours later. Moreover, the merger was only a merger of the parliamentary *kaiha*; the parties remained independent of each other. Yet on the morning of April 25, the Socialists voted in the Diet to make Hata prime minister and expected that their party chairman would become deputy prime minister in the new government. That evening, because of the creation of *Kaishin*, they withdrew from the coalition entirely. Why did proponents of a unified *kaiha*—namely, Democratic Socialist Party Chairman Ouchi, former Prime Minister Hosokawa, and Japan Renewal Party Secretary-General Ozawa—push forward with the unified *kaiha* strategy in spite of the dangers it posed to coalition unity and the survivability of the Hata government?

The motivations for creating a new unified *kaiha* seem to have operated at three different levels. One was a concern to improve the policy-making process in the coalition by reducing the number of *kaiha* that had to be involved in making decisions. A second was a concern about the distribution of cabinet posts in the new Hata government. The third was a concern about building a new party large enough to compete with the LDP for the three hundred seats at stake in the single-member districts of the new electoral system.

Streamlining Decision Making

The Hosokawa government was a coalition of seven parties, each of which had to be consulted and with each of which agreement had to be reached before the government could make any important policy decision. This was a source of intense frustration for Hosokawa and Ozawa. Hosokawa believed that the near impossibility of managing an alliance of seven or more parties was a major factor contributing to his inability to govern more effectively. At one point in the period between the time Hosokawa announced his intention to resign and Hata's election as prime minister, there were as many as twelve *kaiha* in the lower house, the largest number ever, exceeding even the ten *kaiha* that were in the lower house when Japan last had a coalition government, nearly half a century earlier, in 1948.[15] Part of the motivation for creating *Kaishin* was the desire on the part of the non-Socialist coalition leadership to make it possible for the new Hata government to implement more streamlined and effective decision making.

The view that policy coordination was impaired by there being too many *kaiha* was not limited to Ozawa and Hosokawa. Hata, too, was a supporter of a unified *kaiha* in order to facilitate policy making. The question was one of timing. Hata later recalled that

> during the Hosokawa Administration there were about nine groups in the lower house. Because of that, every time something had to be decided, you had to take the issue back to the different *kaiha*. I thought that this was an impossible situation . . . and that it would be better to consolidate them. . . . Since it was probably impossible to create one party all of a sudden, I suggested on television and elsewhere that a new unified *kaiha* be created which would make communication easier and would allow for the *kaiha* leaders to consult and make decisions about policy and other matters. So I myself agreed that such a *kaiha* should be formed. But I had no idea that it would be registered on the very day I was elected prime minister. I knew nothing about it.[16]

Hata, who had been kept in the dark about the decision to create the unified *kaiha*, found out about it only after it had been registered with the Speaker of the house.

Apportioning Cabinet Posts

Real politics is all too often not about edifying causes or about powerful social movements but is dominated by the much less uplifting struggle among politicians for shares, even small and trivial shares, of political power. The story of the formation of the new *kaiha* is a good example. The rush to form a new *kaiha* on the day Hata was made prime minister, and before he formed his cabinet, was because the number of cabinet posts, just as is the case with Diet committee assignments, is based on the proportional representation of *kaiha*.

There are many different mathematical formulae available in the calculation of proportional representation. The most popular one, used in electoral systems around the world and the one that is used extensively in Japan, is known as the d'Hondt formula. It is a formula employed to calculate the distribution of seats in the upper-house proportional-representation district and in the eleven regional proportional-representation districts in the new lower-house electoral system. It is also employed to calculate the distribution of Diet committee assignments, and it was used in determining how to distribute cabinet posts among the parties in the ruling coalition. It is a method of calculating proportional representation that moderately favors the largest party.[17]

The d'Hondt formula is not employed in a rigid manner in determining the distribution of cabinet posts. Bargaining does occur. A party that falls below the threshold to qualify for a cabinet post, for example, may get one anyway because its support proved crucial to the leadership. But the d'Hondt formula *(dontoshiki)* has a significant impact on how power is distributed among coalition parties, or among factions in the LDP in LDP one-party governments. The Socialists were the largest party in the coalition as long as the others were divided into separate *kaiha*. They received six cabinet posts in the Hosokawa cabinet, the largest number of all the parties. The formation of *Kaishin* created a *kaiha* of 130 members, compared with the Socialist Party's 74 members. Now, proportional representation would give *Kaishin* the largest number of cabinet posts. The calculation that appeared in the Japanese press was that it would result in the Socialist Party having two fewer cabinet posts in the Hata administration than it had when Hosokawa was prime minister.[18] It also meant, of course, that the JSP's representation on Diet committees, too, would be reduced.

DSP Chairman Ouchi took the initiative in organizing the *Kaishin*. He had been minister of health and welfare in the Hosokawa government, but now, with Hata about to form a new cabinet, the DSP's one allotted post in the cabinet would rotate to another party member. Contemporary newspaper commentary and interviews with several participants in the events surrounding the formation of *Kaishin* suggest that the DSP chairman believed that if he could demonstrate his ability to bring about the formation of a new unified *kaiha*, he would reinforce his power within his own party, earn the gratitude of Ozawa, and be rewarded with one of the two posts that the Socialist Party would lose. Kozo Watanabe, who was the Japan Renewal Party vice president at the time these events occurred, wrote later that Ouchi was an enthusiastic promoter of the *Kaishin* because he calculated that the application of the d'Hondt formula would bring the new *kaiha* additional seats and thus make it possible for him to remain in the cabinet.[19]

Ouchi's enthusiasm even led him to believe, or at least to claim, that he had secured JSP Chairman Murayama's agreement not to oppose the formation of the new *kaiha*. Hata recalls turning on a television program shortly after he was elected prime minister and watching Ouchi discuss the new *kaiha*. "Listening to him, I felt that this was the real thing. After all, Ouchi was not being secret about it. He was talking on television about getting the Socialist Party's understanding, and Socialist Party members were watching, too. I was impressed that the Socialists would go along. After all, it meant that the JSP's number of cabinet posts, parliamentary vice-ministers, and committee chairmanships all would be reduced."[20] Hata did not know that Murayama had denied that he had said anything to Ouchi to indicate Socialist Party acquiescence to the forming of a unified *kaiha*.

Hata spent the afternoon waiting for Ozawa to give him a list of proposed cabinet ministers. As noted in chapter 2, during the many years that the Tanaka faction, and then its successor, the Takeshita faction, exercised effective power in the LDP while members of other factions took their turn at being prime minister, a pattern of cabinet formation arose in which the secretary-general, who was a Takeshita faction member, put together a list of recommended cabinet ministers that the prime minister then appointed. Ozawa played this role in forming the Kaifu cabinet when he was LDP secretary-general, and now he was responsible for organizing Hata's new coalition government. Hata, not knowing all the trouble that had been sparked by the *Kaishin* affair, waited for the list to arrive. "I had to form a cabinet, but the list of recommended names of cabinet ministers did not come to me. I was wondering what was happening because none of the parties was saying anything to me. When I contacted Ozawa, he said to wait a little longer. I didn't know anything about what was going on concerning the unified *kaiha*. I thought it was just a matter of the time involved in deciding who to make cabinet ministers—of getting the list together. Well, that seemed normal enough; it happens all the time." Hata added ruefully that "if there had been more consultation, if others had been asked to confirm the position of the Socialists, if that effort had been made, things would have turned out differently."[21]

Ozawa did not make that effort. Although he dismisses the idea that the *Kaishin* incident was especially important, maintaining that the Socialists "were looking for a way to make Murayama prime minister,"[22] he doubtless saw the creation of *Kaishin* as an opportunity to strike a fatal blow against the Socialists and consolidate his power over the coalition. Ozawa, as mentioned earlier, was anything but diplomatic in demanding that the Socialist Party support the policy program he drafted for the new government. Yet the Socialists swallowed their pride and agreed to stay in the coalition. Now he apparently concluded that the Socialist Party either would again do the same, in the face of the formation of the unified *kaiha*, or, if it withdrew from the coalition, the party would split, sending many moderate and right-wing Socialists into the new *kaiha*. With that accomplished, Ozawa could once again turn his attention to enticing LDP members to join him and thus control the largest and most powerful political party in Japan.

Ozawa's tactics produced an outcome that was the exact opposite of what he had hoped for. Even those Socialists who had been critical of Murayama and the party leadership and who were most tempted to leave the party now were infuriated by Ozawa's failure to consult with them and by his readiness to treat them as nothing more than pawns in his drive for party consolidation. To leave the JSP now and join the new *kaiha* would give them no bargaining power at all within the coalition. The formation of *Kaishin* produced a new unity in the Socialist Party. Ozawa's remark in the television interview quoted above—that it would be suicide for the JSP to join a coalition government with the LDP—was prophetic.

The Socialists now began to think it would be better to take the chance that alliance with the LDP would be suicidal than simply to do nothing and let the party be destroyed by Ozawa. The *Kaishin* blunder not only made Hata the leader of an unstable minority government; it made allies of the LDP and the JSP and the Sakigake and opened the way to the return of the LDP to power.

The decision to form the *Kaishin* changed the course of Japanese political development, all but pushing the JSP into the arms of a surprised but delighted LDP. If *Kaishin* had not been formed when it was and if the Socialists had remained in the government for some months more, a strong, counterfactual argument can be made that the LDP would not have returned to power at all and that a fundamental restructuring of the party system would have taken place.

The LDP had been faring badly in opposition. Relations among faction leaders and between younger members and the party's old guard were becoming increasingly acrimonious. There had been a slow but steady trickle of defections from the LDP to the coalition. Rumors were rife that more were imminent. Having been elected in a party that monopolized governmental power for nearly forty years, LDP Diet members had developed campaign strategies that were rooted in their ability to deliver concrete benefits to their constituents. Political power was the oxygen that kept the LDP alive. If deprived of this political oxygen for some months longer, many of its Diet members, facing an impending election under the new, predominantly single-member-district, electoral system, might well have concluded they would be better off joining the coalition and running as candidates of a party that was in the government rather than remain in the opposition in the LDP.

The point is not that defections from the LDP would have strengthened the unity of the coalition parties over the long term. At some point, the strains that characterized relations among parties in the coalition probably would have broken it apart. The issue was a matter of timing. If the goal of those with power in the coalition was to weaken the LDP and strengthen their own ranks before calling an election, they should have been willing to pay almost any price to keep peace with the Socialists and hold the coalition together. If they had done so, it is entirely conceivable that the split within the coalition, when it did occur, would have been along a conservative-liberal divide. But Ozawa was determined to bend the Socialists to his will or to drive the party out of the coalition, even if doing so entailed the risk of losing power.

There was nothing inevitable about the LDP's return to power. If the coalition parties had remained in power longer, a possible disintegration of the LDP and subsequent restructuring of the party system might have infused some policy content and a new dynamism into party competition. The constraints of the *kaiha* system, when combined with other factors such as the tradition of proportional representation of *kaiha* in the distribution of cabinet posts and Diet committee seats, and the adoption of a new electoral system that created pressures on parties to consolidate, impelled leaders of the coalition to adopt a strategy that made Hata the head of a minority government. It also opened the door to the LDP's return arm-in-arm with its erstwhile nemesis, the Japan Socialist Party.

The LDP-JSP Historic Compromise

Back in the summer of 1993, as the vote on a nonconfidence motion in Prime Minister Miyazawa approached, many LDP leaders insisted that the party would somehow survive this crisis as it had survived others. Four decades of political power had convinced them that theirs was the one and only natural party of government. One way or another, they believed, either in the interparty bargaining over the nonconfidence motion or, if those negotiations failed, in the bargaining that would follow a general election, they would be able to attract the support of a sufficient number of non-LDP Diet members to enable the LDP to retain its Diet majority.

Now, nearly a year later, with access to government resources that could be used to channel benefits to their supporters shut off and popular support for the party weakened by continuing media criticism of their opposition to reform, LDP leaders were worried that further defections to the ruling coalition might place the party's very existence in jeopardy. Desperate to get back into power as quickly as possible, they were ready to think the unthinkable and do the impossible. The *Kaishin* blunder offered an opportunity that they were determined not to miss.

Now that the uproar created by the formation of the *Kaishin*, the unified *kaiha*, had sent the Socialist Party into the opposition and left Prime Minister Hata presiding over a shaky minority government, LDP leaders began to explore the possibilities of alliance with the JSP, as well as with the Sakigake, which had left the coalition government before the *Kaishin* incident erupted. Some LDP and JSP Diet members, having a common cause in their opposition to electoral-system reform, had begun meeting quietly soon after Hosokawa came to power. They continued to meet after the electoral-reform legislation passed the Diet. Those contacts increased after Hosokawa's resignation, but they shifted from a focus on electoral reform to the issue of whether they might be able to agree on the formation of a coalition government. These discussions moved into a higher gear after the Socialists withdrew from the coalition.

The LDP and JSP had been traditional archenemies, but now that alliance with the Socialists was the only way the LDP could return to power, LDP leaders, who for years had accused the Socialist Party of undermining political stability and compromising the national interest, quite suddenly began to reinterpret postwar Japanese political history. The '55 system was not so much characterized by conflict between the LDP and the JSP, according to the newly popular interpretation, as it was by a kind of division of labor. While the LDP managed the alliance with the United States, the Socialists kept open lines of communication to the Soviet Union and China. As the LDP deepened relations with South Korea, the Socialist Party saw to it that there would be at least unofficial relations with North Korea as well. The LDP and the JSP made a show of their rhetorical and sometimes even physical conflict in publicly visible Diet sessions, but they actually cooperated behind the scenes and developed close personal relations. Koichi Kato, who as chairman of the LDP Policy Affairs Research Council played a crucial role in managing the decision-making process during the time that JSP Chairman Murayama was prime minister, maintained that one important reason they were able to work so well together was because Socialists and LDP members who, like him, were university students in the 1960s, when the student movement was at its strongest, shared a common culture, even if they were on opposite sides of the political barricades at that time.[23]

According to the LDP's new interpretation of postwar history, a division of labor between the two major parties in the '55 system was a consequence of the cold war and the lack of domestic consensus about the constitutional order imposed by the U.S. Occupation after the Second World War. Now that public support for the constitutional order was pervasive and the cold war was over, it should be possible for the LDP and the JSP to forge a historic compromise that would mark the final end of the '55 system. LDP leaders had reinterpreted the past to service their present need to rationalize an alliance with their former adversary. There were people in the party who continued to believe that fundamental philosophical and policy differences separated the LDP and the JSP. But in June 1994, with the opportunity to return to governmental power facing them, few of them voiced these views very loudly.

After bolting Hata's coalition, the Socialists found themselves being courted by both the LDP and the ruling coalition. Coalition leaders expected the LDP to submit a nonconfidence motion in Prime Minister Hata before the Diet session concluded at the end of June. Unless the Socialist Party came back to the coalition, or the right wing of the JSP broke off and joined it, the nonconfidence motion was likely to pass and the Hata government would fall. Hata was hoping the coalition somehow would be able to return the Socialists to the fold before the Diet session ended.

The Socialists responded as might be expected: they encouraged both the LDP and the ruling coalition to compete for their support. By late May, a month after Hata came to office, Socialist Party leaders were speaking publicly about the possibility of joining forces with the LDP.[24] They also said they would consider rejoining the anti-LDP ruling coalition. Their condition for taking the latter course was the resignation of the Hata cabinet so that the Socialist Party could be directly involved in deciding the composition of the new government. They held open the possibility that they would support Hata's reelection as prime minister. Up to this point, Socialist Party leaders still were looking for a way to return to power while retaining their anti-LDP stance.

The ruling coalition, however, was controlled by Ozawa. His strategy and that of Komeito's Chairman Ichikawa remained fixed on the goal of splitting the LDP and either dividing the JSP or forcing the left-wing leadership to forestall a party split by returning to the coalition on Ozawa's terms.[25] Ozawa and Ichikawa said they would rather go into opposition than compromise with the Socialists since they were certain that an LDP-JSP coalition would prove so disastrous that it would lead to the defeat of both parties in the next election.[26] This turned out to be a monumental miscalculation.

Choosing a New Prime Minister

On June 24, the LDP decided to submit a motion of nonconfidence in Prime Minister Hata. Hata announced the resignation of his cabinet the following day before the nonconfidence vote was taken. A vote to elect a new prime minister was scheduled to be held on June 29, the last day of the Diet session. At this point, only days before a new prime minister was to be elected, it was uncertain what alignments would be forged among parties and who the candidates for prime minister would be.

With Ozawa still trying to entice the right-wing Socialists to break away from their party and join the coalition, the LDP decided to do the one thing that would ensure that the Socialist Party would remain unified and would join it in forming a coalition government: it announced on June 28 that it was going to vote the next day for Socialist Party Chairman Murayama for prime minister and that it intended to form a coalition government with the Socialists and the Sakigake. Support among Socialist Party members for rejoining the Ozawa-led coalition government on Ozawa's terms all but disappeared with the prospect that their party's leader would become prime minister. It would be the first time in forty-seven years a Socialist had held the post.

The ruling coalition now made a desperate gambit to hold on to power. On the morning of June 29, the very day on which the vote was to be taken, LDP member Kaifu, the former prime minister, announced that he was opposed to the LDP's decision to support Murayama for prime minister and was going to run against him with the support of the parties in the Hata coalition government. Ozawa had once again cast Hata aside, as he had done when he made the decision to support Hosokawa for prime minister. Ozawa had been secretary-general of the LDP when Kaifu was prime minister; he now was offering Kaifu a chance to recreate that relationship. Kaifu jumped at the opportunity, apparently in the hope that a sufficient number of other LDP members would follow him to give the ruling coalition a lower-house majority and give him a second chance to be prime minister.[27]

The Diet convened on the evening of June 29 to choose a successor to Hata, who had been in office for only sixty-five days. With 253 votes needed for a majority, on the first ballot, Murayama received 241 and Kaifu 220.[28] Twenty-six LDP members and eight Socialist Party members broke with party discipline to vote for Kaifu. Just before ten o'clock that evening, members of the lower house voted in a second and final runoff between the two highest-placed candidates, Murayama and Kaifu. This time, the eight Socialists again voted for Kaifu, but only nineteen LDP members supported him. The Socialist Party chairman became prime minister and the LDP was back in the government after ten months in the political opposition. Everyone, even the leaders of the parties involved, seemed stunned by what had happened.

Voters had not exerted any pressures on parties to cause this realignment; the last time there had been an election for the lower house was when Miyazawa was prime minister. Nor had there been a carefully thought-through strategy to cause it. The LDP had found its way back into power as the result of improvised responses to the tactical mistakes of others.

The Rise and Fall of the New Frontier Party

With the LDP back in power and allied with the Socialists and the Sakigake, the remaining parties that had been part of the Hosokawa and Hata governments moved forward with plans to consolidate their forces into a single party capable of challenging the LDP in the single-member districts of the new electoral system. In December 1994 the parties that were part of the "unified *kaiha*" Kaishin—the Japan Renewal Party, Japan New Party, and Democratic Socialist Party—and the Komeito's lower-house members merged to form the Shinshintō, the New Frontier Party. Kaifu became the party's first president; Ozawa used his perch as party secretary-general to control party affairs. With more than two hundred Diet members, the NFP was the largest party to be formed in postwar Japan other than the LDP itself.

The NFP made a strong showing in the upper-house election held seven months later, in July 1995, and it appeared for a time as though Japanese party politics was being reconstituted into the kind of two-party system that Ozawa and other reformers envisaged. But the cohesion of the NFP was undermined by policy and personality conflicts, especially between Ozawa and other veteran politicians in the party.

Ozawa's seeming willingness to take huge risks and to gamble everything in his quest for political control tended to make some mostly younger politicians his fervent supporters, but it turned others who had been his allies into his enemies. Formerly stalwart supporters deserted Ozawa one after the other. In December 1995, the NFP faced a new election for party president. Hata entered the race, promising that he would not reappoint Ozawa as secretary-general if he were elected. This forced Ozawa, whose preferred mode of operation was to manage political power from behind the scenes, to run against Hata in order to avoid being driven out of the party leadership entirely. Ozawa won the election, but the party was hopelessly divided. A year later, Hata and twelve other NFP members broke away to form their own party. Former Prime Minister Hosokawa eventually left the party as well (and in the spring of 1998 resigned his Diet seat and withdrew, at least for the time being, from active political life). Other NFP members began to drift back to the LDP. By September 1997, twelve NFP members had joined the LDP, making it possible for it to regain a lower-house majority for the first time in more than four years.

Ozawa's hopes of creating a party that could defeat the LDP evaporated. In December 1997, his two-year term as party president concluded, Ozawa once again ran for party president, and once again he won. But the party was so badly split that Ozawa, concluding that there was no point heading a party that he could not completely control, decided to abandon the NFP. In January 1998, within weeks of his election victory, he formed yet another party, the Jiyutō, the Liberal Party. Now with only forty members in his party, Ozawa changed his strategy. Rather than challenge the LDP for power, he would look for an opportunity to form a "conservative-conservative alliance" *(hoho rengō) with* the LDP.

The Rise of the Democrats

The alliance between the LDP, the Socialists, and the Sakigake led to the formation of yet another new political party, the Minshutō, the Democratic Party, comprised mainly of members of the Sakigake and the Socialist Party who were unhappy with their parties' alliance with the LDP. The party was formed in September 1996 largely as the result of the efforts of the Sakigake's Yukio Hatoyama, a well-known and popular politician who was the grandson of the LDP's first prime minister, a Stanford University Ph.D., and an outspoken champion of political reform. Hatoyama at first shared and eventually ceded leadership of the party to another former Sakigake member, Naoto Kan, who had emerged as the most popular politician in Japan. Kan had entered the first Hashimoto coalition cabinet as minister of health and welfare and quickly became something of a national hero by forcing the release of government documents that demonstrated the involvement of his ministry's officials in a scandal involving the importation of HIV-contaminated blood that had infected a large proportion of Japan's hemophiliac population.

As a result of Ozawa's decision to take his supporters into the Liberal Party, the New Frontier Party splintered into six separate groups, most of which, joined by Hata and most of the members of his small party, merged with the Democrats in April 1998. They retained the Democratic Party name, made Kan the president of the new party, Hata its secretary-general, and Hatoyama the deputy secretary-general. The new Democratic Party, with 148 Diet members in December 1998, now comprised the major opposition to the LDP.

The Democrats advocate a reform program that tries to embrace the views of both its former LDP and JSP members. Kan has been fond of citing former Italian Prime Minister Prodi's Olive Tree Alliance as a model for his new Democratic Party (and Prodi compares his Olive Tree Alliance to Tony Blair's New Labour Party in Britain). Kan, in a conversation after Prodi's fall from power, characterized his party's stance with a different, and somewhat more telling, European analogy. The Democratic Party, he said, has to be "the party of Thatcher and Blair." Since the LDP had failed to undertake Thatcherite liberalizing reforms, the Democrats would have to do so when they came to power. They would also simultaneously have to adopt new social-welfare policies—thus the Blair moderation of Thatcherism—to cushion the adverse impact on society's weakest members that would result from increased competition and less government management of the economy.[29]

In truth, it is difficult to identify a Democratic Party common policy agenda. The party encompasses a wide range of somewhat incompatible policy views. The party's platform puts a considerable emphasis on the need to establish a new economic structure based on the "market principle," "individual responsibility," and "individual choice," code words for restructuring the Japanese political economy along contemporary U.S. lines. Yet the Democrats also claim to be to the left of the LDP in their concern for protecting the weak and disadvantaged. The tensions generated by policy differences between former Socialists—and former JSP headquarters staff in the Democratic Party organization—and more conservative politicians, as well as potential conflicts among its key leaders, are an ever present threat to its unity. But unlike the New Frontier Party under Ozawa, the Democratic Party is led by pragmatists who are willing to live with policy ambiguity and endeavor to avoid intraparty power struggles as long as they believe that doing so offers a realistic prospect of coming to power. And in the last year of the twentieth century, it seemed to many Democrats, as explained in the following chapter, that there was good reason to be optimistic about the future.

The Return of the Komeito

The final unraveling of Ozawa's effort to create a unified party to oppose the LDP was the reemergence of the Komeito as an independent party. The Komeito strategy when Hosokawa was in power, as already noted, was to pursue the so-called *"ichi-ichi* line." Then, apparently convinced that the new electoral system created irresistible pressures for party merger, the party leadership decided to merge their party with others to form the New Frontier Party. But it hedged its bets. Only the Komeito members in the lower house and those in the upper house whose terms were expiring at the time of the most immediate triennial election joined the NFP. Other upper-house members and all Komeito members elected to local assemblies became part of a new Komei party that kept the Komeito infrastructure in place.

After the NFP collapsed, the Komei leadership decided to abandon its strategy of joining forces with other parties. It began the process of reintegrating former Komeito members in the lower house in a new Komeito. The process was completed in November 1998. Party leaders who had insisted only a few years earlier that adoption of a new predominantly single-member electoral system made party merger unavoidable now argued with equal conviction that the Komeito should pursue an independent line. They had good reason to change their strategy. By doing so, Komeito leaders, for reasons that are explained in the next chapter, found themselves being courted vigorously by both the LDP and the Democrats and able to exercise more influence over the policy process than at any previous time in their party's history.

From Katayama to Murayama

It is one thing to explain why the LDP was successful in forging an alliance that enabled it to return to power; it is quite another to explain why it was so successful in stabilizing its relationship with the Socialist Party. Unable to cooperate with the conservatives who left the LDP to become leaders in the Hosokawa coalition government, the Socialists yet were able to work together with the conservatives in the LDP. The LDP remained unified and began to consolidate its power. The coalition government that was supposed to mark the end of LDP rule now appeared instead to be an interlude separating LDP rule under the '55 system and LDP rule in a new post '55 political party system.

One factor contributing to the LDP's ability to manage its coalition government relationship with the Socialist Party successfully was its decision to offer the post of prime minister to the Socialist Party's chairman. Putting Murayama at the head of a coalition in which the LDP was the largest party had the effect of largely locking in the Socialists to LDP policy positions. Since each party in the coalition obtained a number of cabinet posts proportional to its Diet-member strength, the LDP dominated the cabinet. It received thirteen cabinet portfolios, the JSP five, and the Sakigake two. The Murayama administration was essentially an LDP government with the Socialist Party chairman as prime minister.

In terms of its dynamics, the Murayama-led coalition government had much in common with the government that was formed when a Socialist had last become prime minister. In June 1947, during the U.S. Occupation, the Socialists joined forces with the conservative Democratic Party and the People's Cooperative Party to take control of the government. The Socialist Party chairman at the time, Tetsu Katayama, became prime minister, but the Diet members in his party were outnumbered by the considerably larger number of members in the conservative parties.[30]

The JSP secretary-general, Suehiro Nishio, a crafty politician who had honed his political skills in the prewar labor movement, and who would later break away from the Socialist Party to form the Democratic Socialist Party, argued that the JSP should participate in the coalition government but should not accept the post of prime minister. Nishio warned that the JSP would become hostage to the policies of the conservative parties because Prime Minister Katayama would be compelled to support the policies proposed by his own, conservative-party-dominated cabinet.[31] The Socialists should join the government, Nishio argued, but put itself in a position where it could make its own demands on a conservative prime minister. The party's powerful left-wing leaders, however, argued that the JSP's chairman should become prime minister or the party should not participate in the government at all.

Nishio's warning was prophetic. Katayama came to power just as the Occupation was shifting to a "reverse course" in its policies, downplaying and in some respects reversing its earlier democratic reforms in favor of an emphasis on economic recovery. The conservatives in the coalition readily agreed with Occupation authorities to support new restrictions on the right to strike of public-sector labor unions. They also supported other policies that had been anathema to the Socialists.

The Katayama government had little choice but to implement this "reverse course." Katayama resigned after a dismal nine months in office, his government finally brought down by a decision by a key JSP left-wing leader who was chairman of the lower-house budget committee to oppose the budget the government had submitted to the Diet. Divided and demoralized, the JSP stayed in power through the seven-month tenure of the successor government of conservative Hitoshi Ashida. The JSP left the government after the Ashida cabinet fell in October 1948, not to return until its chairman Murayama was chosen to be prime minister nearly half a century later.

Murayama found himself in a position similar to Katayama. As prime minister, he was the representative of his cabinet, and the cabinet was dominated by the LDP. When Murayama resigned after a year and a half in office, his party remained in the government, now in a coalition led by LDP President Hashimoto, just as the JSP had remained in the post-Katayama cabinet of conservative party leader Ashida.

In the November 1996 lower-house election, the Socialist Party—which had lost half of its lower-house seats in the preceding election of July 1993, going from 136 in 1990 to 70 in 1993—was decimated. It won only four seats in the single-member districts and eleven in the regional proportional-representation districts. In an attempt to revive the party's fortunes, the party had changed its name to the Social Democratic Party in January 1996. The following September, knowing that a general election was imminent, it had brought back Takako Doi, the popular chair of the party when it enjoyed a brief spurt of public support at the time of the 1989 upper-house election, to be the party's leader. The party continued to languish, however.

With Murayama as prime minister, the LDP and the JSP forged a historic compromise that reflected and confirmed the disintegration of the progressive-conservative cleavage, the defining feature of the '55 system. The essence of this compromise was an agreement explicitly to accept as legitimate the political order that had been enshrined in the postwar constitution and that had evolved over the past nearly fifty years of conservative-party rule. It was an agreement to favor continuity over change and consensus over confrontation.

This compromise put a much heavier burden on the Socialists than it did on the LDP since it obligated the Socialists formally to renounce many if not all of their party's traditional policy positions. Murayama, who had long been identified with the Socialist Party's left wing, responded to the new responsibilities thrust upon him as the nation's leader by separating himself from virtually all the policies that had formed the core of the Socialist Party's platform.

Murayama declared the self-defense forces to be constitutional, the U.S.-Japan security treaty to be indispensable, the national anthem Kimigayo and the Hinomaru national flag to be legitimate, nuclear-energy plants in Japan to be necessary, and an increase in the consumption tax to be unavoidable. He contradicted long-standing Socialist Party policy on each of these issues, and he did so without even going through the motions of having these reversals in official party policy approved by the relevant party organs before he made them. When a party congress was convened in September 1994, three months after Murayama became prime minister, it hastily endorsed the changes in policy that he had initiated and it did so over the protests of a vocal but entirely demoralized minority of the party's true believers.

The relative ease with which Murayama reversed the party's policies, especially on foreign policy, was no doubt facilitated by the fact that he was a leader of the party's left wing. It was as difficult for left-wing Socialists to oppose their leader's embrace of the U.S.-Japan security treaty as it had been for conservative Republicans to oppose Richard Nixon's opening to China.

It is also true, however, that there was less than is generally recognized to the JSP's renunciation of its traditional policy line, and something more than is generally recognized to the LDP side of the compromise. The Socialist Party had retained a radical rhetoric, but it had become in reality a deeply conservative party in its opposition to change in either domestic or foreign policy. By agreeing to support the security treaty with the United States and to recognize the legitimacy of the self-defense forces, the JSP was essentially bringing its official position—its *tatemae,* to use the Japanese term—in line with what had evolved as the Socialists' actual position—its *honne.* What the Socialists demanded in return was that the LDP also commit itself to the status quo—that it unambiguously accept the legitimacy of the postwar constitution, that it not seek radical change in either domestic or foreign policy matters, and that it not take actions that were not supported by a strong public consensus.

This was a compromise that Kono, the liberal president of the LDP at the time, was fully prepared to accept. He had long been opposed to the current of revisionism in the party, to those who advocated a broader Japanese military role, constitutional revision, and a return to so-called traditional values. His enthusiasm for forging a compromise with the Socialists was not strenuously contested by LDP members desperate to regain power at any cost.

Moreover, neither the LDP nor the Socialists, however intense their conflicts may have been in the past, embraced a vision of a Japanese future that was fundamentally at odds with the Japanese present. And that was the secret of their successful collaboration. Ozawa argued that Japan needed radical change, and the more he argued his vision, and the more he insisted that everyone else in his party embrace it as well, the greater the conflicts he generated with the Socialists. The LDP-JSP-Sakigake coalition, by contrast, was built on the basis of a cautious and incremental approach to dealing with pressing domestic economic and social issues and with a changed international system.

In the late 1990s, the Japanese government resisted U.S. demands that it take decisive action in the face of financial and economic crises in Korea and Southeast Asia and the problems in its own financial and economic system. The reason was not that Japanese did not understand what measures were needed to improve their economic situation; nor was it because powerful bureaucrats in the Ministry of Finance prevented the political leadership from doing what it wanted to do. The reason was embedded in the political developments that had brought the LDP back to power. The LDP was constrained by its need to retain the cooperation of the Socialists and the Sakigake, even after those two parties withdrew from the cabinet following the November 1996 lower-house election. It was constrained even more by a perception that the public was ambivalent about basic policy change, recognizing in principle that Japan had to adjust to new international and domestic realities, but being in practice profoundly risk-averse. The LDP-JSP-Sakigake coalition did not inspire the public, but it captured and reflected the ambivalence and caution of the Japanese electorate.

By deciding to forge their historic compromise in support of the status quo, the LDP and the JSP agreed to make the past history. Together, they swept away the debris of postwar ideology, but they were unable to articulate any new goals or vision. There was no larger purpose to cooperation between the LDP and the JSP than to hold political power. The result was a relatively stable government, a flaccid policy response to the internal and external challenges that Japan faced, and an electorate that was critical of the government and nervous about economic conditions, but politically apathetic.

Institutionalizing Cooperation

I once asked former Prime Minister Hosokawa the awkward question of why he thought the LDP and the JSP were able to work well together in contrast to the experience of his own coalition government. He immediately replied that both parties had learned from the experience and the mistakes of his and the Hata administrations. They both recognized the need to *"gaman,"* to be patient, to hold back, to compromise.[32]

Hosokawa's point was well taken. One reason the LDP-JSP-Sakigake alliance succeeded was the high premium that its leaders placed on a process of consultation and compromise. If Ozawa's strategy was to confront the Socialists on every important issue, the LDP's approach was to coopt the Socialists by bringing them around to LDP views through an exhaustive series of committee meetings and informal discussions.

Immediately after coming to power, the LDP, JSP, and the Sakigake signed an agreement called "the Murayama cabinet's three-party policy accord." This accord raised the meaning of the word opportunistic to a new level. The leaders of the three parties agreed to uphold the principles and the policies that been adopted by the parties that had joined together to form the Hosokawa government the previous year.[33] In other words, the LDP had joined the JSP and Sakigake to support an agreement drafted to justify the decision by seven parties, including the JSP and the Sakigake, to form a coalition government *against* the LDP. The accord committed the three parties, including the LDP, to "respect the constitution, and on the basis of broad public support, create a politics for the people and advance the cause of environmental protection and disarmament on a global scale." It also included an addendum to the original 1993 policy accord on "the ruling parties' management of the coalition government." It called for transparent and democratic policy-making procedures and for the establishment of specific new interparty decision-making bodies. These included at the top of the structure a liaison council of top government and party officials,[34] a ruling parties' leaders' committee comprised of the party representatives on the liaison council,[35] and a ruling-party parliamentary executive board that would recommend legislation to these top decision-making organs and deal with Diet-related procedural matters.[36]

The important mechanism created by the new coalition, however, operated below this level. Over the years of LDP power, the party's Policy Affairs Research Council had developed into a complex and differentiated decision-making structure. Through its sections *(bukai)*, which paralleled each of the government ministries, and its special committees and commissions, the PARC coordinated policy making between the party and the bureaucracy, gave each party member an opportunity to participate in the decision-making process on issue areas that were of particular interest or constituency concern, and determined what legislation would be submitted to the Diet. Kato, LDP chairman of the PARC during the time Murayama was in office, took the initiative to create a mechanism for interparty decision making modeled on the LDP's PARC. This amounted to an elaborate and largely successful effort to socialize the Socialists into the LDP's way of making legislative decisions, and to coopt their support for LDP policy positions.

The parties created a Policy Coordination Council *(seisaku chōsei kaigi)*. Three members from each party, including their respective PARC chairmen, served on it. The position of head of the council shifted from one party to the next every two months. The council met twice a week and it became the main venue for negotiating compromises between the parties on legislative matters. Under this council, the parties established nineteen ministry-specific policy-coordination committees *(shōchō betsu chōsei kaigi)* and project teams that were the counterparts to the sections and special committees in the LDP's PARC.

Throughout the life of the Murayama cabinet, the LDP leadership put a great deal of emphasis on discussing policy issues and developing coalition positions in the context of this Policy Coordination Council. The LDP's PARC Chairman Kato in particular was an ardent advocate of a conciliatory "bottom-up" approach to managing relations with the LDP's coalition partners. He was determined to show that his style was better-suited to the new realities of Japanese politics than the kind of confrontational approach that was both employed by Ozawa and supported by conservatives within the LDP. Kato as well as other LDP Diet members and the professional staff of the LDP's PARC were seasoned veterans in the art of policy formulation; they effectively controlled the coalition's policy-making process.

For Socialist Diet members, the Policy Coordination Council provided an opportunity to participate in policy formulation for the first time. They had been excluded from this process during the years that the LDP was the sole party in government, and the Hosokawa coalition government was never able to design an effective decision-making structure. Now, through the council and the ministry-specific policy coordination committees, Socialist Dietmen found themselves deeply involved in policy making.

Policy coordination among the three parties in the coalition proved surprisingly successful. Their task was eased by the fact that coordination had to be managed among only three parties rather than seven, as had been the case with the Hosokawa government. The most critical factors, however, were the LDP's strategic decision to emphasize cooperation and conciliation with the Socialists, and its ability, because of its long policy-making experience, to manage a relatively complex, inter party policy-formulation system.

LDP leaders had made the decision to let nothing drive a wedge between themselves and Prime Minister Murayama's Socialist Party, at least not until the LDP was strong enough to form a government without Socialist cooperation. They never lost sight of their goal, which was to keep Ozawa in the opposition and to delay holding a lower-house election until they felt confident they could increase their party's representation. The LDP leadership stood by Murayama no matter how much public criticism was directed against him for his weak leadership. After the coalition's poor performance in the upper-house election in July 1995, Murayama himself suggested that he should resign and turn over the prime minister's portfolio to LDP President Kono. The LDP insisted that he remain in the post for some months longer.

The decision-making structure that had been established when Murayama became prime minister remained in effect for the duration of the first Hashimoto cabinet—that is, until the November 1996 lower-house election. As a result of the devastating defeat they suffered in that election, both the Socialist Party and the Sakigake withdrew from the cabinet. They continued in coalition with the LDP, however, and continued to participate in the decision-making structures that had been established during the Murayama administration. However, now that the Socialists and Sakigake had so few Diet members, part of the decision-making system became inoperative, resulting, for example, in the abolition of the ministry-specific policy coordination committees. More important, the balance of power within the coalition had shifted so conclusively to the LDP as a result of the election that the entire structure established to facilitate interparty policy coordination became much less significant. The Policy Coordination Council, which had been an important site for policy making during the

Murayama cabinet, now became a committee where decisions made in the LDP's PARC were acknowledged and endorsed by the Socialists and the Sakigake.[37] And when the Socialists and the Sakigake left the coalition in April 1998, before the July upper-house election, the Policy Coordination Council was disbanded.

The policy-making innovations devised during the Murayama cabinet essentially were LDP organizational approaches projected to a supraparty level. Coalition leaders made no attempt to bolster the role of the Diet in decision making because they wanted to avoid having the Diet become a more pivotal arena for policy making and thereby raise the opposition parties' opportunities for influencing the process. As the need for coordination diminished, the organizational mechanisms created to facilitate collaboration were either abolished or atrophied. Decision making reverted to patterns similar to those that prevailed before the LDP lost power in 1993. The innovations in policy making, therefore, left no discernible impact on the political system. They did, however, offer a model for party policy coordination that might be resuscitated if there is coalition government again in Japan.

The LDP's defeat in the 1998 upper-house election—to be discussed in chapter 6—raised the possibility that a new pattern of policy making might emerge. The opposition Democratic Party rejected a revival of *"kokutai* politics" and insisted that it would draft its own legislation and then bargain with the LDP in the Diet, and in the full light of the television cameras, over the shape of the final legislation. If a pattern of compromise openly arrived at in the context of Diet deliberations actually were to materialize, it would mark a sharp break with the combination of collusion and opposition-for-opposition's-sake behavior that characterized the *kokutai politics* of the '55 system.

The LDP: Japan's Natural Party of Government?

The LDP's ability to regain political power and the fragmentation and incoherence of the political opposition stunned observers who just a few years earlier were excitedly writing the LDP's obituary and heralding the arrival of a new politics. Few anticipated that LDP leaders would prove to be as resourceful as they were in finding a way back to power. Even fewer expected that political rivalry among the parties of the coalition that ousted the LDP from power would prove to be so self-destructive.

The LDP, even when it was in opposition, still had advantages over other parties, having been in power for so long. For one thing, it had a nationwide organization. Few LDP members at the prefectural-assembly level or below defected to other parties as a result of the LDP's losing power at the national level. Locally elected LDP politicians had their own, strong, personal bases of support; they did not feel immediate pressure to ally themselves with another party, and in any case other parties did not have local organizations that they could join. This situation might have changed considerably had the LDP been kept out of power for a longer period of time. This again underscores the strategic mistake Ozawa and Hosokawa and the Komeito made, after Hosokawa resigned as prime minister, in not compromising with the Socialists and keeping the LDP out of power.

It bears repeating that voters did not play a direct part in bringing about the stunning reversal in the LDP's fortunes and the disintegration of the New Frontier Party. Voters were disengaged from the struggle for political supremacy among Japan's political elite, and they became by turns disillusioned and disinterested as that struggle unfolded. In local elections held throughout the country in the spring of 1995, voters demonstrated their disillusionment with mainstream political leaders and their parties by electing more mayors and governors who were not supported by any of the parties than had ever before been the case. In the elections for governor in both Tokyo and Osaka, Japan's two largest cities, voters elected former show-business celebrities who eschewed ties with any of the established parties over the former high-ranking bureaucrats who ran with the backing of the LDP.

Voting rates also plummeted. In the 1995 upper-house election, only 44.52 percent of eligible voters cast ballots. It was the lowest voting rate ever recorded in a national election. In the lower-house elections the following year, the first held under the new electoral system, the voting rate was a record low 59.65 percent, the lowest for a lower-house election since the end of the Second World War. In local elections, too, voting rates recorded record low levels. It was 40.8 percent in the March 1992 election for the Chiba prefectural governor.

For several years after the Miyazawa government fell in 1993, parties formed and reformed so rapidly that it was virtually impossible for even the most politically concerned citizen to keep track of the changing names of *kaiha* and parties. Through this period of political turmoil, only the LDP and the Communist Party retained the names that they had before

1993. This may have been a factor of some significance in accounting for the relatively good performance of both of these parties at the polls, although hard data to back up this impression is elusive.

As Japan approached a triennial upper-house election in July 1998, it appeared to many observers that a new era in LDP dominance might be in the making. The situation, however, was highly unpredictable. Public support for parties that were in opposition to the LDP was in the single digits in the spring of 1998, but a majority of Japanese supported no party at all. As long as this *mutōhasō*, the large mass of nonparty supporting voters, did not vote, the revival of LDP hegemony seemed probable. But economic conditions were deteriorating and the LDP, despite its rhetorical support for reform, did not seem to be able to instill confidence in the electorate that it knew how to deal with the situation. The Hashimoto administration's caution and ambivalence mirrored the public mood, but an increasingly nervous electorate wanted a political leadership that was resolute rather than ambivalent. The opposition had reverted to an earlier pattern of waiting for the LDP to get itself into trouble, and much to the surprise of nearly everyone, that is exactly what the LDP did.

Chapter Six

Japan's Uncertain Political Future

The 1998 Upper-House Election Results

In the spring of 1998, with an upper-house election scheduled for July, LDP leaders exuded confidence that their party was on track to reestablish its traditional dominant role. There seemed to be good reason for optimism: the LDP had won several recent local and Diet by-elections and the opposition was fragmented, disoriented, and demoralized. New Frontier Party Diet members had headed off in half a dozen different directions after the party's collapse in January 1997. In April 1998, those who had not already returned to the LDP or gone with Ozawa in his new Liberal Party joined former Socialists and Democratic Socialists and Sakigake members in the Democratic Party. This party, which as mentioned in the preceding chapter had been formed initially in September 1995, was the single largest opposition party now that the New Frontier Party had disintegrated. Its support ratings, as measured by public-opinion polls, however, hovered around a dismal 5 percent. LDP leaders prepared for the election believing that they might recapture an upper-house majority that had been lost in 1989. Seasoned political observers also expected the election to produce significant LDP gains.

These expectations made the election's results all the more shocking. Not only did the LDP fail to take the sixty-eight seats necessary to recover its upper-house majority, it fell far short of winning even sixty seats, which every major newspaper poll had predicted it was likely to win.[1] Only forty-four LDP candidates won, making for the worst upper-house electoral performance by the party in any upper-house election. The LDP failed to win a single seat in Japan's most populous urban prefectures—

Tokyo, Aichi, Osaka, Saitama, Kanagawa, Kyoto, and Hyogo. It won but eleven seats in the national proportional-representation district, just one more than the Democrats.[2]

The Democratic Party received nearly 22 percent of the proportional-representation vote, only three percentage points less than the LDP. The Communist Party won 14.6 percent of the vote, a record high for that party, and the Komei scored a new high in its level of support: 7.7 million voters, some 13.8 percent of those voting, cast their proportional-representation ballots for the Komei. Ozawa's Liberal Party also did well, winning 9.3 percent of the vote in the nationwide proportional-representation district. The only party not benefitting from the anti-LDP vote was the Social Democratic Party. Its 7.8 percent of the nationwide vote was less than half what it obtained in the previous 1995 election.

The election's results—presented in appendix 4—left the LDP, even with the addition to its roster of several independents who had won in the election, with only 104 seats in the 252-member upper house, 23 seats shy of a majority. Its defeat was so total that Prime Minister Hashimoto immediately announced his resignation as LDP party president and as the nation's prime minister, effective as soon as the LDP selected a new party leader and the Diet convened to select a new prime minister.

The Voters' Revolt

The upper-house election came in the midst of Japan's worst economic performance in the postwar period. After seven long years of stagnation, Japan now was in a full-blown recession. Unemployment was more than 4 percent—not a high figure compared with France or Germany and about the same as the "low" unemployment rate in the United States—but the highest official unemployment rate in Japan since comparable figures began to be compiled in the early 1950s.

Adverse economic conditions alone might not have led voters to cast their ballots against the LDP had they believed the government was doing all it reasonably could be expected to do to tackle the nation's economic problems. Prime Minister Hashimoto, however, did not convey an image of confidence and competence. He concluded his election campaign by waffling on the issue of whether he planned to institute a permanent tax cut. It is not that there was overwhelming public support for a permanent tax cut; there is no evidence that there was. But the voters wanted to know that their leader knew what he wanted to do and why he wanted to do it. The impression that voters took with them to the polls was that Hashimoto was ambivalent and indecisive.

Alarmed by the bleak economic news and by the Hashimoto government's inability to articulate a strategy to deal with a worsening economic situation, many voters who otherwise might have abstained turned out to express their lack of confidence in the Hashimoto administration. The voting rate shot up fourteen points from the previous upper-house election, from 44.5 percent in 1995 to 58.8 percent. Exit polls indicated that 56 percent of those who abstained in the 1995 upper-house election and voted this time were supporters of no party—the so-called *mutōhasō*. Among all the *mutōhasō*, again according to exit polls, only 14 percent voted for LDP candidates in the single-member district elections and only 10 percent in the nationwide proportional-representation district.[3]

Apparently, many voters made the decision to vote and to vote against the LDP only toward the end of the campaign, which helps explain why the polls were so far off the mark in predicting the extent of the LDP's defeat. A series of public-opinion surveys taken in Tokyo during July offer an indicator of what was happening. They showed a precipitous decline in LDP support, from 20 percent on July 1 to 14 percent on July 9. The Democratic Party candidate who ended up with the highest vote in Tokyo's four-member district, was supported by only 8 percent of voters in the poll taken on July 1, but by 15 percent on July 9.[4]

The upper-house election was a devastating defeat for the LDP and a repudiation of the Hashimoto government. The long-term implications of the outcome were unclear, however. All opposition parties did well in the election, but their success apparently stemmed from the voters' desire to send a message of protest against the LDP, not from any one of the opposition parties having tapped some new vein of electoral support. According to postelection polls, 57 percent of voters who cast their ballots for the Democratic Party said they did so because there was no other party they wanted to vote for; 23 percent said it was because they found the party's leader, Naoto Kan, to be attractive; and only 8 percent said they voted for the Democratic Party because they thought it could be expected to run the government well.[5]

In addition to the protest vote by the *mutōhasō*, the rout of the LDP largely came at the hands of LDP supporters who decided to vote against their party. Exit polls indicated that only 61 percent of LDP supporters voted for LDP candidates in district elections. Just 58 percent of LDP supporters in cities of more than half a million people voted for the party in the nationwide proportional-representation district. In cities of less than 500,000 people, 37 percent of LDP supporters voted for other parties. Even in the countryside, the vaunted bastion of party strength, about 30 percent of LDP supporters defected to cast their proportional-representation vote for one of the opposition parties.[6] In a postelection poll, 40 percent of LDP supporters indicated that they believed it was good that the LDP had lost the election.[7]

Candidate Strategies

The LDP's misjudgment about the possibility of its recovering an upper-house majority produced tactical mistakes that, it may seem, magnified its losses. It ran thirty-five more candidates in this election than it did in the election in 1995. In that election, it won seats in four of the five three- and four-member districts and in fourteen of the eighteen two-member districts. In the 1998 election, it ran two candidates in four of the five districts that elect three or four members, but won no seats. In Aichi prefecture, for example, it ran two candidates who together received 30 percent of the vote. Both lost, while the winning Democratic Party candidate who won the most votes in the district obtained only 17 percent of the vote. It is entirely conceivable that if the LDP had run only one candidate in each of these three- and four- member districts, it would have won seats. But it was a catch-22: if it ran fewer candidates, it would have no chance of winning enough seats to recover its upper-house majority.

In any case, the LDP's endorsement strategy was not a major cause of the party's defeat. True, it ran two candidates in eight of the eighteen two-member districts and won both seats in only one of those eight districts. But it won one of the two seats in the other seven. In other words, running two candidates in these districts did not produce *tomodaore*, the defeat of both candidates. It could not have won more seats if it had run one instead of two candidates. In each of the five two-member districts where it won no seats, it ran only one candidate. So here as well, defeat could not be blamed on an incautious endorsement strategy.

While tactical error had a minimal impact on LDP losses, however, the opposition parties' running of many former lower-house incumbents who had been defeated in the 1996 lower-house election had the effect of producing opposition-party success that exceeded opposition-party popularity. Seeing little opportunity to recover their lower-house seats in the single-member districts of the new electoral system, some twenty-seven former members of the lower house ran in the upper-house election. Seventeen of them were elected, twelve in prefectural districts and five through proportional representation. In the prefectural district races, these candidates, nearly all of whom had been members of the LDP before 1993, had high personal name recognition. Now only one ran as an LDP candidate. The victory of these former lower-house, mostly conservative, politicians is hardly an indicator of a massive shift in voter support from the LDP to any of the opposition parties. The victory of most of them probably owed a great deal to their name recognition and their command of long-established, personal support organizations in the areas in which they ran.

The most one could conclude from the election was that the public did not like the way the Hashimoto government was dealing with Japan's economic problems. The LDP, then, could take some solace in the results: if the party could stabilize or begin to improve the economic situation, it might regain public support. Its percentage of the proportional-representation vote was only two points lower than in the previous 1995 election, and it won eighteen more seats in the district elections than its nearest competitor, the Democratic Party. Also, support for the opposition was fragmented. The Democratic Party secured fewer seats in 1998 than the New Frontier Party had won in 1995, or the Socialist Party won in 1989. Finally, the LDP could look forward to doing better in those single-member, lower-house districts where LDP candidate organizations were strong, where name recognition was high, and where there was a strong possibility that candidates from several parties would divide the anti-LDP vote.

The election results also held out hope for the opposition parties. If voter disenchantment with the LDP persisted and if the Democrats could succeed in transforming a protest vote against the LDP into positive support for their own party, they stood a good chance of denying the LDP a majority in the next lower-house election. The Democrats had emerged as the party with the most seats in urban Japan. The Communists and Komeito, too, had demonstrated impressive strength among the urban electorate. Postelection opinion polls recorded a surge in Democratic Party popularity. In the single digits in June, and at 16 percent in the first postelection poll, it continued to increase. In early August, it was 20 percent to the LDP's 23 percent. Ominous for the LDP, 35 percent of respondents in this August poll said they wanted the Democrats to win in the next lower-house election. Only 19 percent expressed the hope that the LDP would emerge victorious.[8]

With little prospect that the economic situation would improve dramatically before the next election—which had to be called by October 2000 at the latest—there seemed to be rich opportunities for the opposition to make inroads into LDP strength in the lower house. Only time would tell whether the 1998 upper-house election results were just a warning shot across the LDP bow or marked the beginning of a process of party realignments and coalitions like the one that followed the fall of the LDP government in 1993.

Choosing a New Prime Minister

With Prime Minister Hashimoto's resignation, the LDP had to choose a new party president, a decision to be made by a party conference composed of LDP Diet members and one party representative from each of the forty-seven prefectural chapters. The party had long ago dispensed with a primary system that gave rank-and-file party members a role in choosing the party leader, one that led to the unexpected defeat of Prime Minister Fukuda in 1979 that is recounted in chapter 2. Choosing the party president would be contained within LDP leadership circles and take place in the context of LDP factional politics.

The strongest candidate was Keizo Obuchi, head of the largest and most powerful LDP faction—the one that previously had been led by former Prime Minister Takeshita. Obuchi, as mentioned in chapter 2, had succeeded to the leadership of the faction in December 1993 when Ozawa and Hata split off to form their own faction. Like Takeshita, his former faction boss and political mentor, Obuchi was a consummate political insider. He was adept at managing factional affairs, mediating disputes, and building consensus within the party, but he lacked a strong public profile. He performed credibly as foreign minister in the Hashimoto cabinet, gaining some public applause for his insistence that Japan sign a treaty banning land mines despite apparent opposition from foreign-ministry officials. He also earned the respect of foreign-affairs professionals for his skill in dealing with Russia over the signing of a peace treaty, keeping the negotiations on track.[9]

The selection of a new party president came at a time of leadership change in the LDP's factional organizations. Decisions to support or challenge Obuchi were based largely on calculations of personal advantage by those aspiring to faction leadership and eventually to becoming party president and prime minister. Two top LDP leaders immediately backed Obuchi. One was Koichi Kato, the outgoing party secretary-general and heir apparent to leadership of the faction headed by Miyazawa. The other was Taku Yamazaki, the chairman of the party's Policy Affairs Research Council under Hashimoto and the most likely successor to leadership of the faction led by former Prime Minister Nakasone. An Obuchi administration would leave basic factional relationships in place, enabling both Kato and Yamazaki to consolidate leadership in their respective factions and position themselves to contend for the party presidency after Obuchi's departure.

There were in 1998 at the time of the LDP presidential election four major factions in the LDP—headed by Obuchi, Miyazawa, Nakasone, and a former finance minister, Hiroshi Mitsuzuka. Because Kato and Yamazaki, the two leading figures respectively in the Miyazawa and Nakasone factions, supported Obuchi, his election was a foregone conclusion as long as factional cohesion was maintained. If that cohesion were lost and if Obuchi was denied the party's presidency, the Obuchi faction in all likelihood would splinter and the hopes of Kato and Yamazaki for a smooth transition to leadership of their respective factions would be set back. A general factional reorganization would take place that might give other politicians—ones who at that time seemed to have only a distant opportunity—a chance to contest the party's and the nation's highest position. It was in this context that another top LDP politician, Seiroku Kajiyama, decided to make a bid for the party presidency.

Kajiyama has appeared several times in these pages as a behind-the-scenes wheeler-dealer and quintessential practitioner of *kokutai* politics. In December 1992, he had been one of the key Takeshita faction members who had maneuvered to deny leadership of the faction to Ozawa and to make Obuchi faction chairman. Six months later, he was the LDP secretary-general when the Miyazawa government fell. He served as chief cabinet secretary in the first Hashimoto cabinet, then upon leaving the government he became a vocal critic of Hashimoto's economic policies. He was one of the party's leading advocates of a conservative-conservative alliance *(hoho rengō)* with Ozawa's Liberal Party to replace the LDP's alliance with the Socialists and Sakigake.

Kajiyama was the favorite candidate of the financial markets and the

Japanese business community because he insisted that the next government focus on banking-system reform and economic growth. The press treated Kajiyama's challenge to Obuchi as if it represented a major difference over policy and over leadership style. Kajiyama was portrayed as a forceful, presidential-type of leader; Obuchi was described as a traditionalist with an unexciting, consensus-building style.

In reality, Kajiyama was playing a complex factional game of his own in vintage Japanese political style. He entered the presidential race hoping he could divide the Obuchi faction and draw the support of Nakasone and Miyazawa faction members who opposed Yamazaki and Kato. He also hoped to win support from *hoho rengō* advocates in Mitsuzuka's faction and other LDP Diet members. Even if he failed to win the party presidency, he might sow enough dissension in factional relationships to emerge as a key leader of a new faction and position himself to have major influence in determining who would obtain power in the event Obuchi should stumble.

If Kajiyama was the favorite of the financial markets and business community, a third candidate, Junichiro Koizumi, seemed to be the people's choice. A former minister of posts and telecommunications, Koizumi was well known for having unorthodox views, such as his support for privatizing Japan's postal service. He represented the younger, cosmopolitan, straight-speaking generation of Japanese politicians, and was one of what was known in Japanese political circles as the YKK trio—Yamazaki, Kato, and Koizumi. But with Kato and Yamazaki backing Obuchi, Koizumi's base in the party was the weakest of the three presidential candidates. Even his own Mitsuzuka faction was divided between Koizumi supporters and a group of pro-Kajiyama conservatives.

For about a week preceding the party conference that would pick a new president, the three candidates engaged in a virtually nonstop series of television appearances, joint press conferences, and public debates. Man-in-the-street interviews and nationwide public-opinion polls consistently ranked Koizumi the most popular candidate, with Kajiyama second and the noncharismatic Obuchi a distant third. The press treated the contest like a national presidential election, rather than what it was— an election among LDP members to choose a new party president. In treating the election in this manner, the media unwittingly helped create an impression that the LDP somehow had become more open in the procedures it used to choose its president. The reality was that the LDP was *less* open than it had been at earlier times in its history, when—as noted above—rank-and-file members had a voice in the selection process.

The mass-media's enthusiasm for making this internal LDP decision appear as some kind of public contest was, if nothing else, a reflection of how much American political styles have shaped Japanese perceptions of what it is that constitutes modern and desirable political practice. No one suggested it would have made more sense, given the structure of the Japanese political system, if LDP Diet members had debated policy at a party conference and then chosen their president. Nor did any commentator think to caution the public or to educate people in the financial markets who had suddenly discovered Japanese politics that a leader's success would hinge on his ability to build a consensus in the LDP and find ways to forge compromises with opposition parties that controlled a majority in the upper house. Media coverage did have one positive effect: it forced the candidates to discuss policy issues, which in turn helped educate the public about the seriousness of the economic problems facing the country.

In terms of public popularity, the candidates were ranked in the order of Koizumi, Kajiyama, Obuchi. In terms of power within the party, the ordering was the reverse. The LDP elected Keizo Obuchi its new president, giving him a majority of votes on the first ballot. Kajiyama, finishing second, came in with fewer than half the number of votes Obuchi obtained. Koizumi placed third. On July 24, 1998, Obuchi was elected prime minister, Japan's ninth prime minister in ten years.[10]

The upper-house election defeat was a kind of shock therapy for the LDP. Not only did it force the LDP to change its leadership, but it caused a stunning reversal in the optimistic, even cocky, attitude LDP leaders displayed just a few weeks earlier. The party's new leaders seemed to realize that, if they did not undertake concrete steps to restore the confidence of Japanese voters in the LDP's ability to manage the economy, they would face an angry electorate in the next lower-house election. They also had to worry about the possibility of an internal revolt. If the party's future appeared in jeopardy, Kajiyama and others, who after the election constituted something of a new "anti-mainstream" group in the party, would press for a change in leadership and a more drastic policy agenda. Urban-based members might be tempted to leave the party altogether in order to salvage their own reelection prospects. It was easy to paint a scenario that would recreate the kind of political jockeying that followed the Miyazawa government's collapse in 1993, or produce a punishing defeat for the LDP in the next lower-house election. However, one could also project circumstances that could boost Obuchi's popularity and stabilize LDP power. In a sense, Obuchi's low standing in public opinion was an advantage. Even modest accomplishments were bound to surpass expectations and raise his popularity.

This uncertainty about the future implied something definitive about the past—the era of stable, LDP one-party dominance was irretrievably over. The precise features of the new party system that would replace the '55 system remained unclear. Their eventual shape would be influenced by domestic economic developments, external events and pressures, and international financial-market perceptions of the adequacy of the government's economic policies. How these influences would affect political action would depend on the behavior of political leaders seeking to maximize their opportunities to obtain power. Strategic calculations—whether by Ozawa or the leaders of the Komeito, JSP, and LDP—had shifted dramatically over the course of the 1990s. And as a result of the 1998 upper-house election, they would shift again.

The Obuchi-Ozawa Accord

The LDP's upper-house election defeat and the surprising success of the Democratic Party not only left the Obuchi government without an upper-house majority; it made it impossible for the LDP to put together a coalition that would produce a majority. Alliance with the LDP's former coalition partners, the Social Democrats and the Sakigake, would not suffice. The Sakigake had virtually collapsed (and it would formally dissolve a few months later). Together, the Socialists and the Sakigake held only eighteen seats, including the seats that they had won in the 1995 upper-house election, while the LDP needed at least twenty-three seats to obtain a majority.

In order to be able to pass legislation over the Democratic Party's opposition, the LDP would have to obtain the support of both the Komeito, which had twenty-two seats in the newly elected upper house, and Ozawa's Liberal Party, with its twelve seats. There was little chance, however, that the LDP would succeed in drawing the Komeito into a formal coalition arrangement. Its leaders, after the collapse of the New Frontier Party, had decided to resurrect the old Komeito party name and embark on a new strategy in which they would try to use their position as a swing vote to leverage their position vis-à-vis both the LDP and the Democrats. They were not about to tie their fate to another party, not after their unhappy experience in the New Frontier Party, and not now that the LDP seemed to be in serious trouble with the voters.

Without the participation of the Komeito, there was considerable opposition to alliance with the Liberals among those in the LDP whose support had been crucial to Obuchi in the party presidential election. LDP leaders such as Koichi Kato might have been agreeable to an LDP-Komeito-Liberal alliance since it would give the LDP a clear upper-house majority and would relegate Ozawa to a minor role as leader of the smallest party in the coalition. However, they were opposed to an alliance with the Liberals alone since it would not provide an upper-house majority and it conceivably would put Ozawa in the position of being able to determine the fate of the coalition.

The problems and the dangers that this upper-house situation posed to the Obuchi government quickly became apparent when the government in the fall of 1998 found itself facing a united front among the opposition parties over banking legislation. Led by the Democrats, the opposition parties demanded that the government's proposed legislation to deal with severely undercapitalized and insolvent banks be strengthened, forcing in effect the nationalization of the Long Term Credit Bank. Young LDP Diet members negotiated directly with opposition-party representatives over the details of the legislation, circumventing the formal LDP policy-making apparatus. Facing the certain defeat of the government's bills in the upper house, and a possible revolt by younger members of his own party if he did not compromise, Obuchi capitulated to the opposition's demands.

This experience caused the Obuchi government to redouble its efforts to draw the Komeito and the Liberals away from the Democrats. It agreed to support a Komeito proposal to stimulate consumer demand by issuing vouchers that people could use to make purchases at local stores. And in spite of internal opposition to a coalition with the Liberals, Obuchi and his chief cabinet secretary, Hiromu Nonaka, began speaking out publicly about the desirability of a coalition with the Liberals. The immediate consequence of these efforts was an agreement with the Komeito and with the Liberals on a set of banking bills that provided up to ¥60 trillion (roughly $500 billion) to banks to augment their capital base and to relieve a credit crunch, and to increase deposit-insurance reserves. The legislation passed over the opposition of the Democratic Party.

A persuasive case can be made that the manner in which the Diet initially dealt with banking legislation in the aftermath of the July 1998 upper-house election represented a positive development in Japanese party politics. Compromise between the LDP and the opposition parties produced stronger and better legislation than would have been the case had the LDP won a majority of seats in that race. Led by the Democrats, the opposition demanded greater transparency about the state of banks' loan portfolios and more stringent conditions for the injection of public funds than the LDP wanted to impose.

Opposition party leaders tried to demonstrate their capacity to govern by abandoning an old "opposition for opposition's sake" posture in favor of making detailed and constructive proposals for amending the legislation proposed by the LDP. Young LDP and opposition-party members, drawing on the expertise of specialists in securities companies and elsewhere in the private sector, became important participants in the policy process, while Ministry of Finance bureaucrats were pushed to the sidelines. Debate was public and the legislative process was transparent. As a result, Prime Minister Obuchi, so widely criticized for lacking leadership, accomplished more in just a few months than almost anyone was ready to give him credit for.

LDP leaders, including the prime minister, did not view the situation in such a positive light, however. Without the ability to cobble together an upper-house majority, they would be at the mercy of the Democrats. They doubted that the government would survive if the LDP were forced to capitulate again to the opposition, or if the opposition passed in the upper house another motion of nonconfidence in a cabinet minister as it did in the minister in charge of the defense agency in November 1998.[11] The LDP leadership was desperate to reverse a trend that was reducing the power of the party's senior leaders over policy making in the party itself and that was forcing compromises openly arrived at with opposition party leaders.

Seeking to strengthen his party's position in the upper house, Prime Minister Obuchi forged an agreement at the end of November 1998 with Liberal Party President Ozawa to establish a coalition government. Although an LDP–Liberal Party coalition would not give the LDP a majority in the upper house, it would break the opposition parties' united front. With at least one other party aligned with the LDP, it should be easier, in the estimation of Obuchi's chief strategist Nonaka, to obtain the support of the Komeito on specific legislative bills even if the Komeito did not formally join the coalition.[12] And alliance with the Liberals would bring the LDP to within twelve votes of a majority which, depending on the issue involved, might be secured with the support of conservative independents and minor-party upper-house members.

There was every reason for the Liberals to want to enter into coalition with the LDP. Few of the thirty-five lower-house Liberal Party members had any hope of being elected in single-member districts under the new lower-house election system that their leader Ozawa had been so instrumental in bringing about. The key provision in the accord that Obuchi and Ozawa reached to establish a coalition government was that the two parties would coordinate their candidate endorsements in the next election, giving priority to incumbents. In other words, Liberal Party Diet members who had been elected in single-member districts would run the next time with the support of the LDP. At least this was what was agreed to in November 1998. It remained to be seen whether the parties would still be together at the time of the next election, and whether LDP members who had been planning to run in single-member districts against Liberal Party incumbents would be forced to go along with the Obuchi-Ozawa agreement.

Ozawa insisted that the policy agreement he struck with Obuchi exacted a heavy price from the LDP in return for his agreement to have the Liberals enter a coalition. Their agreement called for reducing the number of cabinet ministers in the next cabinet from twenty to seventeen, shrinking the size of both the lower and upper houses by fifty members each, introducing a system of deputy ministers, and eliminating the practice of having bureaucrats respond to interpolations in the Diet.[13]

Even if all these reforms are realized, which seems unlikely, they are not much to show for the effort to revolutionize Japanese politics that Ozawa ostensibly set out on, almost six years earlier, when he left the Takeshita faction and then bolted the LDP altogether. On the one issue that could have given significant policy meaning to the alliance, Ozawa's proposal for a temporary elimination of the consumption tax, and then its gradual reintroduction as a tax earmarked for social-welfare purposes, the agreement called for nothing more than a general review of the tax. It was followed by quick denials by LDP leaders that they had any intention of reducing, much less eliminating, the consumption tax, even temporarily. LDP leaders also effectively parried another Ozawa demand—that they support an interpretation of the constitution that would permit Japan to send troops to participate as fighting forces in peacekeeping operations authorized by the United Nations Security Council. Ozawa, however, was never one to take a defensive position in political infighting. After signing his agreement with Obuchi, he appeared on numerous Sunday morning TV news interview programs to claim that he had scored a major victory: he had, he said, forced the LDP to agree to his terms in return for his party's support.[14]

To many professionals inside Nagata-chō, both in the LDP and in the Democratic Party and the Komeito, the LDP-Liberal alliance represented Ozawa's surrender. Having failed in his gambit to drive the LDP out of office with a new party under a new electoral system, he was now in effect bringing the Diet members who had stayed with him back to the LDP, and getting little in return except for some face-saving gestures with respect to political reform.

But others wondered whether Obuchi was not taking a dangerous and unnecessary risk bringing Ozawa back into the LDP fold. If the LDP did not do as Ozawa wished, he could leave the coalition, once again standing as the champion of "reform" against an LDP that refused to change, and threaten the continued existence of the Obuchi government. The LDP leadership was gambling that not many Liberal Party members would follow him; their Liberals only hope of being elected depended on getting the agreement of the LDP to support their candidacies. But given Ozawa's penchant for risk-taking and for doing the unexpected, the future of the coalition was anything but certain. And if the alliance were simply a step in the process of reincorporating Ozawa and his supporters into the LDP, then it meant that Ozawa once again would be an important player in the LDP's factional politics.

The LDP-Liberal alliance had the paradoxical effect of weakening support for Obuchi by Yamazaki and Kato, the two leaders who were most important to his success in winning the LDP's presidency and who were most opposed to alliance with Ozawa, while giving greater prominence to Kajiyama and others who had opposed Obuchi's election and who had been advocates of a so-called "conservative-conservative" alliance with Ozawa.

No one could be sure what the voters made of this latest twist in Nagata-chō politics. It seems not to have improved the image of either Obuchi and the LDP leadership or of Ozawa. Beginning with the 1989 upper-house election, when the LDP lost a majority for the first time in its history, and through the three subsequent lower-house and three upper-house elections, up to and including the July 1998 election for

members of the upper house, voters had demonstrated an unprecedented volatility in party support. Now, with its alliance with the Liberals,
the LDP had strengthened its negotiating position perhaps vis-à-vis
other parties in the Diet. There was no reason to believe, however, that
it had strengthened its support among the electorate or that the political
turmoil that was so prominent a feature of politics in the 1990s was about
to end.

The Changing Japanese Voter

Thirty years ago, one of the main questions asked about Japanese voting
behavior was why voting rates were so high. Voting in Japan is not, as it is
in Italy and some other countries, compulsory, yet it was not unusual for
voting rates in national elections to exceed 90 percent in many districts.
The island of Himeshima, sitting off the tip of the Kunisaki Peninsula in
Oita Prefecture, which I visited several times in the late 1960s, is a case in
point. When I called on the mayor of that island village many years ago,
he pointed out the plaques on the walls of his office that had been given
to the village by the Ministry of Home Affairs to commend its citizens
for taking their civic responsibilities seriously and producing some of the
highest voting rates in the country. The voting rate in Himeshima in the
1967 lower-house election was 97.96 percent. Not only did Himeshima's
voters vote, they nearly all voted for the same candidate. In that election,
one LDP incumbent candidate, a native son of the village, won 2,140
votes. The Socialist Party candidate finished second with a grand total of
fifty-four votes. Another LDP incumbent received six votes. And the
third LDP candidate, whose campaign was the object of my field research,
received three votes.[15] Himeshima was an extreme example of a widespread phenomenon. In nonmetropolitan Japan—that is, the Japan that
lay beyond Tokyo, Nagoya, and Osaka—community solidarity and the
ability of people in the local power structure to manipulate networks of
long-existing social relationships to turn out the vote and to turn that
vote out for particular candidates, raised voting rates and support for
hometown LDP candidates to a uniformly high level.

Voting rates are usually associated with political interest, cognition,
and a sense of efficacy: people vote because they are interested in politics,
have knowledge about the candidates, parties, or issues at stake, and
believe their vote is meaningful. High voting rates are supposed to be

an indicator, as the get-out-the-vote campaigns of the Ministry of Home Affairs and Japanese popular wisdom have it, of "high political consciousness."

Yet in Japan in those times, there was something of an inverse correlation between voting rates and political consciousness. While urging voters to vote, the Home Ministry also used a slogan that was telling: "I won't sell my vote for a bribe or out of a sense of obligation" *(baishū ya giri jya uranai kono ippyō)*. For many people, the act of voting was not so much an exercise of individual political choice as much as an expression of solidarity with the community or a way to return a favor *(giri)* incurred to someone who was involved in the election campaign. Each Diet politician developed a campaign organization that relied on town and village assemblymen and other locally prominent individuals who were at the center of extensive and intricate webs of social relationships to "gather the vote" for them.[16]

In the fall of 1996, during the first lower-house election campaign to be held under the new, mixed, single-member-district and proportional-representation, system, I spent several days visiting some of the towns and villages that had been the object of my field research some thirty years earlier.[17] Himeshima was still a beautiful and pristine island. It had an ecologically concerned mayor (the son of the mayor I met in 1967) who had kept resort developers out, instituted a stringent recycling program, and, with the support of the prefectural government's innovative "one village one product movement" *(isson ippin undō)*, had overseen Himeshima's development into the nation's largest center of shrimp farming.

The mayor took me on a tour around the island to show me what had changed since I had been there last. One new addition was a modern and attractive *wakamono yado*, a youth club, that the island's young people could use free of charge. The mayor ruefully noted that the club was almost never used. When I visited Himeshima in the 1960s, the fire-brigade and other traditional young people's groups were vibrant social organizations. Today, young people prefer to stay at home and watch television or go with a friend to a local coffeehouse. Almost the only time the *wakamono yado* was used, the mayor said with a shrug, was for an occasional karaoke party. Moreover, there are far fewer young people in the village to take advantage of the club's facilities than there were thirty years ago. Like nearly every other rural community in Japan, Himeshima has lost population, especially its young population, to Japan's urban centers.

This theme of the weakening of traditional bonds of social cohesion was repeated in other towns and villages I revisited in 1996. Decline of community cohesion has had important political effects. It has diminished the ability of local elites to mobilize the vote for Diet candidates. They can guarantee fewer "hard votes" *(koteihyō)* to the Diet candidate of their choice than was true in years past.[18] There are more floating voters—that is, voters who cannot be counted on to support a particular Diet candidate because of relationships they may have with that candidate's local campaign organizer.

As a result, candidates seem to be spending much more time, energy, and money in trying to reach voters in towns and villages directly, relying less on local politicians and other influentials to mobilize support for them. Thirty years ago it was not uncommon for a candidate's local campaign manager, typically a prefectural or town assemblyman, to insist that the Diet candidate not campaign in his town. His own interests were best served by keeping the Diet candidate dependent on the local machine to deliver the vote. And Diet candidates saw little purpose in spending time campaigning in areas where their campaign managers would in any case deliver their "hard" votes.

This pattern of political campaigning is changing. As the power of local politicians to deliver the vote has declined, Diet candidates have turned their attention more and more to building evermore powerful support organizations, *kōenkai*, to forge direct links between the candidate and voters. The diminished role of local politicians and other community elites in delivering votes for Diet candidates amounts to a weakening of machine politics in rural Japan that is comparable to the weakening of machine politics in U.S. cities earlier in this century. This has not led to a decline in the importance of the *kōenkai*, however. Politicians depend more than ever on their personal, direct links to voters to develop a support network. That has made the *kōenkai* even more important as the centerpiece of many politicians' campaign organization. There is no reason to believe the new electoral system will fundamentally change this organizational staple of Japanese political life.

The weakening of community solidarity and the consequent diminished ability of local elites to gather the vote have lowered voting rates across districts in Japan. If the question thirty years ago was why Japanese voting rates were so high, the question today is why they are almost as low as voting rates are in the United States. Rural Japanese voters turn out in larger numbers to vote than people living in cities, but everywhere people vote less now than they did twenty or thirty years ago. Those voting rates have declined as more and more people slip through the nets of social relationships that candidates traditionally have used to mobilize voter support.

Voters relatively satisfied, or at least not intensely dissatisfied, with the government's performance, are less likely to vote than in the past. Conversely, voting rates in Japan today tend to rise when people are dissatisfied either with the politicians elected in their district and/or with the party in power. As noted earlier, almost all voters who accounted for the fourteen-point jump in the voting rate in the 1998 upper-house election compared with the previous race in 1995 voted against the LDP.

Voting behavior has changed in another important respect. The reason the '55 system lasted for as long as it did was not so much because of the popularity of the LDP as it was the unwillingness of the public to turn government over to the opposition. This produced a logic that seems peculiar in U.S. or western European terms: the LDP tended to do better at the polls at times of economic difficulty and to lose support when times were good. In difficult times, voters were loath to risk turning power over to parties with no experience in governing the country and managing the economy. Support for the LDP increased in the aftermath of the oil shocks of the 1970s precisely because of this risk-averse attitude of the Japanese voting public. When economic tensions eased, voter attention turned to political corruption or inadequate social welfare programs, and public anger on these or other noneconomic matters was expressed at the polls in increased support for opposition parties.

The logic is entirely different now. Japanese voters have become more "normal," in that they tend to vote against a party in power that fails in its economic policies. Japanese are ready to "throw the bums out" if they do not perform well in office. There are two reasons for this change in behavior. One is that in the past, the LDP could attribute the nation's economic problems to external causes, the oil shocks being a prime example. The LDP argument that it was the only party capable of steering the ship of state through troubled waters was one many voters accepted. Responsibility for the "post-bubble" economic problems of the 1990s, however, clearly rested with the government and its policy mistakes. These mistakes did enormous damage to the image of LDP and bureaucratic competence.

There is a second and related reason why voting behavior has become more "normal." Voters no longer fear that anything other than an LDP government might have disastrous consequences. In retrospect, one of the major contributions of the Hosokawa government, perhaps because its accomplishments were so modest, was to disprove LDP warnings that an alternation of parties in power would be destabilizing or have calamitous policy consequences. Hosokawa did not embark upon a radically new domestic policy agenda; nor did he launch Japan off on a wholly different path in foreign affairs; in fact, his administration was a disappointment to those who did expect dramatic changes. But the Hosokawa administration was not a disaster, and it had the salutary effect of energizing the LDP leadership to work hard to recover power. Also, by giving an opportunity for every opposition party except the Communists to participate in government, it effectively changed public perceptions that the LDP was the country's only governmental party and that the role of the opposition is only to protest and put a brake on LDP policies.

Voting behavior appears to have changed in other ways. Party image and the personal appeal of the party leader seem to have a considerably bigger impact on voting behavior now than they did in the past. The reason is that the *mutōhasō*, the electorate supporting no particular party, is larger than it was in the past. A focus on party leadership is not new, but is more important as party identification among the public has declined.

Because of these factors—decline of community solidarity and a consequent reduced ability of local notables to gather and deliver votes to candidates of their choice, increased attention to party and leadership image, the experience of opposition parties in government, and the disappearance of fundamental ideological cleavages and policy differences between the LDP and the opposition—Japan has an electorate whose voting behavior is more volatile than at any time at least since the early 1950s. There is a larger number of voters than before whose propensity to vote increases in direct proportion to their unhappiness with the incumbent governing party's performance.

This volatility both in voting rates and in party support exerts intense pressure on parties and leaders to adopt campaign styles that can attract the support of the nonparty electorate. It has led to expensive and slick party advertising campaigns and a heightened role for television in providing a venue for political discussion. It also is forcing party leaders in power to try to convince the public that they control the bureaucracy and policy making. More than anything else, the decline of party identification and the swings in the voting rate impart a new tension and an unprecedented degree of uncertainty to Japanese politics.

The Circulation of Political Elites

These developments in voting behavior have been paralleled by an unprecedented fluidity in the party affiliations of political elites, the organizational stability of parties, and party alliances. Volatility at the level of the party system has been reinforced by the weak links of loyalty of Diet members to the parties to which they belong, the Communist Party and Komeito being notable exceptions to this general rule.

In the '55 system, with its broad ideological gulf separating the conservative and the progressive camps, there were few opportunities or incentives for politicians to defect from one party to another. Party loyalties were reinforced by politicians' need for factional and party financial backing, in the case of the LDP in particular, and for union and other organizational support in the case of the Socialists. Throughout the years of the '55 system, party loyalties, especially for the LDP, seemed to grow stronger in the sense that fewer and fewer Diet candidates could run successful election campaigns as independents. Party affiliation became a necessary condition of political success. As long as the party system was stable, this produced stable affiliations of Diet politicians to parties.

The situation that emerged in the 1990s is different. All parties with the exception of the Communists no longer represent antithetical ideological positions but operate essentially within the same ideological space. Party affiliation in Japan is determined more than ever before by pragmatic considerations of prospects for electoral success rather than by a belief that a particular party represents a community of shared values and policy goals that distinguish it from other parties. Accordingly, a Diet member's incentives to remain in a particular party are only as strong as the assessment that doing so would enhance the incumbent's reelection prospects.

In the past, one of the important incentives for politicians to remain in the LDP was their dependence on faction and party for financial support. Over time, largely because of changes in the political-funding law making it harder for factions to raise money, politicians increasingly have come to rely on their own fund-raising abilities for the lion's share of their political funds. Faction financial support is important mostly for new candidates and first-term Diet members who have not yet developed sufficient fund-raising capabilities of their own.

Politicians who depend mostly on their own fund-raising abilities stand to lose relatively little in the way of financial support if they quit the

LDP as long as their own key financial backers, who usually are important businessmen in their electoral districts, continue to support them. There are strong incentives for them to continue to do so, assuming that defection is based on a pragmatic judgment about reelection prospects and the opportunity to be part of a governing party.

The 1994 introduction of sizeable public subsidies to all parties further loosened bonds of loyalty of candidates to particular parties. Subsidies are given to parties on the basis of the number of members in them. As long as a Diet member is affiliated with some party, and the party dispenses the subsidy funds to district "branch chairmen," as they all do, a politician can access this source of backing. The Communist Party is the sole exception: that party's policy is not to accept its allotted share of the public subsidy. This provision for public financing discourages politicians from running as independents, but it does not induce party loyalty.

As mentioned above, Diet members' organizational support is based on personal *kōenkai* structures within a party-franchise system rather than on strong local party organization and strong identification with a party by voters: this further erodes incentives for party loyalty. Other things being equal, an incumbent who concludes that defection might attract more nonparty affiliated floating voters without threatening his *kōenkai* organizational support or financial backing would be quite tempted to leave his party.

But other things are not equal in politics. Calculations of risk and benefit to be derived from defecting are always complex and subtle. Although a politician might conclude that he or she would be better off in a different party, that party might already have a candidate in that election district. The point is not that politicians necessarily will defect from the LDP or from other parties, but that the situation is unstable. This instability compounds the sense of uncertainty and the anything-can-happen political mood in Japan.

Volatility and uncertainty at the level of the party system also has been heightened by the defection of many of the LDP's most attractive and best-known leaders. To people familiar with the personalities in Japanese politics, the list of former LDP members now outside the party reads like a roster of political stars. It includes among others former prime ministers Hosokawa, Hata, and Kaifu, former LDP secretary-general Ozawa, former finance minister Takemura, Yukio and Kunio Hatoyama, grandsons of the LDP's first prime minister. These defections have left the LDP with only a small circle of politicians whose reputation for leadership is nationwide and has set back the party's attempts to convey an image of being in tune with the modern electorate. The presence of so many well-known former LDP leaders in other parties helps give these parties an image of competence and makes an alternation of power seem less risky. Thus it contributes to the volatility in voting behavior noted earlier.

Under the previous electoral system of multimember districts and single-entry ballots, a voter dissatisfied with the LDP government might vote for an LDP newcomer or an "anti-mainstream" LDP member running in his district. In the single-member districts of the new system, a vote against the government in power is necessarily a vote for another party. The new system encourages voting behavior that turns elections into assessments of the performance of the incumbent government. Given current public perceptions of the inadequacy of that performance, this system increases the likelihood of continued turmoil in party politics.

Uncertainties about voting behavior and the potential for further restructuring of the party system have created pressures on the policy-making system as well. There are pressures for change at the level of policy making and policy ideas that, combined with the volatility of voting behavior and party behavior, help create a situation of great uncertainty and ferment. On the threshold of a new century, there seems to be general agreement that Japanese policy-making processes need to be reformed and that policies that have undergirded the Japanese political economy for the past half century have to be changed.

Reforming the Policy-making System

Government policy making under the '55 system took place in the context of an implicit public consensus that the state's role in pursuing the national goal of rapid economic development was to be more than serving as umpire for the private market economy, simply insuring that everyone observes the rules of the game and does not impede the free movement of capitalism's invisible hand. The business community and the public at large expected that the state would be, and should be, an important and active partner in the grand national project of creating an economy second to none.

Relations between bureaucrats and politicians under the '55 system were complex and relations between state and society imposed significant limitations on state power. The power of the Japanese state was not that of the command economies of the Communist bloc, nor that of the authoritarian developmental states of Korea or Taiwan. The refractive state in Japan interacted with powerful organizations in the private sector as it sought to bend demands emanating from society to accord with its own sense of values, preferences, and priorities: there was a constant process of consultation and negotiation.

Analysts who have defined Japan as the exemplar of state-led capitalist development and as possessing a quintessential "strong state" invariably have underestimated the power of interest groups, and of public pressure exercised through citizen movements and elections, to force the state to adopt policies that government officials thought were unwise, and to thwart government efforts to adopt policies that the public thought were undesirable. On the other hand, those who have argued that society was in charge in Japan have tended to describe the state as little more than a facilitator of private-sector efforts to limit excessive competition, fix prices, and provide for the orderly exit of noncompetitive firms from the market. An emphasis on the power of the market over the state (even when recognizing that the state was active rather than passive in playing its facilitator role) often has been accompanied by an underestimation of the state's autonomous power and the refractive elements of its processing of social demands. Japan is an example of a political economy that has been characterized by a strong state *and* a strong society.

Within the state itself, the effective functioning of this system required a division of labor and considerable coordination between the LDP and the bureaucracy. The ruling party's leadership has defined broad policy goals, whether it be the "Yoshida line" of alliance with the United States, a limited defense role and a focus on economic growth, the "double the income" policies of Ikeda in the 1960s, the redistributive policies of Tanaka in the 1970s, or the administrative reform program of Nakasone in the 1980s. The bureaucracy retained a great deal of authority over decisions precisely because it did not frontally challenge these goals or the LDP's power to make them. Bureaucrats might have tried to sabotage particular policies, but they were careful to avoid taking public positions that would threaten LDP interests and lead to confrontation with the ruling party.

So long as the bureaucracy's actions supported LDP policy goals, the LDP had little incentive to seek alternative sources of policy-relevant information, ideas, or expertise from outside the bureaucracy. The Japanese bureaucracy, which drew its elite members from among the best and brightest that Japan's higher-education system produced, served in effect as the LDP's think tank.

The LDP's Policy Affairs Research Council, with its array of sections, special commissions, and committees, became increasingly enmeshed in policy making, but without developing a large staff of policy experts of its own. The relationship of government bureaucrats to PARC politicians was not unlike that of congressional staffers to members of the U.S. Congress in respect to providing information and analysis and drafting specific policy proposals. As long as LDP rule was stable, this system operated relatively smoothly.

The end of one-party dominance and the conflicting views that emerged in the 1990s over economic policy and structural reform exposed the inherent weaknesses of this policy-making system. Unlike the loyalty of congressional staffers in the United States to the congressmen who employ them or that of White House staffers to the president, Japanese bureaucrats' loyalties are not to politicians or parties. Their loyalties are to the ministries that employ them.

The issue is not whether or not political leaders in Japan have the power to impose their policy decisions on the bureaucracy. In a showdown between ministers and ministries or between the Diet and the bureaucracy, the constitutional structure puts power squarely in the hands of Japan's elected representatives. The issue is not about formal power, but about capabilities. Japanese political parties have woefully little in the way of an autonomous capability to formulate legislation. Neither parties nor individual Diet members employ policy experts to any significant degree. There is not, as there is in the United States or the Republic of Korea and other countries, a tradition of recruiting people from universities and the private sector for public service.

Cabinet ministers rotate frequently, and the ruling party does not infiltrate ministries with political appointments as is the case in the United States. The only politicians inside ministries other than the minister are parliamentary vice-ministers, usually one per ministry, almost all of whom are first- and second-term Diet members. The post of parliamentary vice-minister has served mostly as a vehicle for educating backbenchers about policy issues and for developing their personal ties with ministry bureaucrats and with the interest groups that form the ministry's clientele.

The common practice in Diet interpolations is for ministers to read responses scripted by bureaucrats to questions submitted in advance and to rely on bureaucrats themselves to respond to questions of a technical nature. Recent developments have challenged that system. These include demands by reform-minded politicians for more open debate in the Diet, for economic policies not necessarily supported by the bureaucracy, and the use of language that is persuasive to domestic and foreign audiences, without the circumlocutions typical of bureaucrat-drafted statements.

Politicians in the LDP as well as in the opposition parties have found it convenient to engage in "bureaucrat bashing." They have complained that the bureaucracy exercises powers that should be in the hands of politicians. This is a convenient way for political leaders to avoid taking responsibility for failed policies that would not have been adopted without their approval. It also raises the question of whether and how political parties plan to develop a policy-making capability not so heavily dependent on bureaucratic expertise. The efforts undertaken so far by the LDP and other parties to develop more of an autonomous policy-making capability have been modest, to say the least. They are also based upon premises that are questionable at best.

In the early 1990s, for example, the Diet passed legislation to enable each member of the Diet to employ a "policy assistant" whose role supposedly was to give policy advice. The idea was borrowed from U.S. congressional practices, but it hardly seems to be a sensible way to strengthen political control over the bureaucracy in a system characterized by strong party discipline and cabinet government. The relationships of politicians to parties and of parties to the government have much more in common with western European countries than they do with political practices in the United States. Those leaders who created a modern state in nineteenth-century Japan were deeply influenced by Prussia and by France, and that history influences Japanese institutions to the present day. In Germany, each political party has attached to it a major research foundation supported partially by public funds. Such a system would seem to offer a more appropriate model for Japan than the one in the United States, where Congress has developed a huge bureaucracy of its own in order to secure its independence from the executive.

The lack of an autonomous capacity for developing policies is an even more serious problem for parties that are not in power. Opposition parties do not have access to bureaucratic expertise, nor do they have a research capability of their own. Moreover, there is a relative scarcity of institutions in civil society that play the role that, in the United States and some other countries, think tanks play in the policy process and in providing expertise to parties when they are in opposition. Universities have only recently begun to develop graduate programs of "policy studies," and there are few career paths outside of the government's administrative bureaucracy for people interested in issues of public policy. Consequently there is a relative scarcity of public intellectuals to debate important public policy issues.

The policy-making infrastructure problem is compounded by the readiness of Japanese politicians, whether in the LDP or in the other parties, to adopt a literal interpretation of the term "small government" and to define the primary goal of administrative reform to be a reduction the number of government employees. Prime Minister Hashimoto promised to reduce the number of government personnel by at least 10 percent over ten years. During the LDP presidential contest that followed the Hashimoto resignation, Obuchi called for a 20 percent reduction and Koizumi touted a whopping 50 percent over ten years. Democratic Party leader Naoto Kan, the Liberal Party's Ozawa, and other party leaders have made similar cost-cutting and personnel-reduction pledges.

It is puzzling why there should be such a focus on reducing the number of government employees; after all, Japan has the smallest government among the industrialized democracies and the fewest government officials relative to population size of any OECD country. The Japanese government employs 6 percent of the total labor force, whereas the figure is 14 percent for the United States, 17 percent for G-7 countries on average, and 19 percent for OECD countries.[19] Shrinking the bureaucracy without reducing the discretionary authority of an even smaller corps of bureaucrats and without developing other nongovernmental institutions with policy-making capabilities seems a peculiar approach to administrative reform. To the extent that reform of the bureaucracy in Japan aims to introduce new procedures for reducing bureaucratic discretionary authority and for improving transparency, it may require more, not fewer, officials.

Banking-system reform is a case in point. Disclosure of the full extent of banks' bad-loan problems is essential to restore the health and credibility of Japan's financial sector. Since bank managers themselves are unlikely to admit the full extent of their own mistakes, intrusive, thorough, and sustained investigation of the banks' loan portfolios by government examiners is imperative. In June 1998, the government established a Financial Supervisory Agency (FSA) to do just that. However, only 400 officials were assigned the FSA. According to *Yomiuri Shimbun* data, the number of bank examiners in the FSA and in the local bureaus of the Finance Ministry totaled 621—a figure that can be compared with that for the United States of an estimated 8,000 bank examiners at the state and federal level.[20] A lead story on the front page of the *Asahi Shimbun* in August 1998 was a report that the FSA had proposed doubling the number of officials working in the FSA and local branches of the Finance Ministry by 2001.[21] Even if the government adopts this plan, it still seems grossly inadequate to instill confidence that the government would be able to carry out its commitment to take prompt and decisive action to resolve the problems in Japan's financial sector. Nonetheless, the *Asahi Shimbun*, in a commentary on the decision that also appeared on the front page, pointed out that the Obuchi administration now had to show how it was going to square this increase in the number of local MoF and FSA personnel with the government's plan to reduce the size of the bureaucracy by 4 percent between 1997 and 2001 and Obuchi's promise to reduce it by 10 percent in ten years.[22]

The more the government shifts away from its traditional "partnership" with the private sector to a neutral, regulating "umpire" role, the greater will be the pressures to expand rather than contract the size of the bureaucracy. Yet "small government," in the sense of a government of few people rather than a government of fewer powers, has become a goal every party has embraced as its own. The mass media has climbed aboard this small-government bandwagon in a manner reminiscent of its enthusiasm for electoral reform earlier in the decade. "Small government" has become the litmus test for any bona fide political reformer. In earlier days, to be against electoral reform was to violate the canons of Japanese political correctness; and so it is now to speak out against small government. Nearly everyone is for small government, whether or not it makes any sense for Japan.

It would be foolish for Japan to adopt reforms that simply serve to undermine the morale or lessen the quality of people who opt for careers in Japan's elite bureaucracy. Modern societies need competent and dedicated bureaucrats. It is pointless, too, to undertake reforms that leave bureaucrats with much the same powers they now exercise. Politicians' and media enthusiasm for shrinking the government, however, threatens to bring about precisely such an outcome; that is, a smaller and less-competent bureaucracy with excessive power. Plans to reduce the number of ministries by nearly half may cut some costs, but consolidating bureaucratic agencies and creating new and larger ones will not necessarily diminish bureaucratic power, and it will make political control more, not less, difficult.

New and more stringent restraints on amakudari, whereby bureaucrats leave the government well before reaching the legal retirement age to parachute into comfortable and powerful posts in the private sector and in public corporations, would be a meaningful reform. It also would be expensive, for it would mean keeping the highest-paid civil servants longer on the government payroll. Elimination of the practice of bureaucrats testifying in the Diet on behalf of the government also might be a useful reform. But to be successful, the deputy ministers who would replace the bureaucrats would need access to expertise that is autonomous of the bureaucracy—otherwise they would do little more than read scripts bureaucrats prepare for them. Introduction of such a system would also involve some increase in government expenditures. To be meaningful, moreover, it would require parties to change their operating procedures in fundamental ways, bringing an end to, for example, the practice of appointing cabinet ministers on the basis of factional affiliation and number of terms served rather than on the basis of knowledge and talent. There is scant evidence that the LDP or other parties are prepared to move far in this direction.

Changes in bureaucratic organization that would alter the relationship of the bureaucracy to political parties and of the state to society would have profound consequences. Probably for that reason, and despite the popularity of the slogan of "administrative reform," LDP leaders have been hesitant to curtail the prerogatives of the bureaucracy drastically, preferring instead to talk of the need for a reduction in costs. Other parties, since they are in the opposition and do not have to work with the bureaucracy, are less constrained in their attacks. Should they, however, come to power without having put in place new systems for managing the policy process, they will face much the same dilemma the Hosokawa coalition government confronted. They will be reluctant to depend heavily on the bureaucracy for fear they will be coopted by bureaucratic interests and yet unable to work without it.

Rethinking Policy Ideas

Japanese political leaders throughout Japan's modern history have framed choices of basic national direction in terms of what was required to accommodate Japan to the prevailing "trends of the times." In the Meiji period, the answer was to build a "rich nation, strong army" *(fukoku kyōhei)* to ward off Western imperialism and to have Japan be accepted as a modern nation. After the Second World War, the answer that Prime Minister Yoshida crafted was to accept democracy, to be in alliance with the United States, and to concentrate the nation's energies and resources on economic development. Conventional Japanese wisdom today, as noted in chapter 1, is that Japan at the end of the twentieth century faces a challenge no less daunting than those it confronted during the Meiji era and in the immediate postwar period.

It is hardly surprising, given the seriousness of Japan's financial and economic problems, the long-term challenges presented by the aging of its population, and the uncertainties that pertain to its future international position that its leaders would favor a political vocabulary that, as I have already pointed out, evokes a sense of danger and crisis and the need for unity in the face of virtually insurmountable challenges. There are, and there have been for many years, countless publications in Japan on the theme "Can Japan survive?" Can it survive the cold war, the oil shocks, U.S. protectionism, globalization . . . ? One can finish the sentence with almost any object of choice.

In the LDP presidential election following Prime Minister Hashimoto's resignation in July 1998, all three candidates resorted to doomsday rhetoric in describing Japan's current plight. Japan would "sink," Kajiyama repeatedly warned, unless it embarked on a program of radical reform. Japan would have "no tomorrow" *(asu wa nai)*, Obuchi gloomily predicted, unless it fundamentally changed its ways of doing things. The Japanese people could not avoid feeling "pain," Koizumi proclaimed, if they wanted Japan to survive. The logic of the '55 system that guided the behavior of LDP leaders was rooted in the belief that the more people were convinced that the difficulties the country faced were serious and the result of forces beyond the government's control, the more likely they would be to support their party. In 1998, LDP leaders, still captured by this logic, continued to employ a gloom-and-doom rhetoric, seemingly oblivious to the possibility that the public would hold them and their party responsible for having created the situation that they now decried

To take the rhetoric of Japanese leaders at face value, one has to conclude that there is virtual unanimity among them, and among the mass media as well, that Japan must revolutionize its current socioeconomic system. It was nearly impossible in Japan in the late 1990s to find leaders with positive things to say about the Japanese system—a rather remarkable phenomenon considering that only a decade earlier Japanese political leaders and opinion makers were touting the Japanese model as superior to the kind of capitalism practiced in the West.

It is difficult not to be skeptical about this rhetoric. There seem to be few politicians, or newspaper editorial writers, who are not ready to run away from this language of radical change when asked directly whether it would mean abolishing the lifetime employment system—including a given editorial writer's own lifetime employment arrangement—and accepting a society with wider income disparities. The public mood throughout the 1990s, as this book has emphasized, was conservative rather than revolutionary. Despite the rhetoric of "individual choice" popular with political reformers and anxiety about the future among the public, there was little apparent support for replacing a system that emphasized social equality with a more rough-edged economic competition that would clearly differentiate winners and losers.

The result has been a yawning gap separating the reform policies of the Japanese government from the reform rhetoric of Japan's political leaders. While the rhetoric has been bold, the policy response has been hesitant. A combination of bureaucratic intransigence, the power of vested interests, public resistance to undoing the system that brought Japan its postwar success, and a fundamental lack of confidence or conviction among the political leadership in the radical reforms they were proposing have conspired to produce policy measures that are faint echoes of the political rhetoric that those leaders regularly employ.

This gap has had several negative consequences. One of the most important is that Japanese have become so used to hearing politicians speak of crisis that they tend to discount their warnings heavily, thereby increasing the probability that they would be slow to react to a truly threatening situation. Such was the case with respect to Japan's banking system and economic problems in the 1990s. When, toward the end of the decade, the public did begin to accept the seriousness of the situation, the result was such a loss of consumer confidence, coupled with nervousness about the future, that the government's efforts to stimulate domestic demand seemed to have little effect: voters opted to increase their savings rather than their spending.

Japanese political leaders seemed unaware that the impact of their language on general public attitudes was to reinforce public support for holding on to known and tried ways of doing things and, at the same time, to make the public ever more pessimistic that Japan would be able to recover its former vitality and strength. Political leaders in a sense were all too skillful at reflecting the ambiguity, ambivalence, and resistance to anything more than cautious incremental change that characterized public opinion.

Leaders in the LDP and in the opposition parties had become so intent on attacking the past policy failures of the bureaucrats and the weaknesses of the '55 system that they seemed almost uniformly unable to conjure up a positive vision of the future. It is hardly surprising that none of them was able to ignite much enthusiasm among the electorate. It is puzzling why political leaders believe that their dark imagery would somehow draw public support to them when the evidence is fairly convincing that Japanese voters, like voters elsewhere, look for leaders who can offer a positive and hopeful message. Japan's two most popular postwar prime ministers, Kakuei Tanaka and Morihiro Hosokawa, in their very different ways inspired the public with a future-oriented outlook and a fundamental optimism. Tanaka attracted the nickname "computerized bulldozer" for his enthusiasm for barreling ahead with his grand design to remodel the Japanese archipelago, and Hosokawa's entire demeanor conveyed an image of freshness and change. Yet at the end of the 1990s, this kind of leadership seemed strangely absent from the Japanese political scene.

Future Prospects

For the future, the foregoing suggests that the most likely scenario is one of incremental, rather than radical, policy change. Unless Japan faces a truly catastrophic economic situation marked by double-digit unemployment rates, and a crisis in its external relations, political competition will take place at the center. The inescapable pressures of global market forces will continue to push the Japanese economy in the direction of greater openness and less regulation. Those whose interests are threatened by such trends are certain to mount a formidable political effort to contain them, but they will face strong countervailing pressures. Political parties will have to appeal to an electorate that exhibits low levels of party support, that is less enmeshed than before in the webs of social ties that provide the foundation for traditional machine politics, and that seems determined to punish ruling parties that fail to produce effective policies.

It is highly improbable that political parties will array themselves on either side of a sharp cleavage line defined in terms of differences in fundamental economic policy orientation, with internationalists in one party competing against supporters of protectionism in another, for example. No political party in Japan that aspires to hold political power will position itself unambiguously on one side or the other of such a dividing line. In the United States, neither the Democratic nor the Republican Party does so, and there are far fewer incentives to do so in Japan, where social cleavages in general are less distinct and where there are few political leaders—toward either right or left—who advocate such a clear-cut policy choice.

Perceptions of self-interest are complex. People are as concerned about job security and about their incomes as producers as they are about their expenditures as consumers. Leaders of globally competitive companies that also enjoy large domestic market share are hesitant to speak out publicly and forcefully for radical economic changes and incur the wrath of Japanese who would be hurt by these changes and who buy their products. At the same time, there is grudging recognition among those who benefit from trade protection and government regulation, that Japan has to become a more open and less regulated economy to survive in an era of economic globalization. It is inconceivable that any major political party would advocate an economic program that represents only constituencies interested in protection against imports and continued access to government subsidies. To do so would be to consign itself to a marginal political status.

The upshot of these conflicting pressures will be support for incremental change. The change is certain to bring about substantial reforms, in terms of political and bureaucratic practices and organization and in the structure of the Japanese political economy, over time. The reforms will do so more slowly and much less thoroughly, however, than many observers believe is desirable.

What might upset a prognosis of incremental change and political competition within a rather narrow political spectrum would be sharply deteriorating domestic economic conditions coupled with a crisis in Japan's external relationships, involving in particular a worsening of relations with the United States. Such a development is not high on a list of probabilities nor is it entirely implausible. It was all too evident at the end of the 1990s that there was intense frustration and anger within the U.S. government over the failure of the Japanese government to move forward more forcefully with banking-reform policies and with fiscal policies to generate growth in the economy. There was deep resentment among Japanese leaders over incessant public criticism of Japan by high-ranking U.S. government officials. There also was evident in Japan concern that the United States was not focusing sufficient attention on its security and political relationships with Japan as it pursued strategic engagement with China. Indeed, more than differences over economic policies, the emergence of fundamental differences between the United States and Japan over issues relating to national security potentially could polarize public opinion in Japan and generate intense political conflict.

Even within a scenario of incremental change and essentially centrist politics, there is room for a strengthening of political forces pulling both right and left. It is difficult to imagine a sequence of events that would make the Left as powerful a force in Japanese politics in coming years as it was in the early years of the '55 system, when there was a strong left-dominated Socialist Party. It is entirely conceivable, however, that the Communist Party will become more popular with voters looking to cast a protest vote against the mainstream parties.

The Japan Communist Party, as noted earlier, did well in the 1998 upper-house election. It has a pragmatic leadership and stands apart from other parties in many ways, including having the highest percentage of women Diet members of all parties.[23] In terms of economic and social policy, it has been almost alone in refusing to jump aboard the bandwagon of deregulation and liberalization and remains a steadfast advocate of strong welfare-state policies. On foreign policy, it has moderated its opposition to Japan's security alliance with the United States, announcing after the July 1998 upper-house election that it was ready to "freeze" its position on the security treaty, meaning that it would not insist on treaty abrogation if it participated in a coalition government.[24] The JCP also moved quickly after that election to reestablish relations with China. A week after the July election, the party's chairman led a delegation to Beijing where he reestablished formal relations with the Chinese Communist Party—relations that had been broken off at the height of the Cultural Revolution in 1966.[25]

The JCP, however, remains a Communist Party, and that sets narrow limits on its growth potential. Rather than the kind of strong Communist subculture that has characterized countries such as France or Italy, there is in Japan instead a deep reservoir of suspicion about the party and its real intentions. Moreover, Marxism is no longer strong in the intellectual community and among students, nor in the labor movement, as it was in the 1950s and 1960s. If the JCP were to move too far in the direction of accommodating the views of mainstream parties in order to position itself for participation in a coalition government, or if it were to change its name as the Italian Communists have done (and which JCP leaders insist they have no intention of doing), it would run the danger of losing its appeal to those wanting to lodge a protest.

The Japan Communist Party enjoyed a period of significant growth in the late 1960s and 1970s. It tripled the number of its lower-house seats between the elections of 1967 and 1969, and more than doubled their number again in 1972, when it won thirty-eight seats and 10.5 percent of the popular vote. The party seems to have entered another period of growth in the late 1990s, although the new electoral system with its predominance of single-member districts makes it very difficult for the Communists to win as many seats as they did under the previous electoral system, even if it obtains a comparable share of the popular vote.

Intensified economic difficulties and heightened tensions with the United States, far more than encouraging greater support for the Communists or other left-wing parties, is likely to result in the emergence of a New Right in Japan. This conceivably might be in the form of an independent party on the LDP's right, or if the New Right is successful in taking control of the LDP's leadership, it might provoke a party split that would result in more moderate members of the party leaving the LDP. A New Right would advocate a program of domestic reform to be sure, but its major focus almost certainly would be on issues of national security, emphasizing the importance of Japan strengthening its own military capabilities and pursuing a more autonomous foreign policy. It is entirely conceivable that pressures from both right and left would converge on favoring the reduction and eventual elimination of the U.S. military presence in Japan. The difference between them would be whether Japan should strengthen its own military capabilities and expand the roles and missions of its military forces. But there inevitably would be an underlying commonality in their promise to stop permitting outsiders to "push us around."

If a New Right were to emerge in the form of a new political party, or if it were in effect to secure control over the LDP and drive others out of the party, it would have an impact on politics and on foreign policy for which there is no precedent in the postwar period. The Communist Party and the Left more generally have been part of the political scene in Japan ever since the end of the Second World War. The Right was so discredited by the war, however, that it has not been a significant independent factor in postwar politics. To the extent that the Right has been active politically, it has operated within the confines of the LDP, where it has had to moderate its positions and accept policies—support for U.S. foreign-policy positions, a minimal defense capability, and acceptance of the so-called "MacArthur Constitution"—to which it is opposed. The emergence of a New Right as an independent political force, in other words, would represent an important new phase in Japanese politics. Depending on circumstances surrounding its emergence, it conceivably could have a significant impact on Japanese government policy, especially with respect to security relations with the United States and foreign affairs more generally.

To raise these cautionary notes and engage in crystal ball gazing is to underscore the uncertainties inherent in contemplating Japan's political future. It would be foolish, given the past decade of political turmoil, the serious economic problems Japan confronts, and the fluidity of international relationships in post–cold war East Asia to claim to be able to anticipate political developments with the same degree of confidence as was possible in the 1970s or 1980s. But there does seem to be good reason nonetheless to anticipate fundamentally centrist politics, continued political turmoil as a new party system struggles to take shape, and incremental change that will foster adjustment to a new, post catch-up, phase of economic development.

Contrary to the currently popular view that it is about to "sink" unless it drastically changes course, Japan is likely to survive this current difficult period to remain a powerful economy and a strong democracy. Japan has a strong and resilient society that rests on a bedrock of social trust— a sense of community and common destiny that provides a great amount of what has recently come to be called "social capital." This social capital is a source of cohesion and collective energy. There also has developed in Japan a complex system of social, economic, and political institutions that force government to respond to pluralistic and competing interests and that counters pressures for radical, destabilizing change. Admittedly, such a system does not easily respond to problems with the alacrity that critics, foreign governments, and financial markets demand; nor does it insure that the wisest course will be followed by policy makers. It puts a high premium on consensus building. It makes policy making a messy affair of compromise among competing interest groups and political parties.

However, it also puts an enormous amount of pressure on political leaders to do what is needed to convince voters that the leadership is doing a competent job. The logic of Japanese politics is different today from what it was under the '55 system, even if the logic of Nagata-cō, the inside-the-beltway kind of thinking among the political elite, retains ties to that earlier period that are all too strong. Old verities—a prestigious and competent bureaucracy, a public consensus on national goals, one-party dominance, an opposition that opposes for opposition's sake and does not offer a credible alternative to the party in power—are gone. Japanese political leaders face a voting public that will hold them accountable for their performance in office. Leaders who fail to instill confidence in the electorate that they are successfully managing the nation's affairs will be voted out of office. This has not been the logic of Nagata-chō, but it is the logic, and the strength, of Japanese politics at the end of the twentieth century.

Appendixes

Appendix 1
The Changing Party System 1955-1999

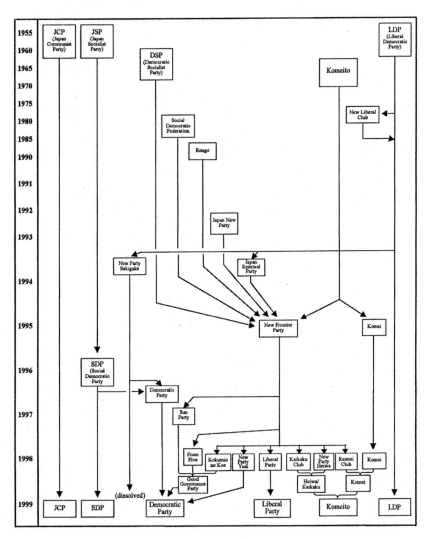

Appendix 2
Japanese Prime Ministers 1945–1998

Years Served	Name	Dates Served
1945	Haruhiko Higashikuni	Aug. 17, 1945–Oct. 9, 1945
1945–1946	Kijuro Shidehara	Oct. 9, 1945–May 22, 1946
1946–1947	Shigeru Yoshida	May 22, 1945–June 1, 1947
1947–1948	Tetsu Katayama	June 1, 1947–May 10, 1948
1948	Hitoshi Ashida	Mar. 10, 1948–Oct. 19, 1948
1948–1954	Shigeru Yoshida	Oct. 19, 1948–Dec. 10, 1954
1954–1956	Ichiro Hatoyama	Dec. 10, 1954–Dec. 23, 1956
1956–1957	Tanzan Ishibashi	Dec. 23, 1956–Feb. 25, 1957
1957–1960	Nobusuke Kishi	Feb. 25, 1957–July 19, 1960
1960–1964	Hayato Ikeda	July 19, 1960–Nov. 9, 1964
1964–1972	Eisaku Sato	Nov. 9, 1964–July 7, 1972
1972–1974	Kakuei Tanaka	July 7, 1972–Dec. 9, 1974
1974–1976	Takeo Miki	Dec. 9, 1974–Dec. 24, 1976
1976–1978	Takeo Fukuda	Dec. 24, 1976–Dec. 7, 1978
1978–1980	Masayoshi Ohira	Dec. 7, 1978–July 17, 1980
1980–1982	Zenko Suzuki	July 17, 1980–Nov. 27, 1982
1982–1987	Yasuhiro Nakasone	Nov. 27, 1982–Nov. 6. 1987
1987–1989	Noboru Takeshita	Nov. 6, 1987–June 3, 1989
1989	Sosuke Uno	June 3, 1989–Aug. 9, 1989
1989–1991	Toshiki Kaifu	Aug. 9, 1989–Nov. 5, 1991
1991–1993	Kiichi Miyazawa	Nov. 5, 1991–Aug. 9, 1993
1993–1994	Morihiro Hosokawa	Aug. 9, 1993–Apr. 28, 1994
1994	Tsutomu Hata	Apr. 28, 1994–June 30, 1994
1994–1996	Tomiichi Murayama	June 30, 1994–Jan. 11, 1996
1996–1998	Ryutaro Hashimoto	Jan. 11, 1996–July 30, 1998
1998–	Keizo Obuchi	July 30, 1998–

Appendix 3
Lower-House Elections

Party	Votes	% of Vote	Seats	Candidates
February 18, 1990				
LDP	30,315,417	46.1	275	338
JSP	16,025,472	24.4	136	149
DSP	3.178,949	4.8	14	44
JCP	5,226,986	8.0	16	131
Komeito	5,242,675	8.0	45	58
Minor and Ind.	5,714,805	8.7	26	233
Total	65,704,304	—	512	953
July 18, 1993				
LDP	22,999,646	36.6	223	285
JSP	9,687,588	15.4	70	142
DSP	2,205,682	3.5	15	28
JCP	4,834,587	7.7	15	129
Komeito	5,114,351	8.1	51	54
Shinseito	6,341,364	10.1	55	69
Nihon Shinto	5,053,981	8.1	35	57
Sakigake	1,658,097	2.6	13	16
Minor and Ind.	4,908,843	7.8	34	175
Total	62,804,139	—	511	955
October 20, 1996, Single Member Districts				
LDP	21,836,089	38.6	169	288
JSP	1,240,649	2.2	4	43
Shinshinto	15,812,322	28.0	96	235
JCP	7,096,781	12.6	2	299
Democratic Party	6,001,664	10.6	17	143
Sakigake	727,644	1.3	2	13
Minor and Ind.	3,813,272	6.7	10	85
Total	56.528,421	—	300	1106
October 20, 1996, Proportional Representation Districts				
LDP	18,205,955	32.8	70	327 (260)*
JSP	3,547,240	6.4	11	48 (43)*

Party	Votes	% of Vote	Seats	Candidates	
Shinshinto	15,580,053	28.0	60	133	(7)*
JCP	7,268,743	13.1	24	53	(31)*
Democratic Party	8,949,190	16.1	35	159	(141)*
Sakigake	582,093	1.0	0	11	(9)
Minor and Ind.	1,435,921	2.6	0	77	
Total	55,569,195	—	200	808	

*Number of candidates who also ran in single-member districts

SOURCE: Figures for 1990–1993 elections from Ishikawa Masumi, *Sengo Seiji Shi*, (Tokyo: Iwanami shoten, 1995), pp. 234–235. Figures for 1996 election from *Asahi Shinbun.*

Appendix 4
A. Upper-House Elections, Proportional Representation

PARTY	VOTES	% OF VOTE	SEATS	CANDIDATES
July 6, 1986				
LDP	22,132,573	38.6	22	25
JSP	9,869,088	17.2	9	18
DSP	3,940,325	6.9	3	17
JCP	5,430,838	9.5	5	25
Komeito	7,438,501	13.0	7	17
Minor and Ind.	8,551,417	14.9	4	141
Total	57,362,742	—	50	243
July 23, 1989				
LDP	15,343,455	27.3	15	25
JSP	19,688,252	35.1	20	25
DSP	2,726,419	4.9	2	17
JCP	3,954,408	7.0	4	25
Komeito	6,097,971	10.9	6	17
Rengo				0
Minor and Ind.	8,360,823	14.9	3	276
Total	56,171,328	—	50	385
July 26, 1992				
LDP	14,961,199	33.3	19	27
JSP	7,981,726	17.8	10	25
DSP	2,255,423	5.0	3	17
JCP	3,532,956	7.9	4	25
Komeito	6,415,503	14.3	8	17
Rengo				0
Nihon Shinto	3,617,246	8.1	4	16
Minor and Ind.	6,184,644	13.8	2	202
Total	44,948,697	—	50	329
July 23, 1995				
LDP	11,096,972	27.3	15	29
JSP	6,882,919	16.9	9	18
JCP	3,878,955	9.5	5	25
Shinshinto	12,506,322	30.8	18	30

(*continued on following page*)

Party	Votes	% of Vote	Seats	Candidates
Sakigake	1.455,886	3.6	2	10
Minor and Ind.	4,852,206	11.9	1	69
Total	40,673,260	—	50	181

July 12, 1998

Party	Votes	% of Vote	Seats	Candidates
LDP	14,128,719	25.2	14	30
SDP	4,370,761	7.8	4	17
Democratic Party	12,209,685	21.7	12	25
JCP	8,195,078	14.6	8	25
Komei	7,748,301	13.8	7	18
Liberal	5,207,813	9.3	5	12
Sakigake	784,591	1.4	0	3
Minor and Ind.	3,492,075	6.2	0	28
Total	56,137,023	—	50	158

B. Upper-House Elections, Prefectural Districts

July 6, 1986

Party	Votes	% of Vote	Seats	Candidates
LDP	26,111,258	45.1	50	58
JSP	12,464,578	21.5	11	40
DSP	2,643,370	4.6	2	10
JCP	6,617,486	11.4	4	46
Komeito	2,549,037	4.4	3	4
Minor and Ind.	7,552,497	13.0	6	105
Total	57,938,226	—	76	263

July 23, 1989

Party	Votes	% of Vote	Seats	Candidates
LDP	17,466,406	30.7	21	53
JSP	15,009,451	26.4	26	30
DSP	2,066,533	3.6	1	8
JCP	5,012,424	8.8	1	46
Komeito	2,900,947	5.1	4	5
Rengo	3,878,783	6.8	11	12
Minor and Ind.	10,565,089	18.6	12	131
Total	56,899,633	—	76	285

Party	Votes	% of Vote	Seats	Candidates
July 26, 1992				
LDP	19,711,045	43.4	50	55
JSP	5,846,238	12.9	12	18
DSP	1,039,979	2.3	1	3
JCP	4,817,001	10.6	2	46
Komeito	3,550,060	7.8	6	6
Rengo	4,399,684	9.7	0	22
Nihon Shinto				0
Minor and Ind.	6,019,180	13.3	6	161
Total	45,383,187	—	77	311
July 23, 1995				
LDP	10,557,547	25.4	31	37
JSP	4,926,003	11.8	7	22
JCP	4,314,830	10.4	3	47
Shinshinto	11,003,681	26.5	22	32
Sakigake	1,059,353	2.5	1	5
Minor and Ind.	9,711,623	23.4	12	232
Total	41,573,055	—	76	386
July 12, 1998				
LDP	17,252,329	30.8	31	58
SDP	2,403,649	4.3	1	21
Democratic Party	9,063,939	16.2	15	23
JCP	8,758,759	15.7	7	45
Komei	1,843,479	3.3	2	2
Liberal	980,249	1.8	1	9
Sakigake				0
Minor and Ind.	15,633,653	27.9	19	158
Total	55,936,057	—	76	316

SOURCE: Figures for 1986-1992 elections from Ishikawa Masumi, *Sengo Seiji Shi*, pp. 258–63; figures for the 1995 and 1998 elections from Asahi Shinbun.

Notes

INTRODUCTION

1. Japanese names appear in the text with the given name followed by the family name. Citations of Japanese-language sources, however, follow the Japanese practice of placing the family name first. Macrons are not used on personal names, nor on words that regularly appear in English, such as Komeito.

2. Several politicians remained active during the war outside the government-created IRAA. They were elected without its recommendation in the 1942 election and went on to be important political leaders in the postwar period. In addition to Miki, the list includes Ichiro Hatoyama, the LDP's first prime minister; Ichiro Kono, one of the LDP's early faction bosses, political mentor to Prime Minister Nakasone, and father of Yohei Kono, who appears later in this book as the first president of the LDP-in-opposition; and Suehiro Nishio, postwar Socialist Party leader and founder of the Democratic Socialist Party.

3. "Institutions" include organizations such as political parties and party factions, sets of formal rules such as those pertaining to the electoral system, time-sanctioned standard operating procedures, and accepted ways of doing things that are the product of custom and precedent. Peter Hall's oft-cited definition ("formal rules, compliance procedures, and standard operating practices that structure the relationship between individuals in various units of the polity and economy") is similar, but I want to emphasize more the importance of informal institutions. As broad as it is, my concept of "institution" is narrower than the one offered by Douglass North, which is so limitless in scope as to have virtually no discriminatory power at all: to wit, "Institutions are the rules of the game in a society, or, more formally, are the humanly devised constraints that shape human interaction." Peter Hall, *Governing the Economy* (New York: Oxford University Press, 1986), p. 19; Douglass C. North, *Institutions, Institutional Change and Economic Performance* (Cambridge: Cambridge University Press, 1990), p. 3.

4. Theda Skocpol, perhaps the best known of the non-Marxist "structuralists," argues that "any valid explanation of revolution depends upon the analyst's 'rising above' the viewpoints of participants" to emphasize "objective relationships and conflicts among variously situated groups and nations, rather than the interests, outlooks, or ideologies of particular actors in revolutions." However, not every revolutionary situation produces a revolution, and studies of revolution that lack revolutionaries, or studies of any political event that lack actors, are bound to miss a rather important part of the story. Theda Skocpol, *States and Social Revolutions: A Comparative Analysis of France, Russia and China* (Cambridge: Cambridge University Press, 1979). pp. 18 and 29; cited in Mark I. Lichbach, "Social Theory and Comparative Politics," in Mark Irving Lichbach and Alan S. Zuckerman, *Comparative Politics: Rationality, Culture, and Structure* (Cambridge: Cambridge University Press, 1997), p. 248.

5. Ira Katznelson, "Structure and Configuration in Comparative Politics," in Lichbach and Zuckerman, *Comparative Politics,* p. 83.

6. Jonathan Lynn, *The Complete Yes, Prime Minister: The Diaries of the Right Hon. James Hacker,* Jonathan Lynn and Anthony Jay, eds. (New York: Harper & Row, 1981).

7. Hugh Byas, *Government by Assasination,* (New York: Knopf, 1942).

8. Andrew Gordon, *The Evolution of Labor Relations in Japan: Heavy Industry 1853–1955* (Cambridge: Harvard Unversity Press, 1988), p. 83.

9. Ibid.

10. Andre Seigfried, quoted in Jonathan Rauch, *The Outnation: A Search For the Soul of Japan* (Boston: Harvard Busines School Press, 1992), p. 117.

11. Lucian Pye, *Asian Power and Politics: The Cultural Dimensions of Authority* (Cambridge: Belknap Press, 1985), p. 65.

12. The anthropologist Clifford Geertz refers to enduring values, inherited myths, language, styles of social intercourse, the "webs of significance" human beings have spun and in which they are suspended that provide a framework, a context, for interpreting behaviors, institutions, or processes. He cites another anthropologist's listing of eleven other definitions of "culture." Clifford Geertz, *The Interpretation of Cultures* (New York: Basic Books, 1973), pp. 4–5, 14.

13. Gabriel A. Almond and G. Bingham Powell, *Comparative Politics: A Developmental Approach* (Boston: Little Brown, 1966), p. 23.

14. Philippe C. Schmitter and Terry Lynn Karl, "What democracy is . . . and is not," *Journal of Democracy* 2, no.3 (1991), p. 81.

15. Otto Kirchheimer, "The Transformation of the Western European Party Systems," in Joseph La Palombara and Myron Weiner, eds., *Political Parties and Political Development* (Princeton: Princeton University Press, 1966), pp. 177–200.

16. Richard S. Katz and Peter Mair, "Changing Models of Party Organization and Party Democracy: The Emergence of the Cartel Party," *Party Politics* 1, no.1 (1995): 5–28.

17. Robert Michels argued nearly a century ago that in large organizations there was an "iron law of oligarchy" that made it inevitable political party leaders would pursue their own interests rather than those of the people who supported and elected them to party and public office. But Michels assumed that parties would continue to maintain a posture of representing particular social groups and propounding discrete political ideologies. He did not anticipate that even parties of the left would give up this pose in favor of portraying themselves as pragmatic parties of all the people. See Robert Michels, *Political Parties: A Sociological Study of the Oligarchical Tendencies of Modern Democracy* (New York: Free Press, 1962; orig. ed., 1914).

18. Anthony Downs, *An Economic Theory of Democracy* (New York: Harper & Row, 1957), p. 25.

19. Chūma Hiroyuki, "Keizai kankyo no henka to chūkō nensō no chokin zōka," in Chūma Hiroyuki and Suruga Terukazu, *Koyō kankō no henka to josei rōdō* (Tokyo: Tokyo Daigaku Shuppankai, 1997), pp. 47ff. For example, among college-educated workers aged fifty-five to fifty-nine, in companies employing more than five thousand people, lifetime employees were 29 percent in 1980 and 65 percent in 1994. Among college-educated workers aged forty to forty-four, roughly the same percentage enjoyed lifetime employment in 1994 as in 1980. See also Inoki Takenori and Higuchi Yoshio, *Nihon no koyō system to rōdō shijō* (Tokyo: Nihon Keizai Shimbun, 1995).

20. Peter Hartcher, *The Ministry: How Japan's Most Powerful Institution Endangers World Markets* (Cambridge: Harvard Business School Press, 1998), p. 69.

CHAPTER ONE

1. Korekiyo Takahashi also became finance minister after having served several years earlier as prime minister. Takahashi is credited with rescuing Japan from a financial collapse when he became finance minister in 1927 (he served several times from 1927 to 1936).

2. Edwin O. Reischauer, "The Broken Dialogue with Japan," *Foreign Affairs* (October 1960): 13.

3. Ibid.: 13.

4. Ibid.: 17.

5. Herbert Passin, "The Sources of Protest in Japan," *American Political Science Review* 61, no. 2 (June 1962): 393.

6. George Packard, *Protest in Tokyo* (Princeton: Princeton University Press, 1966), p. 103.

7. Ishida Hirohide, "Hoshuseitō No Bijon," *Chūō Kōron* (January 1963).

8. Watanuki Jōji, *Nihonjin no Senkyo Kōdō* (Tokyo: Tokyo Daigaku Shuppankai, 1968); Miyake Ichirō, *Seitō shiji no bunseki* (Tokyo: Sobunsha, 1985).

9. Miyake Ichirō, *Nihon no Seiji to Senkyo* (Tokyo: Tokyo Daigaku Shuppankai, 1995).

10. Joji Watanuki, "Patterns of politics in present day Japan, " in Seymour Martin Lipset and Stefan Rokkan, eds., *Party Systems and Voter Alignments* (New York: Free Press, 1967), pp. 447–66.

11. Harold R. Kerbo, *Social Stratification and Inequality* (New York: McGraw Hill, 1991), pp. 454–57; Malcolm Sawyer, "Income Distribution in OECD Countries," *Economic Outlook* (July 1976); Yasuba Yasukichi and Inoki Takenori, eds., *Nihon Keizaishi 8: Kōdo Keizai Seichō* (Tokyo: Iwanami shoten, 1989).

12. Yasusuke Murakami, "The Age of New Middle Mass Politics: The Case of Japan," *Journal of Japanese Studies,* 8, no. 1 (winter 1982): 29–72.

13. Prime Minister's Office, *Gekkan Yoron Chōsa,* May 1985.

14. Economic Planning Agency, *Shohisha dantai kihon chōsa kekka,* 1997, cited in Steven K. Vogel, "When Interests Are Not Preferences: The Cautionary Tale of Japanese Consumers," *Comparative Politics* (January 1999): 187–207.

15. Prime Minister's Office, *Gekkan Yoron Chōsa,* March 1998. The satisfaction level fell in 1997 but was still high at 65 percent, the same level it had been in the late 1980s.

16. *Asahi Shimbum,* May 3, 1998.

17. The following table summarizes those polls for the years indicated. The table is adapted from Miyake Ichirō, *Nihon no Seiji to Senkyo* (Tokyo: Tokyo Daigaku Shuppankai, 1995), p. 180.

Asahi Shimbun Opinion Polls

	LDP				JSP			
	'72	'86	'89	'90	'72	'86	'89	'90
Totals	36	37	26	39	18	10	22	19
Sex:								
Male	39	41	30	42	19	11	23	19
Female	34	34	22	36	17	9	21	19
Age:								
20-24	27	28	15	30	18	7	21	19
25-29	30	29	15	30	20	9	20	20
30-34	32	30	16	29	21	10	22	21
35-39	33	32	19	31	23	11	23	19
40-49	37	36	25	39	21	12	23	20
50-59	43	42	30	44	16	12	25	20
60--	45	46	36	48	9	8	19	16

Occupation:	LDP				JSP			
White Collar	31	32	21	34	23	12	24	22
Industrial Work	23	31	19	33	28	14	27	23
Service Work	31	34	22	37	19	10	23	19
Self-Employed	46	47	36	49	11	5	16	13
Farm	52	56	41	58	10	6	17	11
Other	36	35	26	38	12	11	23	20

18. *Jiji Tsūshin yoron chōsa*, November 1995.

19. *Yomiuri Shimbun*, April 22, 1998.

20. *Asahi Shimbum*, May 20, 1998.

21. Ikuo Kabashima and Yoshito Ishio, "The Instability of Party Identification among Eligible Japanese Voters: A Seven-wave Panel Study 1993–96, *Party Politics* 4, no. 2 (1998): 151–76.

22. Kevin P. Phillips, *The Politics of Rich and Poor: Wealth and the American Electorate in the Reagan Aftermath* (New York: Random House, 1990), p. ix.

23. Ronald Dore, *Flexible Rigidities: Industrial Policy and Structural Adjustment in the Japanese Economy 1970–80* (Stanford: Sanford University Press, 1986).

24. Kakuei Tanaka, *Building a New Japan: A Plan for Remodeling the Japanese Archipelago* (Tokyo: Simul Press, 1969).

25. Ichiro Ozawa, *Blueprint for a New Japan: Rethinking of a Nation* (Tokyo: Kodansha International, 1994). For an effusive U.S. journalist view of Ozawa, see Edward W. Desmond, "Ichiro Ozawa: Reformer at Bay," *Foreign Affairs* (September/October 1995): 117–31. For a more balanced but quite favorable view of this "Gorbachev of Japan," see Jacob Schlesinger, *Shadow Shoguns: The Rise and Fall of Japan's Postwar Political Machine* (New York: Simon & Schuster, 1997).

26. On Japan as a global civilian power, see Yoichi Funabashi, "Japan and the New World Order," *Foreign Affairs* (winter 1991-1992): 58–74; Kuriyama Takakazu, "Gekido 9onendai to nihon gaiko⁻ no shintenkai," *Gaikō Forum* (May 1990).

27. The phrase "small and sparkling" was used by Masayoshi Takemura. See his *Chiisakutomo kirarito hikaru kuni Nihon* (Tokyo: Kobunsha, 1994).

28. For Japan as an Asian power and exponent of Asian values, Kobayashi Yotaro, "'Sai ajia-ka' no susume," *Foresight* (April 1991): 44–46; Yoichi Funabashi, "The Asianization of Asia," *Foreign Affairs* (November/December 1993): 75–85; Ogura Kazuo, "'Ajia no fukken' no tame ni," *Chōō Kōron* (July 1993): 60–73.

29. Komatsu Sakyo, *Nihon Chinbotsu* (Tokyo: Kobunsha, 1973); *Japan Sinks*, Michael Gallagher, trans. (New York: Harper & Row, 1976).

30. Gerald L. Curtis, *The Japanese Way of Politics* (New York: Columbia University Press, 1988), pp. 49–61.

31. Yasuo Suwa, "Enterprise-based Labor Unions and Collective Agreements," *Japan Institute of Labor Bulletin* 31, no. 9 (1992): 1. The comparable figure for the United States in the same year was 14.2 percent.

32. Theodore Cohen, *Remaking Japan: The American Occupation as New Deal*, Herbert Passin, ed. (New York: Free Press, 1987), p. 191.

33. Ibid., pp. 277–300.

34. Ehud Harari, *The Politics of Labor Legislation in Japan* (Berkeley: University of California Press, 1973), pp. 66–78.

35. Figures from Department of Labor statistics and "US Private Sector Trade Union Market Share Falls to 95-year Low," *Labor Market Reporter* (May 1998).

36. Japan Ministry of Labor, *Rōdō kumiai kisō chōsa*, June 30, 1997, mimeo.

37. Suwa, "Enterprise-based Labor Unions," p. 1.

38. See Ronald Dore, *Land Reform in Japan* (London: Oxford University Press, 1959).

39. Frank J. Schwartz, *Advice and Consent: The Politics of Consultation in Japan* (Cambridge: Cambridge University Press, 1998), p. 217.

40. Japan Defense Agency, *Defense of Japan* (Tokyo: Japan Times, 1987), p. 302.

41. Curtis, *The Japanese Way of Politics*, p. 59.

42. Schwartz, *Advice and Consent*, p. 259.

43. Ibid., p. 215.

44. Elliott A. Krauss, *Death of the Guilds: Professions, States, and the Advance of Capitalism, 1930 to the Present* (New Haven: Yale University Press, 1996).

45. Donald R. Thurston, *The Interests of Teachers: A Study of the Japan Teachers' Union* (Princeton: Princeton University Press, 1970).

46. Takahashi Atsutarō, "Nikkyōso no rosen tenkan, kibishii tairitsu izuko," *Asahi Shimbun*, February 9, 1998, p. 9.

47. *Sankei Shimbun*, June 12, 1997.

48. Tiana Norgren, "Abortion Before Birth Control: The Interest Group Politics behind Japanese Reproduction Policy," *Journal of Japanese Studies 24*, no. 1, (1998): 72–74, 83–85.

49. William Steslick, *Doctors in Politics: The Political Life of the JMA* (New York: Praeger, 1973), p. 56; Stephen Anderson, *Welfare Policy and Politics in Japan: Beyond the Developmental State* (New York: Paragon House, 1993), p. 126.

50. Krauss, *Death of the Guilds*, p. 45.

51. Japan Medical Association, "Nihon ishikai kaiinsū no suii," mimeo, December 1, 1997.

52. John Creighton Campbell and Naoki Ikegami, *The Art of Balance in Health Policy: Maintaining Japan's Low Cost, Egalitarian System,* (New York: Cambridge University Press, 1998).

53. Ibid.

54. Gerald L. Curtis, "Big Business and Political Influence," in Ezra Vogel, ed., *Modern Japanese Organization and Decision Making* (Berkeley: University of California Press, 1975).

55. Inoguchi Takashi and Iwai Tomoaki, *Zokugiin no Kenkyū: Jimintō Seiken o Gyūjiru Shuyakutachi* (Tokyo: Nihon Keizai Shimbunsha, 1987); Satō and Matsuzaki, *Jimintō Seiken* (Tokyo: Chūōkoronsha, 1986).

56. David Riesman and Evelyn Thompson Riesman, *Conversations in Japan: Modernization, Politics, and Culture* (Chicago: University of Chicago Press, Midway reprint, 1976), p. 202; cited in Andrew Barshay, "Postwar Social and Political Thought, 1945–1990," in Bob Tadashi Wakabayashi, *Modern Japanese Thought* (Cambridge: Cambridge University Press, 1998), p. 331.

57. Gerald L. Curtis, *Nihon No Seiji o Dō Miru Ka?* (Tokyo: Nihon Hōsō Shuppan Kyōkai, 1995), pp. 109–19.

58. John C. Campbell, "Bureaucratic Primacy: Japanese Policy Communities in an American Perspective," *Governance* 2, no. 1 (1989): 86–94.

59. Chalmers Johnson, *MITI and the Japanese Miracle: The Growth of Industrial Policy, 1925–1975* (Stanford: Stanford University Press, 1982).

60. Mark Ramsayer and Frances McCall Rosenbluth, *Japan's Political Marketplace* (Cambridge: Harvard University Press, 1993).

61. The classic statement of "the traveling problem"—of stretching concepts to create pseudo-equivalences—is Giovanni Sartori, "Concept Misformation in Comparative Politics," *American Political Science Review* 64, no. 4 (1970): 1033–53.

62. Mark Ramsayer, in an essay on public choice, presents the logic of a theory derived entirely from observations of U.S. legislative behavior and applies it to Japan as though it has universal validity; for example, "when constituents don't much care about an issue, rational politicians will likely trade their vote on it for a vote on something their constituents do care about." It is puzzling why scholars who know something about Japan, and presumably know that party discipline is observed in Diet voting, would embrace theoretical assumptions that make no sense at all in Japan. See J. Mark Ramsayer, "Public choice," *The Coarse Lectures*, Chicago Law and Economics Working Paper no. 24, University of Chicago Law School, winter 1995.

63. Michio Muramatsu and Ellis S. Krauss, "The Conservative Party Line and the Development of Patterned Pluralism," in Yasuba Yasukichi and Kozo Yamamura, eds., *The Political Economy of Japan* (Stanford: Stanford University Press, 1987).

64. John O. Haley, "Governance by Negotiation: A Reappraisal of Bureaucratic Power in Japan," *Journal of Japanese Studies* 13, no. 2: 343–57.

65. Richard J. Samuels, *The Business of the Japanese State: Energy Markets in Comparative and Historical Perspective* (Ithaca: Cornell University Press, 1987).

66. Gary D. Allinson, "Introduction: Analyzing Political Change: Topics, Findings and Implications and Citizenship, Fragmentation, and the Negotiated Polity," in Gary D. Allinson and Sone Yasunori, eds., *Political Dynamics in Contemporary Japan* (Ithaca: Cornell University Press, 1993).

67. Shumpei Kumon, "Japan as a Network Society," in Shumpei Kumon and Henry Rosovsky, eds., *The Political Economy of Japan: Cultural and Social Dynamics* (Stanford: Stanford University Press, 1992).

68. Daniel I. Okimoto, *Between MITI and the Market: Japanese Industrial Policy for High Technology* (Stanford: Stanford University Press, 1989).

69. See, for example, Kent Calder, *Strategic Capitalism: Private Business and Public Purpose in Japanese Industrial Finance* (Princeton: Princeton University Press, 1993); Robert M. Uriu, *Troubled Industries: The Political Economy of Industrial Adjustment in Japan* (Ithaca: Cornell University Press, 1998); Schwartz, *Advice and Consent*.

70. Patricia Maclachlan, "The Politics of Consumer Protection in Japan: The Impact of Consumer Organizations on Policy-making," dissertation, Columbia University, 1996.

71. Peter Evans, "The State as Problem and Solution: Predation, Embedded Autonomy, and Structural Change," in Stephan Haggard and Robert R. Kaufman, *The Politics of Economic Adjustment: International Constraints, Distributive Conflicts, and the State* (Princeton: Princeton University Press, 1992).

72. When Prime Minister Obuchi formed his government in July 1998, he appointed two outgoing cabinet ministers as parliamentary vice-ministers, in the Ministry of Finance and the Ministry of Foreign Affairs. Since "parliamentary vice-minister" did not seem to reflect their high status adequately, in November 1996 the Japanese government formally changed their English title to "state secretary." The Japanese term, *seimu jikan*, remains the same, and all other *seimu jikan*, who are still officially "parliamentary vice-ministers" in English, are first- and second-term Diet members. *Asahi Shimbun*, November 20, 1996.

CHAPTER TWO

1. The article was Tachibana Takashi, "Tanaka Kakuei kenkyū—sono kin'myaku to jin'myaku," *Bungei Shunjū* (November 1974).

2. Yohei Kono interview, date uncertain.

3. See *Asahi Shimbun*, September 8, 1993.

4. This argument is offered by several scholars. See, for example, Gary Cox and Frances Rosenbluth, "Anatomy of a Split: The Liberal Democrats of Japan," *Electoral Studies* 14: 35–71; Itō Mitsutoshi, "Jimintō geya no seiji katei," in Nihon Seiji Gakkai, ed., *Nenpō Seijigaku: 55nen taisei no hōkai* (Tokyo: Iwanami Shoten, 1996), pp. 109–28; Masaru Kohno, *Japan's Postwar Party Politics* (Princeton: Princeton University Press, 1997).

5. These scandals are discussed in my *Japanese Way of Politics*, pp. 160–64.

6. For an account of Kawasaki vice-mayor Komatsu's involvement with Recruit and for a summary of the early stages of the Recruit scandal in English, see *Japan Times*, December 3, 1988. For a comprehensive account of the scandal in Japanese, see Asahi Shimbunsha Shakaibu, *Dokyumento Rikurūto Hōdō* (Tokyo: Asahi Shimbunsha, 1989).

7. This politician, Takao Fujinami, resigned from the Diet after being indicted, but after being found innocent by the Tokyo district court in September 1994, he reentered politics and won a seat in the lower-house election in November 1996. Less than a year later, the Tokyo High Court reversed the lower-court ruling, sentencing Fujinami to a three-year suspended prison term and a fine of ¥42.7 million. Fujinami remained in the Diet while he appealed his conviction.

8. He was convicted and given a three-year suspended sentence and fined ¥18.35 million.

9. According to Tachibana Takashi, Tanaka made up the name *yami sho gun* for himself. See Tachibana Takashi, *Yami Shōgun, Tanaka Kakuei no Sakubo , Rokkiido Saiban Bōchōki* (Tokyo: Asahi Shimbunsha, 1983), p. ii. For an excellent study of Tanaka's shadow shogun role, see Schlesinger, *Shadow Shoguns*.

10. Takeshita interview, April 25, 1997; Tokyo.

11. Ozawa explains his position on these and other issues in Ozawa, *Blueprint for a New Japan*.

12. A listing of the members is found in Shiota Ushio, "Dokyumento Keiseikai ga wareta hi," *Bungei Shunjū* (December 1992): 132.

13. Takeshita interview, April 25, 1997.

14. Hata interview, April 24, 1997; Tokyo.

15. See, for example, Ozawa Ichirō, "Wareware wa naze kaikaku wo mezasu ka," *Bungei Shunjū* (December 1992): 136–49.

16. One astute observer of the scene was Takao Iwami, a well-known political commentator with a long career covering LDP politics for the *Mainichi Shimbun*. Writing in the weeks before Obuchi's choice as faction leader, Iwami reported that the Takeshita faction was moving in the direction of expelling the Ozawa group. "That probably will lead to the split of the LDP. As the pressure on the Ozawa group steadily increases, things will move toward Ozawa's defection from the LDP and the formation of a new party. Since I believe that is the first step toward political reform, I'm looking forward to it happening." See Iwami Takao, Matsuzaki Minoru, and Hayashi Shigezo, "Daibunretsu, saisaiken no makubiraki," *Bungei Shunjū* (December 1992): 115.

17. See *Asahi Shimbun*, March 19, 1993.

18. Miyazawa's comments on the television program are quoted in Tase Yasunori, *Sōri Daijin no Za* (Tokyo: Bungei Shunjū, 1995), p. 194.

19. Hata interview, April 24, 1997.

20. Miyazawa interview, June 16, 1997; Tokyo.

21. Miyazawa's published reflections on why he was unable to live up to his public commitment to pass reform legislation and how he still felt more like a bureaucrat than a politician can be found in Miyazawa Kiichi, *Shin Goken Seigen—21 seiki no Nihon* (Tokyo: Asahi Shimbunsha, 1995).

22. Miyazawa interview, June 16, 1997.

23. See Tase Yasuhiro, *Sōri Daijin no Za*, pp. 182–88.

24. Hata interview, April 24, 1997.

25. Miyazawa interview, June 16, 1997.

26. Koichi Kato interview, April 22, 1997; Tokyo.

27. Hata interview, April 24, 1997.

28. Hata interview, April 24, 1997.

CHAPTER THREE

1. For example, Margaret Levi argues that "it is not difficult" to define preferences in many instances because all it requires is "a fairly straightforward observation of what is of principal concern to the class of actors under consideration. . . . In the case of government actors, the presumption is that they want to stay in power." Margaret Levi, "A Model, a Method, and a Map: Rational Choice in Comparative and Historical Analysis," in Lichbach and Zuckerman, *Comparative Politics*, p. 24.

2. This decision was made in the wake of a scandal involving an effort by the Komeito to stop publication of a book critical of the Soka Gakkai. This was the so-called "obstruction of free speech and publication incident" (*genron, shuppan bōgai jiken*). The book at issue was political commentator Fujiwara Hirotatsu's *Sōka Gakkai O Kiru*, published in English as *I Denounce Soka Gakkai* (Tokyo: Nisshin Hōdō, 1970).

3. *Asahi Shimbun*, March 4, 1997, evening ed. AERA Henshūbu, *Sōka Gakkai Kaibō* (Tokyo: Asahi Shimbunsha, 1996).

4. See, for example, *Asahi Shimbun*, February 21, 1996.

5. See, for example, the comments of Komeito chairman Ichikawa in *Asahi Shimbun*, September 15, 1993. Ichikawa argued that the movement toward a two-party system was inevitable and that both the Komeito and the Soka Gakkai would suffer if they did not adopt a strategy that accepted this reality. *Asahi Shimbun*, September 15, p. 7.

6. Hosokawa Interview, June 1993, Tokyo. In an interview on April 24, 1998, Takemura also recalled that he and Hosokawa entered negotiations over coalition formation after the July 1993 election with the intention of combining their two parties into one.

7. The inaugural meeting of the Utopia Political Study Group on September 2, 1988, at which I happened to be the guest lecturer, is reported in *Asahi Shimbun*, September 3, 1988.

8. In Japanese, this is the *ryōin giin sōkai*, which actually includes a representative from each prefectural chapter as well as all the LDP members of the lower and upper houses.

9. Takemura interview, April 24, 1998; Tokyo.

10. Hosokawa interview, July 1, 1997; Tokyo.

11. Hosokawa interview, July 1, 1997.

12. Hosokawa interview, July 1, 1997.

13. The coalition also was joined by a group of upper-house members who had been elected in the 1989 election with the backing of the Rengo labor federation and formed a parliamentary caucus (*kaiha*) in the upper house. This is why in Japanese the coalition is referred to as "seven parties and one parliamentary caucus" (*nanaseitō ichikaiha*). See chapter 5 for a discussion of the significance of the *kaiha* institution.

14. Quoted in Schlesinger, *Shadow Shoguns*, p. 266.

15. Ozawa interview, April 28, 1997; New York City.

16. Takemura Masayoshi, *Chiisakutomo Kirarito Hikaru Kuni Nihon*.

17. Iwai Tomoaki, *Rippō Katei* (Tokyo: Tokyo Daigaku Shuppankai, 1988), pp. 133–34; Yajima Kōichi, *Kokkai* (Tokyo: Gyōken Shuppankyoku, 1987), pp. 131–32.

18. Koichi Yamamoto, quoted in Yomiuri Shimbun Chōsa Kenkyū Honbu, *Nihon no Kokkai: Shōgen, Sengo Gikai Seiji no Ayumi* (Tokyo: Yomiuri Shimbunsha, 1988), p. 159.

19. This observation is based on an analysis of the biographical data of all LDP *kokutai* chairman from 1955 to 1993. The exception was Kaneshichi Masuda, a former vice-minister of the prewar home ministry, who served as LDP *kokutai* chairman for six months in 1960.

20. Ken'ichiro Sato interview, December, 1996; Tokyo.

21. Information in this section on the coalition government's formal decision-making structure draws heavily on Nakano Minoru, "Seikai Saihenki no Rippō Katei: Henka to Renzoku," *Leviathan* 18 (1995): 71–95.

22. Ibid: 75.

23. Nakano makes much the same point: "[A]nother aspect of the reality [of the decision making system] is that the influence of the so-called *ichi-ichi* line, the strong alliance between Ichiro Ozawa, the secretary general of the Shinseito⁻, and Yuichi Ichikawa the chairman of the Komeito, who provided the core support for the Hosokawa government, was entirely outside the organizational framework of the government's various policy making processes." Nakano adds that Ozawa's personal power was so great that it produced a situation in which the old

wine of LDP boss politics was now inside the new bottle of a non-LDP coalition government. Ibid: 76.

24. According to contemporary newspaper accounts and my interviews with Takemura and Hosokawa, Ozawa suddenly appeared at the prime minister's residence on December 30, 1993—the day that his patron Kakuei Tanaka died—to demand that Hosokawa fire Takemura as chief cabinet secretary. When Hosokawa refused, Ozawa stormed out and then refused to talk to anyone for days on end. Neither Hosokawa nor Hata nor anyone else could reach him even by telephone. Recalling the incident three years later, Hosokawa remarked that Ozawa often engaged in similar behavior. He would fail to show up for a meeting and then disappear for days at a time. Hosokawa likened his behavior to that of a child who gets mad when things do not go his way, hides in a closet, and refuses to come out. Hosokawa interview, July 1, 1997.

25. According to Hosokawa, two days before he announced his resignation, on April 6, 1994, JSP Chairman Murayama and two other Socialist Party leaders called on Hosokawa to ask him not to send Hata, who was then foreign minister, to the signing in Marrakesh, Morocco, of the Uruguay Round treaty that was scheduled to be held on April 10. They warned that if Hata went there and signed the treaty that the six JSP members of the cabinet would resign. Hosokawa reminded them that they had agreed the previous December 15, after Hosokawa had accepted a lot of their conditions and negotiated on the phone with the Japanese government representative in Geneva until three o'clock in the morning, to support the government on liberalizing the rice market, the key issue for Japan in the negotiations. Now, Hosokawa said, he told them to go ahead and resign if that is what they wanted to do. He said that he was proud of his decision to open the rice market and that it was all right with him if his government fell on this issue. Hosokawa interview, July 1, 1997.

26. The two facilities that are referred to in English as the prime minister's residence are in fact separate places: the *kantei* is where the offices of the prime minister, the chief cabinet secretary, and staff are located, and where cabinet meetings are held; the official private residence, where prime ministers sometimes but not always live, is called in Japanese the *sōri kōtei*.

27. Hosokawa interview, September 28, 1993; New York City.

28. The politics of this issue is well explained in Junko Kato, *The Politics of Bureaucratic Rationality: Tax Politics in Japan* (Princeton: Princeton University Press, 1994).

29. Hosokawa interview, May 9, 1994. Three years later, Hosokawa remembered it somewhat differently. He said he had opposed the tax-increase proposal to the very end but had to accept the decision once it was made by an ad hoc

committee the coalition parties had set up to decide the issue and that Ozawa chaired. Hosokawa interview, July 1, 1997.

30. *Asahi Shimbun*, Feburary 3, 1993, evening ed.

31. For an analysis of when foreign pressures works and when it does not, see Leonard J. Schoppa, *Bargaining with Japan: What American Pressure Can and Cannot Do* (New York: Columbia University Press, 1997).

32. Hosokawa interview, July 1, 1997.

33. The Japanese government refused to place rice under a tariff system and instead agreed to a quota that amounted to 4 percent of Japan's total rice consumption in 1995 and to raise that figure to 8 percent by 2000. The accord is to be renegotiated that year, and Japan is committed to raise further the import share unless it shifts to a tariff scheme.

CHAPTER FOUR

1. The articles in Hideo Otake's edited volume on the 1996 lower-house election, the first election to be held under the new system, make the same point. The volume's title well expresses it: *How Electoral Reform Boomeranged: Continuity in Japanese Campaigning Style*. Hideo Otake, ed. *How Electoral Reform Boomeranged: Continuity in Japanese Campaigning Style* (Tokyo: Japan Center for International Exchange, 1998).

2. The original statement that plurality systems tend to produce two-party systems is in Maurice Duverger, *Political Parties and Their Organization and Activity in the Modern State* (New York: Wiley, 1959). Duverger's later comment about electoral systems being only one factor among many influencing the shape of the party system is in Maurice Duverger, "Duverger's Law: Forty Years Later," in Bernard Grofman and Arend Lijphart, eds., *Electoral Laws and Their Political Consequences* (New York: Agathon Press, 1986), p. 70. The best assessment of the impact of electoral systems on party systems is found in the writings of Giovanni Sartori. See in particular "The Influence of Electoral Systems: Faulty Laws or Faulty Method?" in Grofman and Lijphart, *Electoral Laws*, pp. 43–68, and Giovanni Sartori, *Comparative Constitutional Engineering: An Inquiry into Structures, Incentives and Outcomes*, 2nd ed. (New York: New York University Press, 1997). Other important sources include Douglas Rae, *The Political Consequences of Electoral Laws*, rev. ed. (New Haven: Yale University Press, 1971); William H. Riker, "The Two-party System and Duverger's Law: An Essay in the History of Political Science," *American Political Science Review* 76 (December 1982): 753–66; Gary W. Cox, *Making Votes Count: Strategic Coordination in the World's Electoral Systems* (New York: Cambridge University Press, 1997); Vernon Bognador and David Butler, eds., *Democracy and Elections: Electoral Systems and Their Political Consequences* (New York: Cambridge University Press, 1983).

4. The Politics of Electoral Reform

3. There were 295 single-member districts, 68 two-member districts, and 11 three-member districts. See Ōtake Kuninori, *Wakariyasui Kōshoku Senkyohō*, 9th ed. (Tokyo: Gyōsei, 1997), p. 37.

4. Amendments to the election law in 1986 and 1992 created two six-member districts and eight two-member districts in an effort to reduce the disparities in the weight of the vote between the country's most- and least-populated districts.

5. A representative example of the views of home ministry bureaucrats is provided by Furuya Keigi, a former vice-minister of home affairs and LDP member of the upper house in "A Memorandum on the Medium-size Election District System." See Furuya Keigi, "Chūsenkyokusei ni kansuru oboegaki," *Jichi Kenkyū* 7, no. 5 (1994): 3–20.

6. Andrew Nathan, "The Legislative Yuan Election in Taiwan: Consequences of the Electoral System," *Asian Survey* 33 (April 1993): 424–38.

7. Eric P. Moon and James A. Robinson, "Single Vote Multi-member Election Districts in Taiwan, 1995: A Replication of Nathan's 1992 Inquiry," *American Journal of Chinese Studies* 4, no.2 (1997): 131–46; Eric P. Moon, "Single Non-transferable Vote Methods in Taiwan, 1996," *Asian Survey* 37, no. 7 (1997): 652–68.

8. Quoted in Tanaka Munetaka, *Seiji Kaikaku Rokunen no Dōtei* (Tokyo: Gyōsei, 1997), p. 229. This volume is an invaluable documentary history of political reform over the six years from the Recruit incident to the adoption of political-reform legislation in 1994.

9. Ibid.

10. Constitutional revision requires an affirmative vote by two-thirds of the members of both houses of the Diet and by a majority of voters casting ballots in a national referendum.

11. See Furuya (note 5): 15–17.

12. Tanaka, *Seiji Kaikaku Rokunen no Dōtei* , p. 29.

13. For example, see the comments by the chairman of the fifth election system advisory council about the obstructionist role played by the political parties' "special delegates" in *Asahi Shimbun*, November 3, 1967.

14. The eighth advisory council had twenty-seven members. Its chairman was the president of the Yomiuri Shimbun and the vice chair was the dean of the law faculty at Tokai University. Members included university professors, journalists, businessmen, a retired official from the home ministry, and another from the Cabinet Legislation Bureau. None except for the two retired bureaucrats was an expert on electoral systems. The advisory council was staffed by bureaucrats from the Ministry of Home Affairs, the ministry responsible for election supervision.

15. See *Asahi Shimbun*, November 3, 1967.

16. These editorials are reproduced in Tanaka, *Seiji Kaikaku Rokunen no Dōtei*, pp. 132–33.

17. The *Asahi Shimbun* editorial of July 28, 1993 is reproduced in Tanaka, *Seiji Kaikaku Rokunen no Dōtei* p. 211; the *Mainichi Shimbun* editorial of the same day is reproduced, ibid., p. 213.

18. Hosokawa interview, July 1, 1997.

19. The LDP came up with an ingenious formula to weight the system in favor of the single-member districts. Voters would have only one ballot in the LDP proposal. On it they would write the name of a candidate running in a single-member district. The candidate with a plurality of votes would win in the district election. The vote would then be calculated in terms of the party affiliation of the candidates and parties be allotted seats on a proportional-representation basis. A voter could cast a ballot for a candidate not affiliated with a political party in the single-member district, but that vote would be discarded in calculating party proportional representation. A voter also could cast a vote for a party running a proportional-representation list but without a candidate in the voter's single-member district. This vote would be discarded in calculating the outcome of the district race. Serious doubts were expressed at the time whether the courts would have upheld this system as constitutional since it had the effect of denying the vote to some voters in the election of single-member-district candidates and denying it to others with respect to proportional representation.

20. A private group known as the League for Political Reform weighed in with its own proposal for a mixed system of single-member and proportional-representation districts. This group's formal name was Seiji Kaikaku Suishin Kyo-gikai but was generally referred to as the Minkan Seiji Rinchō, or Citizen's Political Reform Council. It included senior business and labor-union leaders as well as a number of well-known public personalities. They embraced all of the conventional arguments about the need for electoral-system change in order to improve Japanese politics, and their pronouncements contributed to the public pressure on party leaders to come to an agreement on a new electoral system. The organization's views are explained in "Seiji kaikaku suishin kyōgikai kinkyū teigen, Nihon seiji no kiki to seiji kaikaku no michisuji," *Chūō Kōron* (December 1992), and *Nihon kaikaku no bijyon, minkan seiji kaikaku taikō* (Tokyo: Kōdansha, 1993).

21. Herbert Passin, "The House of Councillors: Promise and Achievement," in Michael K. Blaker, ed., *Japan at the Polls: The House of Councillors Election of 1974* (Washington, D.C.: American Enterprise Institute, 1976).

22. Tanaka, *Seiji Kaikaku Rokunen no Dōtei*, p. 304.

23. There had been only two previous joint conference committees. One was held in 1950 and concerned local-government taxes. The other was held in 1951 and concerned the food-control law. Neither of these two conference committees had been able to produce an agreement. See *Yomiuri Shimbun*, January 22, 1994.

According to article 84 (1) of the Diet Law, a joint conference committee consists of ten members of each house. According to precedent rather than law, members of the committee are appointed (by the respective house Speakers) from among those parties that voted for the legislation in the lower house and from those that voted against it in the upper house. To report out a bill, the joint conference committee requires a two-thirds affirmative vote of its members.

Lower-house Speaker Doi appointed to the joint committee three JSP members, two from the Japan Renewal Party, two Komeito members, and one each from the Sakigake, the Japan New Party, and the Democratic Socialist Party. Eight LDP members, one Communist, and one member of a non-party-aligned group called the Niin Club comprised the upper-house membership of the conference committee. The seventeen upper-house Socialists who voted against the legislation were not represented on the committee, since only members of parties that opposed the legislation were eligible to serve.

24. For an account of the ten-point agreement, see ibid., pp. 306–12.

25. Tanaka, *Seiji Kaikaku Rokunen no Dōtei*, p. 316.

26. For details, see ibid., pp. 321–26.

27. Its seven members included a former president of Keio University, a former director of the Diet library, a professor of politics at Waseda University, a former vice-minister of the home ministry, a freelance journalist, a professor emeritus of law at Tokyo University, and a former director of the cabinet-legislation bureau.

28. Nonetheless, the maximum imbalance between districts in the new law when it came into effect was 2.137 between Shimane 3, the least populated, and Hokkaido 8, the most populated. There were twenty-eight districts where the weight of each vote was more than twice the weight of the vote in Hokkaido 8. By March 1998, as a result of population movements, the maximum imbalance (now between Kanagawa 14 and Shimane 3) was 2.4 and there were seventy-four districts that exceeded the "less than two to one" stipulation. See *Asahi Shimbun*, August 8, 1998. The law provides for an independent commission to recommend district changes after each ten-year national census, but the Diet has the power to decide whether or not to accept the changes recommended.

29. For details, see my discussion of the idea of the Japanese modern political party in *The Japanese Way of Politics*, pp. 157–91.

30. Jichishō Senkyobu Hen, *Kaisei Kōsenhō ni yoru Shūgiin Senkyo no Tebiki* (Tokyo: Gyōsei, 1996), pp. 413–19. In November 1998, the Osaka District Court voided the election victory of a candidate elected in the 1996 lower-house election because a member of his headquarters staff had been found guilty of violating the election law. This Diet member had run both in the Wakayama 3 single-member district and on the LDP's Kinki regional proportional-representation-district list.

He had been defeated in the single-member district but elected on the party list. As a result of his expulsion from the Diet, the next-ranked candidate in the proportional-representation district assumed his seat while the expelled candidate was banned from running for the lower house from the Wakayama 3 district for five years. *Asahi Shimbun*, November 11, 1998.

31. See, for example, the case studies of election campaigning under the new electoral system in Otake, *How Electoral Reform Boomeranged.* For an in-depth case study of LDP campaign organization in Tokyo under the new electoral system, see Cheol-hee Park, *Electoral Strategies in Urban Japan: How Institutional Change Affects Strategic Choice,* dissertation, Columbia University, 1998.

32. *Asahi Shimbun*, October 23, 1996.

CHAPTER FIVE

1. Yagi Tadashi, "Kensho⁻: Renritsu Jidai no Kaiha Kessei," *Gikai Seiji Kenkyū,* no.37 (March 1996): 25.

2. In January 1998, the upper house introduced a new electronic roll-call system, called a "pushbutton system." The procedures for calling for a roll call remain the same, but instead of recording votes by having each member walk to the front of the chamber, the new system records each member's vote by means of an electronic device installed in the member's desk. In the past, only about 10 percent of upper-house votes were roll-call votes. Since the new system will be less time consuming, there has been some speculation that there will be an increase in roll-call voting and that it will increase the independence of upper-house members. There are no plans to introduce this system into the lower house.

3. Shūgiin, Sangiin, *Gikai Seido Hyakunenshi, Gikai Seido Hen* (Tokyo: Okurashō Insatsu Kyoku, 1990), p. 211.

4. Mainichi Shimbun Seijibu, *Kokkai Hyakunen* (Tokyo: Gyōken, 1990), pp. 248–49.

5. Ibid., p. 249.

6. Shūgiin, Sangiin, *Gikai Seido Hyakunenshi*, p. 212.

7. Ibid., p. 213.

8. Mainichi Shimbun Seijibu, *Kokkai Hyakunen*, pp. 248–51.

9. Iwai Tomoaki, *Rippō Katei* (Tokyo: Tokyo Daigaku Shuppankai, 1988), p. 134.

10. "'Hata Shushō' No Furyoku," *Sunday Mainichi*, May 1, 1994, p. 26.

11. See *Nihon Keizai Shimbun*, April 22, 1994.

12. Ibid.

13. See *Nihon Keizai Shimbun*, April 23, 1994.

14. Quoted in Yagi, "Kenshō," p. 12. See also his comments quoted in *Asahi Shimbun*, April 26, 1994.

15. See *Asahi Shimbun*, May 26, 1994; also Yagi, *Kensho⁻*, p. 11.

16. Interview with Tsutomu Hata, April 24, 1997; Tokyo.

17. The d'Hondt method for calculating proportional representation divides the parties' votes by successive divisors of 1, 2, 3, 4, and so on, allocating seats to the party with the highest average at each step of the process. For an explanation of how it favors larger parties, see Rein Taagepera and Matthew Soberg Shugart, *Seats and Votes: The Effects and Determinants of Electoral Systems* (New Haven: Yale University Press, 1989), p. 32.

18. See, for example, *Nihon Keizai Shimbun*, April 26, 1994.

19. Watanabe Kōzō, "Hata mo Ozawa mo Baka o Yatte Kureta Yo," *Bungei Shunjū* (February 1997): 360–65. See also Tase Yasuhiro, "'Seikyoku Konton,' Uzumaku Omowaku," *Nihon Keizai Shimbun*, April 27, 1994.

20. Hata interview, April 24, 1997.

21. Hata interview, April 24, 1997.

22. This comment, and the remark that the *Kaishin* was something that Ouchi was responsible for, were made in a conversation I had with Ozawa in New York City on April 28, 1997. Hosokawa, who along with Ouchi and Ozawa, was a key figure in the *Kaishin* incident, also downplayed its importance. He allowed that it triggered the JSP decision to leave the coalition, but believes that a split would have happened anyway, since the JSP and the LDP "had already begun secret negotiations." Hosokawa interview, July 1, 1997; Tokyo. See also his comments in *Asahi Shimbun*, May 31, 1994. Hosokawa is no doubt right about the LDP-JSP discussions, but the issue, as mentioned earlier, was precisely one of timing. Koichi Kato, who became LDP secretary-general under Prime Minister Hashimoto, claims that he was in fact one of the key participants on the LDP side in the secret negotiations that Hosokawa was referring to. According to Kato, there had been contacts between the JSP and the LDP as far back as December 1993—just a few months after Hosokawa came to office—which were aimed at trying to see if there were ways to prevent electoral-system revision. When Hosokawa resigned, the talks turned to the possibility of forming a coalition to take power. See Katō Kōichi and Gerald Curtis, "Jimintō ittō shihai wa, kokumin no sentaku ka," *Chūō Kōron* (September 1997): 28–30.

23. Ibid., pp. 30–31.

24. See *Asahi Shimbun*, May 25, 1994.

25. See *Asahi Shimbun*, May 31, 1994.

26. Ozawa and Ichikawa's comments about the possibility of going into opposition are reported in *Asahi Shimbun*, June 28, 1994.

27. Kaifu later told me that he was opposed to Murayama because he knew from his own experience as minister of education, when Murayama protested the use of the Japanese flag in public schools, how much Murayama's views differed

from the LDP. When I noted that Murayama and the LDP seemed to get along fine after he became prime minister, Kaifu said, "I didn't know that would happen. To be honest, I didn't imagine that he would do just as the LDP wanted." Kaifu interview, July, 1997; Tokyo.

28. The Communist Party chairman, Tetsuzō Fuwa, got fifteen votes, five votes were for Yohei Kono, and there were twenty-three invalid ballots.

29. Naoto Kan interview, November 25, 1998, Tokyo.

30. The Socialists were the largest party in the coalition with 143 lower-house members. The Democrats had 126 and the People's Cooperative Party 31. The Liberal Party, with 131 lower-house members, did not join the coalition, but it voted for Katayama for prime minister. See Evelyn S. Colbert, *The Left Wing in Japanese Politics* (New York: Institute for Pacific Relations, 1952), p. 217.

31. See Nishio Suehiro, *Nishio Suehiro No Seiji Oboegaki* (Tokyo: Mainichi Shimbunsha, 1968), p. 61ff.

32. Hosokawa interview, July 1, 1997.

33. Specifically, the policy accord committed the three parties to "continue and develop" the "agreement with respect to a coalition government" and "the eight-party memorandum"—documents signed on July 29, 1993. Jimintō Seimu chōsakai, *Murayama Naikaku no Santō Gōi no Jitsugen Jōkyō,* June 29, 1994, mimeo.

34. The liaison council *(seifu-yotō shunō renraku kaigi)* included on the government side the prime minister and several other cabinet ministers. The LDP was represented by its secretary-general, the chairmen of the executive board *(sōmuka)i*, the policy affairs research council *(seimu chōsakai)*, and the Diet management committee *(kokkai taisaku iinkai)*, and the chairman and secretary-general of the upper house LDP *kaiha.* Diet members holding comparable positions in the JSP and the Sakigake also served on the committee. In all, there were seven LDP, six JSP, and five Sakigake members. The committee met every Monday.

35. This committee was called the *yotō sekininsha kaigi.* It met each week just prior to the liaison-council meeting.

36. This *innai yotō sōmukai* had ten LDP, seven JSP, and three Sakigake members.

37. I am indebted to several staff members of the LDP's PARC for information about the structure of the decision-making system in the Murayama and Hashimoto governments.

CHAPTER SIX

1. A survey of the projections of all these polls is reported in *Asahi Shimbun,* July 13, 1998.

2. The upper-house electoral system is similar to the new one in the lower house in that it combines proportional representation and districts in which vot-

ers cast ballots for individual candidates. However, there is one nationwide pro-portional-representation district, rather than the eleven regional proportional-representation districts in the lower house. Each prefecture constitutes a district where voters cast ballots for individual candidates. Unlike the lower house, where all districts electing individual candidates are single-member, there are twenty-four single-member districts, eighteen two-member districts, and five three- and four-member districts in the upper house. A total of 252 members sit in the upper house, 100 elected in the proportional representation district, and 152 in prefectur-al districts. Half of the members are elected every three years for six-year terms.

3. *Asahi Shimbun,* July 13, 1998.

4. *Asahi Shimbun,* July 14, 1998.

5. *Asahi Shimbun,* July 15, 1998.

6. *Asahi Shimbun,* July 13, 1998.

7. *Asahi Shimbun,* July 15, 1998.

8. *Asahi Shimbun,* August 3, 1998.

9. Japan and the Soviet Union had signed a normalization agreement in 1956 formally ending the state of hostilities between the two countries. Negotiations to sign a formal peace treaty broke down over the issue of sovereignty over islands north of Hokkaido. Signing a formal peace treaty before the year 2000 was a major foreign-policy goal of the Hashimoto government.

10. For those who have lost track, the list that begins with Takeshita in 1989 includes Uno, Kaifu, Miyazawa, Hosokawa, Hata, Murayama, Hashimoto, and Obuchi. See appendix 1 for a listing of Japan's postwar prime ministers.

11. The nonconfidence motion was in response to the exposure of a corruption scandal involving defense procurement. Although the minister himself was not involved, passage of the motion was intended to force him to take responsibility for the actions of his subordinates. Although upper-house motions of nonconfi-dence are not binding, the minister resigned his position rather than provoke a confrontation between the LDP and the opposition parties.

12. Hiromu Nonaka interview, November 20, 1998; Tokyo.

13. *Asahi Shimbun,* November 23, 1998.

14. Ozawa's comments were reported widely in the press the following day. See, for example, *Asahi Shimbun,* November 26, 1998.

15. See my *Election Campaigning Japanese Style* (New York: Columbia University Press, 1971), pp. 52–53.

16. For a more extensive exposition, see, ibid., pp. 38–41.

17. This sentimental journey was arranged by the *Asahi Shimbun,* and my observations about what had and had not changed in campaign practices over the intervening years appeared in a three-part series in the newspaper. See "Daigishi no tanjo" no ima," *Asahi Shimbun,* August 28, 30, 31, 1996.

18. On the concept of the hard vote, see my *Election Campaigning,* pp. 38ff.

19. OECD, "Public Sector" data, *National Accounts* (Paris: OECD, 1998).

20. *Yomiuri Shimbun,* August 6, 1998.

21. The total number of officials in local MoF bureaus and in the FSA was approximately fifteen hundred, so the plan called for increasing that number to three thousand. How many of these three thousand officials would be bank examiners was unclear.

22. *Asahi Shimbun,* August 15, 1998.

23. Thirty percent of JCP lower- and upper-house members are women. With 6.5 percent of Diet seats, the JCP accounts for 22 percent of all female members of the Diet.

24. *Asahi Shimbun,* August 16, 1998.

25. *Asahi Shimbun,* July 22, 1998.

Selected Bibliography

Allinson, Gary D. "Introduction: Analyzing Political Change: Topics, Findings and Implications and Citizenship, Fragmentation, and the Negotiated Polity." In Gary D. Allinson and Sone Yasunori, eds., *Political Dynamics in Contemporary Japan*. Ithaca: Cornell University Press, 1993.

Almond, Gabriel A., and Sidney Verba. *The Civic Culture: Political Attitudes and Democracy in Five Nations*. Princeton: Princeton University Press, 1963.

Almond, Gabriel A., and G. Bingham Powell. *Comparative Politics: A Developmental Approach*. Boston: Little, Brown, 1966.

Anderson, Steven. *Welfare Policy and Politics in Japan: Beyond the Developmental State*. New York: Praeger, 1992.

Asahi Shimbunsha Shakaibu. *Dokyumento Rikuriūto Hōdō*. Tokyo: Asahi Shimbun, 1989.

Bognador, Vernon, and David Butler, eds. *Democracy and Elections: Electoral Systems and Their Political Consequences*. New York: Cambridge University Press, 1983.

Byas, Hugh. *Government by Assassination*. New York: Knopf, 1942.

Calder, Kent. *Strategic Capitalism: Private Business and Public Purpose in Japanese Industrial Finance*. Princeton: Princeton University Press, 1997.

Campbell, John Creighton, and Naoki Ikegami. *The Art of Balance in Health Policy: Maintaining Japan's Low Cost, Egalitarian System*. New York: Cambridge University Press, 1998.

Campbell, John Creighton. "Bureaucratic Primacy: Japanese Policy Communities in an American Perspective," *Governance* 2, no.1 (1989).

Chūma Hiroyuki, and Suruga Terukazu. *Koyō kankō no henka to josei rōdō*. Tokyo: Tokyo Daigaku Shuppankai, 1997.

Cohen, Theodore. *Remaking Japan: The American Occupation as New Deal*. ed. Herbert Passin, New York: Free Press, 1987.

Colbert, Evelyn S. *The Left Wing in Japanese Politics*. New York: Institute for Pacific Relations, 1952.

Cox, Gary W. *Making Votes Count: Strategic Coordination in the World's Electoral Systems*. New York: Cambridge University Press, 1997.

Cox, Gary W., and Frances Rosenbluth. "Anatomy of a Split: The Liberal Democrats of Japan," *Electoral Studies*, vol. 14 (1985).

Curtis, Gerald L. *Election Campaigning Japanese Style*. Columbia University Press, 1971.

———. *The Japanese Way of Politics* New York: Columbia University Press, 1988.

———. "Big Business and Political Influence." In Ezra Vogel, ed., *Modern Japanese Organization and Decision Making*. Berkeley: University of California Press, 1975.

———. *Nihon No Seiji O Dō Miru Ka*. Tokyo: NHK Shuppankai, 1996.

Dore, Ronald. *Flexible Rigidities: Industrial Policy and Structural Adjustment in the Japanese Economy 1970–80*. Stanford: Stanford University Press, 1996.

———. *Land Reform in Japan* London: Oxford University Press, 1959.

Downs, Anthony. *An Economic Theory of Democracy*. New York: Harper & Row, 1957.

Duverger, Maurice. *Political Parties and Their Organization and Activity in the Modern State*. New York: Wiley, 1959.

———. "Duverger's Law: Forty Years Later." In Bernard Grofman and Arend Lijphart, ed., *Electoral Laws and Their Political Consequences*. New York: Agathon Press, 1986.

Evans, Peter. "The State as Problem and Solution: Predation, Embedded Autonomy, and Structural Change." In Stephan Haggard and Robert R. Kaufman, *The Politics of Economic Adjustment: International Constraints, Distributive Conflicts, and the State*. Princeton: Princeton University Press, 1992.

Fujiwara Hirotatsu. *Sōka Gakkai O Kiru*. Published in English as *I Denounce Soka Gakkai*. Tokyo: Nisshin Hodo, 1970.

Funabashi, Yoichi. "Japan and the New World Order." *Foreign Affairs* (winter 1991/1992).

———. "The Asianization of Asia," *Foreign Affairs* (November/December 1993).

Furuya Keigi. "Chūsenkyokusei ni kansuru oboegaki," *Jichi Kenkyū* 7, no.5, 1994.

Geertz, Clifford. *The Interpretation of Cultures*. New York: Basic Books, 1973.

Gordon, Andrew. *The Evolution of Labor Relations in Japan: Heavy Industry 1853–1955*. Cambridge: Harvard University Press, 1988.

Haley, John O. "Governance by Negotiation: Reappraisal of Bureaucratic Power in Japan." *Journal of Japanese Studies* 13, no.2 (1987).

Hall, Peter. *Governing the Economy*. New York: Oxford University Press, 1986.

Harari, Ehud. *The Politics of Labor Legislation in Japan.* Berkeley: University of
    California Press, 1973.
Hartcher, Peter. *The Ministry: How Japan's Most Powerful Institution Endangers
    World Markets.* Cambridge, Harvard Business School Press, 1998.
Inglehart, Ronald. *The Silent Revolution in Europe: Changing Values and Political
    Styles among Western Publics.* Princeton: Princeton University Press,
    1977.
Inoguchi Takashi. "Conservative Resurgence under Recession: Public Policies
    and Political Support in Japan." In T. J. Pempel, ed., *Uncommon Democ-
    racies: The One-Party Dominant Regimes.* Ithaca: Cornell University
    Press, 1990.
Inoguchi Takashi, and Iwai Tomoaki. *Zokugiin no Kenkyū: Jimintō Seiken o
    Gyūjiru Shuyakutachi.* Tokyo: Nihon Keizai Shimbunsha, 1987.
Inoki Takenori, and Higuchi Yoshio. *Nihon no Koyō System to Rōdō Shijō.* Tokyo:
    Nihon Keizai Shimbun, 1995.
Ishida Hirohide. "Hoshuseitō No Bijyon." *Chūō Kōron* (January 1963).
Itō Mitsutoshi. "Jimintō geya no seiji katei." In Nihon Seiji Gakkai, ed., *Nenpō
    Seijigaku: 55nen taisei no hōkai* Tokyo: Iwanami Shoten, 1996.
Iwai Tomoaki. *Rippō Katei.* Tokyo: Tokyo Daigaku Shuppankai, 1988.
Iwami Takao, Matsuzaki Minoru, and Hayashi Shigezō. "Daibunretsu,
    saisaiken no makubiraki." *Bungei Shunjū* (December 1992).
Japan Defense Agency. *Defense of Japan.* Tokyo: Japan Times, 1987.
Jichishō Senkyobu Hen. *Kaisei Kōsenhō ni yoru Shūgiin Senkyo no Tebiki.* Tokyo:
    Gyōsei, 1996.
Johnson, Chalmers. *MITI and the Japanese Miracle: The Growth of Industrial Poli-
    cy, 1925–1975.* Stanford: Stanford University Press, 1982.
Kabashima, Ikuo, and Yoshito Ishio. "The Instability of Party Identification
    among Eligible Japanese Voters: A Seven-Wave Panel Study 1993–6."
    Party Politics 4, no.2 (1998).
Katō Ko¯ichi, and Gerald Curtis. "Jimintōittō shihai wa, kokumin no sentaku
    ka." *Chūō Kōron* (September 1997).
Kato, Junko. *The Politics of Bureaucratic Rationality: Tax Politics in Japan.* Prince-
    ton: Princeton University Press, 1994.
Katz, Richard S., and Peter Mair. "Changing Models of Party Organization and
    Party Democracy: The Emergence of the Cartel Party." *Party Politics* 1,
    no.1 (1995).
Kerbo, Harold R. *Social Stratification and Inequality.* New York: McGraw Hill,
    1991.
Kirchheimer, Otto. "The Transformation of the Western European Party Sys-
    tems." In Joseph La Palombara and Myron Weiner, eds., *Political*

    Parties and Political Development. Princeton: Princeton University Press, 1966.

Kobayashi Yōtarō. "'Sai ajia-ka' no susume." *Foresight* (April 1991).

Kohno, Masaru. *Japan's Postwar Party Politics.* Princeton: Princeton University Press, 1997.

Komatsu Sakyo, *Nihon Chinbotsu.* Tokyo: Kobunsha, 1973. *Japan Sinks.* trans. Michael Gallagher. New York: Harper & Row, 1976.

Krauss, Elliott *A. Death of the Guilds: Professions, States, and the Advance of Capitalism, 1930 to the Present.* New Haven: Yale University Press, 1996.

Kumon, Shumpei. "Japan as a Network Society." In Shumpei Kumon and Henry Rosovsky, eds., *The Political Economy of Japan: Cultural and Social Dynamics.* Stanford: Stanford University Press, 1992.

Kuriyama Takakazu. "Gekidō 90 nendai to nihon gaikō no shintenkai." *Gaikō Forum* (May 1990).

Lichbach, Mark Irving, and Alan S. Zuckerman. *Comparative Politics: Rationality, Culture, and Structure.* Cambridge: Cambridge University Press, 1997.

Lynn, Jonathan. *The Complete Yes, Minister: The Diaries of a Cabinet Minister by the Right Hon. James Hacker.* Jonathan Lynn and Anthony Jay, eds. New York: Harper & Row, 1981.

Maclachlan, Patricia. *The Politics of Consumer Protection in Japan: The Impact of Consumer Organizations on Policy Making.* Dissertation, Columbia University, 1996.

Mainichi Shimbun Seijibu. *Kokkai Hyakunen.* Tokyo: Gyōken, 1990.

Michels, Robert. *Political Parties: A Sociological Study of the Oligarchical Tendencies of Modern Democracy.* New York: Free Press, 1962 (originally published in 1914).

Miyake Ichiro. *Nihon no Seiji to Senkyo.* Tokyo: Tokyo Daigaku Shuppankai, 1995.

———. *Seitō shiji no bunseki.* Tokyo: Sobunsha, 1985.

Miyazawa Kiichi. *Shin Goken Sengen—21 seki no Nihon.* Tokyo: Asahi Shimbunsha, 1995.

Moon, Eric P. "Single Non-transferable Vote Methods in Taiwan, 1996." *Asian Survey* 37, no. 7 (1997).

Moon, Eric P., and James A. Robinson. "Single Vote Multi-member Election Districts in Taiwan, 1995: A Replication of Nathan's 1992 Inquiry." *American Journal of Chinese Studies* 4, no.2 (1997).

Murakami, Yasusuke. "The Age of New Middle Mass Politics: The Case of Japan." *Journal of Japanese Studies,* 8, no.1 (1982).

Muramatsu, Michio, and Ellis S. Krauss. "The Conservative Party Line and the Development of Patterned Pluralism." In Yasukichi Yasuba and Kozo

Yamamura, eds., *The Political Economy of Japan.* Stanford: Stanford University Press, 1987.

Nakano Minoru. "Seikai Saihenki no Rippō Katei: Henka to Renzoku." *Leviathan* vol. 18 (1995).

Nathan, Andrew. "The Legislative Yuan Election in Taiwan: Consequences of the Electoral System." *Asian Survey* 33 (April 1993).

Nishio Suehiro. *Nishio Suehiro No Seiji Oboegaki.* Tokyo: Mainichi Shimbunsha, 1968.

Norgren, Tiana. "Abortion Before Birth Control: The Interest Group Politics behind Japanese Reproduction Policy." *Journal of Japanese Studies 24,* no.1 (1998).

North, Douglass C. *Institutions, Institutional Change and Economic Performance.* Cambridge: Cambridge University Press, 1990.

Ogura Kazuo. "'Ajia no fukken' no tame ni." *Chūō Koron* (July 1993).

Okimoto, Daniel I. *Between MITI and the Market: Japanese Industrial Policy for High Technology.* Stanford: Stanford University Press, 1989.

Ōtake Kunimori. *Wakariyasui Kōshoku Senkyohō.* Ninth edition. Tokyo: Gyōsei, 1997.

Otake, Hideo, ed. *How Electoral Reform Boomeranged: Continuity in Japanese Campaigning Style.* Tokyo: Japan Center for International Exchange, 1998.

Ozawa, Ichiro. *Blueprint for a New Japan: Rethinking of a Nation.* Tokyo: Kodansha International, 1994.

———. "Wareware wa naze kaikaku wo mezasu ka." *Bungei Shunjū* (December 1992).

Packard, George. *Protest in Tokyo.* Princeton: Princeton University Press, 1966.

Park, Cheol-hee. *Electoral Strategies in Urban Japan: How Institutional Change Affects Strategic Choice.* Dissertation, Columbia University, 1998.

Passin, Herbert. "The Sources of Protest in Japan." *American Political Science Review* 61, no.2 (June 1962).

———. "The House of Councillors: Promise and Achievement." In Michael K. Blaker, *The House of Councillors Election in 1974.* Washington, D.C., American Enterprise Institute, 1976.

Phillips, Kevin P. *The Politics of Rich and Poor: Wealth and the American Electorate in the Reagan Aftermath.* New York: Random House, 1990.

Pye, Lucian. *Asian Power and Politics: The Cultural Dimensions of Authority.* Cambridge: Belknap Press, 1985.

Rae, Douglas. *The Political Consequences of Electoral Laws.* Revised edition. New Haven: Yale University Press, 1971.

Ramsayer, Mark. "Public choice," *The Coarse Lectures.* Chicago Law and Economics Working Paper no.24. University of Chicago Law School, winter 1995.

Ramsayer, Mark, and Frances McCall Rosenbluth. *Japan's Political Marketplace.* Cambridge: Harvard University Press, 1993.

Rauch, Jonathan. *The Outnation: A Search for the Soul of Japan.* Boston: Harvard Business School Press, 1992.

Reischauer, Edwin O. "The Broken Dialogue with Japan." *Foreign Affairs* (October 1960).

Reisman, David, and Evelyn Thompson Reisman. *Conversations in Japan: Modernization, Politics and Culture.* Chicago: University of Chicago Press, Midway Reprint edition, 1976.

Riker, William H. "The Two-party System and Duverger's Law: An Essay in the History of Political Science." *American Political Science Review*, vol. 76 (December 1982).

Samuels, Richard J. *The Business of the Japanese State: Energy Markets in Comparative and Historical Perspective.* Ithaca: Cornell University Press, 1987.

Sartori, Giovanni. "Concept Misformation in Comparative Politics." *American Political Science Review*, vol. 64 (December 1970).

———. *Comparative Constitutional Engineering: An Inquiry into Structures, Incentives and Outcomes.* Second edition. New York: New York University Press, 1997.

Satō Seizaburo, and Matuszaki Tetsuhisa. *Jimintō Chōchōki Seiken no Kaibō.* Tokyo: Chūō Kōron, 1984.

Sawyer, Malcolm. "Income Distribution in OECD Countries." *Economic Outlook* (July 1976).

Scalapino, Robert, and Junnosuke Masumi. *Parties and Politics in Contemporary Japan.* Berkeley: University of California Press, 1962.

Schlesinger, Jacob. *Shadow Shoguns: The Rise and Fall of Japan's Postwar Political Machine.* New York: Simon & Schuster, 1997.

Schmitter, Philippe C., and Terry Lynn Karl. "What Democracy Is . . . and Is Not." *Journal of Democracy* 2, no.3 (1991).

Schoppa, Leonard J. *Bargaining with Japan: What American Pressure Can and Cannot Do.* New York: Columbia University Press, 1997.

Schwartz, Frank J. *Advice and Consent: The Politics of Consultation in Japan.* Cambridge: Cambridge University Press, 1998.

Shiota Ushio. "Dokyumento Keiseikai ga wareta hi." *Bungei Shunjū* (December 1992).

Shūgiin, Sangiin. *Gikai Seido Hyakunenshi, Gikai Seido Hen.* Tokyo: Okurashō Insatsu Kyoku, 1990.

Skocpol, Theda. *States and Social Revolutions: A Comparative Analysis of France, Russia and China.* Cambridge: Cambridge University Press, 1979.

Steslick, William. *Doctors in Politics: The Political Life of the JMA.* New York: Praeger, 1973.

Suwa, Yasuo. "Enterprise-based Labor Unions and Collective Agreements." *Japan Institute of Labor Bulletin* 31, no. 9 (1992).

Taagepera, Rein, and Matthew Soberg Shugart. *Seats and Votes: The Effects and Determinants of Electoral Systems.* New Haven: Yale University Press. 1989.

Tachibana Takashi. *Yami Shōgun. Tanaka Kakuei no Sakubō. Rokkiido Saiban Bōchōki.* Tokyo: Asahi Shimbunsha. 1983.

————. "Tanaka Kakuei kenkyū—sono kin'myaku to jin'myaku. *Bungei Shunjū* (November 1974).

Takemura Masayoshi. *Chiisakutomo Kirarito Hikaru Kuni Nihon.* Tokyo: Kobunsha. 1994.

Tanaka, Kakuei. *Building a New Japan: A Plan for Remodeling the Japanese Archipelago.* Tokyo: Simul Press, 1969.

Tanaka Munekata. *Seiji Kaikaku Rokunen no Dōtei.* Tokyo: Gyōsei, 1997.

Tase Yasuhiro. *Sōri Daijin no Za.* Tokyo: Bungei Shunjū, 1995.

————. "'Senkyoku Konton,' Uzumaku Omoiwaku." *Nihon Keizai Shimbun* (April 27, 1994).

Thurston, Donald R. *The Interests of Teachers: A Study of the Japan Teachers' Union.* Princeton: Princeton University Press, 1970.

Uriu, Robert M. *Troubled Industries: The Political Economy of Industrial Adjustment in Japan.* Ithaca: Cornell University Press, 1998.

Vogel, Steven K. "When Interests Are Not Preferences: The Cautionary Tale of Japanese Consumers." *Comparative Politics* (January 1999).

Wakabayashi, Bob Tadashi, ed. *Modern Japanese Thought.* Cambridge: Cambridge University Press, 1998.

Watanabe Kōzō. "Hata mo Ozawa mo Baka o Yatte Kureta Yo." *Bungei Shunjū* (February 1997).

Watanuki Jōji. *Nihonjin no Senkyo Kōdō.* Tokyo: Tokyo Daigaku Shuppankai, 1968.

————. "Patterns of Politics in Present Day Japan." In Seymour Martin Lipset and Stefan Rokkan, eds., *Party Systems and Voter Alignments.* New York: Free Press, 1967.

Yagi Tadashi. "Kenshō: Renritsu Jidai no Kaiha Kessei." *Gikai Seiji Kenkyū,* no.37 (March 1996).

Yanaga, Chitoshi. *Big Business in Japanese Politics.* New Haven: Yale University Press, 1968.

Yasuba Yasukichi, and Inoki Takenori, eds. *Nihon Keizaishi 8: Kōdō Keizai Seichō.* Tokyo: Iwanami, 1989.

Yomiuri Shimbun Chōsa Kenkyū Honbu. *Nihon no Kokkai: Shōgen, Sengo Gikai Seiji no Ayumi.* Tokyo: Yomiuri Shimbunsha, 1988.

Index

Index Compiled by Fred Leise

Economic concerns, influences, 72, 208–209, 211

Economic development, 53, 71

Economic policy orientation, 237–238

Economic reform, 72–73

Economy; in 1980s, 20–21; in 1990s, 21–22, 73

Elections; 1958, 31; 1986, 32, 34, 62; 1989, 48; 1993, 62, 101; spring 1995, 204; July 1995, 192; November 1996, 197, 202; linked system *(heiyōsei)*, 150; lower house, chart of results, 247, 248; upper house, chart of results, 249–251; voting rates, 204; *See also* 1993 election; 1998 elections; Voters

Electoral districts, 146

See also Electoral reform; Mixed system of electoral districts; Multi-member districts; Single-member districts

Electoral reform; adoption, 160; defeat of, in upper house, 159; effects of 1994 legislation, 35–36, 122, 138–139; LDP's position after, 167; Ozawa's views on, 89; Ozawa's *vs.* Takemura's views on, 115; as pawn in Takeshita faction/Ozawa power struggle, 153; popular mood in early 1990s, 144; possible alternatives (1972), 149–150; pressures for, 137–140; purposes, 138; reasons for revisions, 139; relationship to political reform, 145, 167, 170; short-term impact, 139; as surrogate for Takeshita leadership struggle, 92; underlying political problem against (in 1989), 150

See also Medium-size-election-district system; Mixed system of electoral districts; Political reform; Propor-

tional-representation districts; Single-member districts

Electoral reform, politics of; drawing district lines, 161; Electoral-system Advisory Council, 148–152; entanglement in LDP factional power struggle, 92–93; Hosokawa legislation, 156; Hosokawa reform, 154–157; origins of the mixed system, 145–148; possibilities for further reform, 167–170; proposals under Takeshita, 149; reasons for parties' maneuvers, 156–157; revival of Hatoyama's reform proposal, 152–154; search for the modern party, 163–166; upper-house autonomy, 157–160; *See also* Political reform

Electoral systems, 139

See also Medium-size-election-district system; Mixed system of electoral districts; Proportional- representation districts; Single-member districts

Electoral-system Advisory Council law, 148; *See also* Electoral reform

Electoral-system advisory councils *(senkyo seido shingikai)*, 148–152; eighth advisory council, 150–151, 160, 266n14; fifth advisory council, 149; seventh advisory council, 149–150

Electoral-system Investigative Council, 151

Electoral-system reform. *See* Electoral reform

Electoral-system specialists, 139

End of Liberal Democratic Party dominance. *See* Liberal Democratic Party, end of dominance

Ezoe, Hiromasa, 74–75

development of policy-making capabilities, 231; extra-social position, 18; future differences in economic policy orientation, 237–242; gain in power after WWI, 175; history of development, 245f; influence of special interests on, 44; interparty relations, 117–118; loss of influence, 16–17; move from two-party to multiparty system, 31–33; possibilities of two-party system, 166–167; public financing of, 165–166, 227; reemergence after WWII, 175; relationship to the state, 17; search for the modern party, 163–166; shifting positions on electoral reform, 145; turmoil after 1993, 172, 204–205; *See also* Catchall parties; Conservative Party; Japan Communist Party; Japan Socialist Party; Komeito; Labour Party; Liberal Democratic Party; New Frontier Party; Sakigake; *entries beginning "Party"*
Partisanship, 34
Party affiliation, 25–26, 226; *See also* Parties (political)
Party caucuses. *see Kaiha*
Party consolidation, 166
Party image, 225
Party labels, 26
Party loyalty, 33–35, 226–227, 227
Party politics, 218
Party representatives, 149
Party support, 220–221
Party system, 163, 227, 245f
Passin, Herbert, 29
Peacekeeping operations, 219–220
Peak organizations (interest groups), 43, 55; *See also* Keidanren

Pessimism index, 33
Phillip, Kevin, 37
Pluralism, 35
Plurality systems, 139, 144
Policy Affairs Research Council (PARC), 117, 151, 201, 230
Policy assistants, 231
Policy Board, 120–121
Policy coordination, 183; *See also* Policy making
Policy Coordination Council *(seisaku chōsei kaigi)*, 201, 202–203
Policy deliberation committee *(seisaku shingikai)*, 178
Policy ideas; future prospects, 237–242; rethinking, 234–237
Policy making; basis in public consensus, 40; changes in, after 1998 election, 218; changes in 1990s, 40; in coalition government, 117, 120–121; four pillars of, 39–40; during LDP reign, 117–118; post-'55 system, 63; public/private relations, 59–60; role of interest groups, 43; *See also Kokutai;* Policy-making syste
Policy tribes *(zoku)*, 36
Policy-coordination committees *(schocho betsu chōsei kaigi)*, 201
Policy-making system; commonality with European countries, 231; pressures for change on, 228; reformation of, 228–234; weaknesses, 120, 230; *See also* Policy making
Political Affairs Research Council, 84
Political appointments in bureaucracy, 230
Political candidates. *See* Candidates
Political consciousness, 222
Political corruption. *See* Corruption

Studies of the East Asian Institute

Selected Titles

Trans-Pacific Racisms and the U.S. Occupation of Japan, by Yukiko Koshiro.
New York: Columbia University Press, 1999

Bicycle Citizens: The Political World of the Japanese Housewife, by Robin LeBlanc.
Berkeley: University of California Press, 1999

Alignment despite Antagonism: The United States, Japan, and Korea, by Victor Cha.
Stanford: Stanford University Press, 1999

*Contesting Citizenship in Urban China: Peasant Migrants, the State and Logic of the
Market*, by Dorothy Solinger. Berkeley: University of California Press,
1999

Order and Chaos in the Works of Natsume Soseki, by Angela Yiu. Honolulu:
University of Hawai'i Press, 1998

Driven by Growth: Political Change in the Asia–Pacific Region, 2nd edition, edited
by James W. Morley. Armonk, NY: M. E. Sharpe, 1998

Japan's Total Empire: Manchuria and the Culture of Wartime Imperialism, by Louise
Young. Berkeley: University of California Press, 1997

Troubled Industries: Confronting Economic Change in Japan, by Robert Uriu.
Ithaca: Cornell University Press, 1996

Tokugawa Confucian Education: The Kangien Academy of Hirose Tanso (1782–1856),
by Marleen Kassel. Albany, NY: State University of New York Press,
February 1996

The Dilemma of the Modern in Japanese Fiction, by Dennis C. Washburn. New
Haven: Yale University Press, 1995.

The Final Confrontation: Japan's Negotiations with the United States, 1941, edited
by James W. Morley. New York: Columbia University Press, 1994.

Landownership under Colonial Rule: Korea's Japanese Experience, 1900–1935, by Edwin H. Gragert. Honolulu: University of Hawaii Press, 1994.

Japan's Foreign Policy after the Cold War: Coping with Change, Gerald L. Curtis, ed. Armonk, NY: M.E. Sharpe, 1993.

The Writings of Koda Aya, a Japanese Literary Daughter, by Alan Tansman. New Haven: Yale University Press, 1993.

The Poetry and Poetics of Nishiwaki Junzaburo: Modernism in Translation, by Hosea Hirata. Princeton University Press, 1993.

Social Mobility in Contemporary Japan, by Hiroshi Ishida. Stanford: Stanford University Press, 1993.

Sowing the Seeds of Change: Chinese Students, Japanese Teachers, 1895–1905, by Paula S. Harrell. Stanford: Stanford University Press, 1992.

Explaining Economic Policy Failure: Japan and the 1969–1971 International Monetary Crisis, by Robert Angel. New York: Columbia University Press, 1991.

Race to the Swift: State and Finance in Korean Industrialization, by Jung-en Woo. New York: Columbia University Press, 1991.

Competitive Ties: Subcontracting in the Japanese Automotive Industry, by Michael Smitka. New York: Columbia University Press, 1991.

Financial Politics in Contemporary Japan, by Frances Rosenbluth. Ithaca: Cornell University Press, 1989.

Education in Japan, by Richard Rubinger and Edward Beauchamp. New York: Garland Publishing, Inc., 1989.

Aftermath of War: Americans and the Remaking of Japan, 1945–1952, by Howard B. Schonberger. Kent, OH: Kent State University Press, 1989.